Narrative Power

Narrative Power
The Struggle for Human Value

Ken Plummer

polity

First published in 2019 by Polity Press

Polity Press
65 Bridge Street
Cambridge CB2 1UR, UK

Polity Press
101 Station Landing
Suite 300
Medford, MA 02155, USA

ISBN-13: 978-1-5095-1702-2 (hardback)
ISBN-13: 978-1-5095-1703-9 (paperback)

A catalogue record for this book is available from the British Library.

Library of Congress Cataloging-in-Publication Data

Names: Plummer, Kenneth, author.
Title: Narrative power : the struggle for human value / Ken Plummer.
Description: Cambridge, UK ; Medford, MA, USA : Polity Press, 2018. |
  Includes bibliographical references and index.
Identifiers: LCCN 2018023141 (print) | LCCN 2018038956 (ebook) | ISBN
  9781509517060 (Epub) | ISBN 9781509517022 | ISBN 9781509517039 (pb)
Subjects: LCSH: Narrative inquiry (Research method) | Power (Social sciences)
  | Sociology--Biographical methods.
Classification: LCC H61.295 (ebook) | LCC H61.295 .P58 2018 (print) | DDC
  001.4/33--dc23
LC record available at https://lccn.loc.gov/2018023141

Typeset in 10.5 on 12 pt Plantin by Servis Filmsetting Ltd, Stockport, Cheshire
Printed and bound in the UK by TJ International Limited

For further information on Polity, visit our website: politybooks.com

Stories animate human life: that is their work. Stories work with people, for people, and always stories work on people, affecting what people are able to see as real, as possible, and as worth doing or best avoided . . . A good life requires living well with stories. When life goes badly, a story is often behind this too . . . Narrative makes the earth habitable for human beings.

Arthur Frank, *Letting Stories Breathe*

That every individual life between birth and death can eventually be told as a story with beginning and end is the prepolitical and prehistorical condition of history, the great story without beginning and end. But the reason why each human life tells its story and why history ultimately becomes the storybook of mankind, with many actors and speakers and yet without any tangible authors, is that both are the outcomes of action.

Hannah Arendt, *The Human Condition*

Every conflict is in part a battle over the story we tell, or who tells and who is heard.

Rebecca Solnit, *Hope in the Dark*

Contents

Prologue: Going Backstage

Once upon a time, there was the story. Like you, I have lived all my life with stories. It is an almost universally recognized fact that what makes our humanity distinct from other life on Planet Earth is our ability to tell and listen to stories. What is less universally recognized is that we are also thinkers about the power of our stories: we do not just tell and listen, we also reflect upon them and act with them. Stories help us to imagine, animate and value human life. We live our lives between stories of imagination and stories of reality: call this, if you like, *the reality puzzle*. This book provides some further ways to reflect on these flowing stories: I ask how power shapes stories, how stories shape power and how understanding the way all this works might help move us towards better worlds for all.

From the slow evolution of the face-to-face local oral cultures of antiquity to our currently dazzling moments of global digitalism that convulse us with rapidly fragmenting, fast-speed, niched networked tweets, we have always been the animal living with narrative power. We dwell across the globe in a vast multitude of complex interconnecting reflective storied social worlds. Our narratives are continually born, sparkle, flicker, silence and die; some get remembered. Our everyday lives are influenced, shaped and even coerced, by the storied actions of others. They become saturated in everyday political relations. And this is a basic puzzle: just how do we human beings come to dwell within this *story–power dialogue,* and what does it do to humane governance and us?

A life in stories

I guess I started being interested in narrative power when I was about 15. As an unread working-class teenage boy and young man born in Wood Green, London, I struggled for a few years with the possibility of being homosexual. This was England in the early 1960s and homosexuality was stigmatized as sin, sickness, crime and tragedy. (It still is today in much of the world.) Everywhere I turned, I heard stories and saw images that suggested my being was a problem and I was doomed for a tragic existence. My life became a dialogue with queer stories. Watching the film *Victim* in 1961 displayed this only too clearly. Here was the story of a life of queer-bashing, blackmail, therapy, prison, darkness, sorrow and ultimately suicide. If I was to believe this dominant powerful narrative of the day, could this well be my own pathetic life story? Maybe. If I had been born any earlier, this may have been my fate, as it certainly was for a great many. But I was also a child of the countercultural 1960s and challenging counternarratives were in the making. Among these was the emerging powerful, positive story of Gay Pride and Gay Rights: 'Sing if you're glad to be gay, sing if you are happy that way.' A few lawyers were beginning to tell new stories to change the law; some psychiatrists were reworking their scripts of sickness into health; and a new language and culture of stories was starting to be told that gave us new visions. A new narrative, and imagery, were in the making and I was living them: the 'Coming Out as Gay or Lesbian' story became a growing genre of writing and film and eventually appeared in many countries across the world. Slowly, new possibilities were being sensed. I seized the moment, as we say, and started to refashion my little youthful life and world through these new tales. My life was not to be downtrodden: I was not going to live in the closet; I was going to make sure I could lead a life where I could be an out gay man. And this is more or less what happened, and very quickly. The old story was discarded, the new one shaped and adopted. The counter-stories of social movements changed my life. But I also learnt that stories are never finished – there is a kaleidoscope of sensibilities around them, and they will keep moving on.[1]

Retrospectively, I can see unfolding in all of this a major genre of storytelling, which has sculptured many little lives and big political moments: a self-fulfilling narrative. Stories become grounded in everyday life, have consequences, shape outcomes, change lives and sometimes become self-amplifying: telling the story helps bring about what it tells. This means we had better be careful what stories we tell. I was lucky to find new stories in the making: the old ones would have made my life very unhappy. I slowly learnt that stories have a history, and their right moment matters a great deal.

And, indeed, since the mid-1970s, I have spent a life academically engaged with stories. Initially examining a wide range of stories about the sexually diverse, I argued for the significance of narrative and story research as a powerful method for the social sciences (in my first publications 'Doing Life Histories' (Faraday and Plummer, 1979) and *Documents of Life* (Plummer, [1983] 2001)). Over the subsequent years, I have increasingly tried to develop an approach that is less concerned with literary narrative and more with the sociological, ethical and political importance of storytelling and listening: there is an ecology of narratives in which stories are assembled, understood, given value and lived through our actions in the world. This was most clearly set out in my book *Telling Sexual Stories* (Plummer, 1995), which offered a sociology of stories and then applied it to the field of sexualities.

And so it seems that I have been living with narrative power all my life, even if I did not quite realize it at the time; and it has now become the prime focus of this study. This new book has been simmering within me for many years. My question, simply put, is: How does narrative shape power and how does power shape narrative? My focus is on power–narrative interaction, a dialogue in which each feeds on the other, is emergent and generates change. I ultimately look to a world where narrative acts and narrative power make for better worlds. As they have for me.

Both narrative and power have existed everywhere since the beginning of human time. They are ubiquitous, and at the start of the twenty-first century there is an explosion of new forms. As I was writing this book, there was never a day when issues of narrative power were not prominent: Trump's 'fake media', the Brexit divide, terrorist stories, 'Putin', the clash over the environment, the refugee crisis, Syria, Yemen, the dangers of the digital world of tweets and surveillance, the emergence of the story of 'Trans', the sexual harassment stories of #MeToo and Weinstein, Hollywood and the UK Parliament. As each of them flagged a significant *narrative crisis or muddle*, I wondered whether there had there been any progress in our narrative understanding and skills since Aristotle's famous discussion of rhetoric and poetics (Aristotle, 1991, 1996). They provided little hope that a civilized, caring modern narrative world was at work here. And yet, at the same time, every day I exchanged good stories with people of all kinds, watched videos, read books, visited art galleries, went to the theatre, listened to music and experienced the omnipresent joy of narratives at their best.

Taking a stance

Folk have written a lot about stories, life stories, narratives, discourse and what is often called 'narratology'. My focus here is selective: on how stories work socially and politically, highlighting the generic features that underpin a great many different stories. I will mention many tales, but I have no space to illustrate any of them in great detail. Readers looking for extended discussions of any specific story will not find them. (I have chosen, for example, largely to bypass Trump and Brexit where there is already a huge industry discussing them.) Nor am I concerned with fiction. My main focus is on *tales of suffering in documentary reality*: these stories are grounded in real life. There will be leakage all around – indeed, the very distinction of what is reality and what is fiction will become central as we move on. I also write at a time of cataclysmic change: digital stories are reworking classical storytelling. I live myself as a migrant in time. Having lived half my life with the classical modern narrative, I have since lived in a world where digital narratives have rapidly taken over. I now stand at this vital threshold and confront it as best I can.

Within this study, two rather different books jostle to appear. First, I attempt to produce a grounded, intellectually serious account of *narrative power*, highlighting its many elements but especially the idea of *narrative actions*. I do this by looking at a range of stories that give us down-to-earth problems to think about, and using them to suggest a few wider patterns.

This is how the book starts and ends; and along the way you will be introduced to a wide array of stories. But second, the book is also a very personal one. It is driven by my own personal, political and normative concerns about human suffering, the struggle for human value, and the precarious narrative muddle we keep making for ourselves.

Each chapter is discrete and problem-focused – drawing out its own questions, examples and ideas. Underpinning all this is a critical humanist stance: a stance that is analytic, theoretical, methodological, ethical and political.[2] It simply takes the complex, grounded human life as a key starting point, even as it must also immediately be located in its insignificance in a vast pluriverse of time and space. Ultimately, it links to progressive egalitarian, humanitarian and caring values and politics: here are emancipations that lead globally to a better world for all and not just the few. As people make their own narratives – but not usually in moments and structures of their own choosing – a politics of empowerment and an enhancement of lives become possible, creating new opportunities for better worlds. I recognize there are no grand truths, no grand theories, no grand narratives and no grand answers in this politics of narrative humanity – even though we have often to act as if there are. Our human world and our humanity are an indelibly risky business. Even as stories are there to help us, they are perpetually fragile.

The stories to come

We will see over and over again a standard catechism of stories. They establish scenes, characters, values and plots with beginnings, middles and endings: themes are established, troubles developed, and ultimately some kind of resolution is attained. This seems to be a basic universal grammar of storytelling. And I have set this book up in this classical mode. But my tone and moods change as the stories unfold.

I start with an Overture of *puzzlement and vision:* with a range of illustrative stories around human suffering that will give a good sense of issues and motifs to come. In Act 1, I set the scene by providing a more formal and abstract statement of the key features of narrative power (chapter 2). I then look at a few of the major stories of power and set them in dialogues with the power of stories (chapter 3). In Act 2, I look at the fragility of our narratives and how this arises from five key sources. I now become more *concerned* and *critical* as I examine areas where human beings suffer while doing narrative work: through narrative inequality (chapter 4); through a changing media, especially the riskiness of narrative digitalism (chapter 5); through the different dangers of living with complex modern narrative states (chapter 6); through a troubling reality puzzle which makes the line between truth and fiction a universal, historical problem (chapter 7); and, finally, through the contingencies that shape our stories over time (chapter 8). Act 3 then suggests the possibility of narrative hope – a better world of stories that can be shaped by a politics of narrative humanity. This final section (chapter 9) then becomes much more explicitly *normative and political,* looking for re-valuations, imaginaries and new political acts in a world fast heading along a road to disaster. We need a better narrative world: here I highlight the importance of developing narrative wisdom and narrative trust, making modest grounded proposals for a new politics of narrative humanity as we move into a digital and cosmopolitan world.

Ultimately, the book leads to a series of meditations about what humanity values – in a world that has now been reduced to an overwhelming crass economic and commercial narrative of life. The book becomes a re-valuation: a critical, analytic provocation, providing tools for making sense of narratives now, and to dream afresh about what could be done in the future – the futures of stories in a challenged world. My tale is a tale of how bad stories can drive out good stories, of how many 'stories of the good' get silenced, but how eventually good stories may just triumph. In the closing chapter, I am ultimately asking the big question: How can we build sustainable stories that support the progress of our world and our humanities?

Overture: In the Beginning

In the beginning
There was the story.
A story of suffering;
And a story of hope.

1
Narratives of Suffering

Six Stories in Search of a Better World

We think we understand each other, but we never really do.
Luigi Pirandello, *Six Characters in Search of an Author*

Narratives are the Wealth of Nations. At birth, we enter a world of perpetual storytelling that has long preceded us. Soon our childhoods become full-time training grounds for early dialogues with others: for making new words, learning to listen, interpreting others. We then live our adult lives acting in dialogues with the stories of others as we struggle with meaning, sense and value. And one fine day, as we reach our deathbeds, so our own life stories may weave into the memories, the hauntings, the obituaries for others. Even as we leave the continual Grand Narrative Dialogue procession behind us, it will most surely continue without us. Every day, a life will entail an immersion in a steady stream of grounded telling and listening to stories in their rich multiplicity of forms. Societies become the vibrant spaces where people go about constructing and reconstructing stories: today, yesterday and tomorrow. Never the one and only story – the fixed and unitary tale does not exist – our stories will change, fragment, multiply, disperse.

The multiplicities and complexities of narrative

The range of the stories we confront is truly astounding: we dwell in worlds of narrative differences, narrative pluralism, narrative polyphony that have been much studied.[1] Difference is the name of the game: varieties of form, structures and contents within storytelling, and multiple audiences in the outer world who make very different senses of the tales. As we start to examine issues of narrative power, we always need to keep in mind this grand diversity of narrative.

Stories exude from past myths, epics, legends, folklore, fairy tales and the grand millennia-old religious tracts, but they can also be found today in the contemporary banalities of mundane scribbles on bathroom walls, Post-it labels and everyday tweets. Stories can harbour grand narrative forms (tragedy, comedy, romance, melodrama, satire, farce) alongside little lesser ones (jokes, anecdotes, gossip). Our clothes, our fashions and our artefacts can and do tell the stories of our homes and lives. There are our 'documents of life': the autobiographies and life stories, the obituaries and the tombstones, the oral histories and the family histories, the 'truth commissions' and the 'memory sites', the desert island discs and the playlists, the diaries and letters, the podcasts and the blogs. There are the *Bildungsroman*, the genealogies, the therapeutic self-testimonials, the memoirs and the auto/ethnographies. There are visual narratives: in art, sculpture, stained-glass windows, architecture, photographs, film and video. Musical narratives – from baroque tales through love songs to aggressive rap – are everywhere. The brand and the logo bring new stories to the commercial world of neo-liberal markets. And more: nowadays our storytelling has exploded beyond the old technologies of film and television into digital life – social media, digital games and the digital narratives of Twitter, Facebook, YouTube, Instagram and the rest. Stories are multiple and multitudinous, arriving in many shapes and forms, speaking of many different things, appearing across all forms of media.

Above all, they weave and interconnect with truth and fiction, each creating a vast inter-textual panorama in which we come to dwell, suggesting a key contrast: that of a *fiction–reality continuum*, a reality puzzle, through which we can appraise stories for being more or less realistic or true to life. They hold one key to the emplotment, ordering and unlocking of the vast complexities and flows of our unique human lives.

On Stories and Narratives

To be clear at the outset: a narrative is not quite the same thing as a story. There is a long-standing terminological muddle here that may never be completely resolved, and, in truth, the two ideas merge with each other so much that the distinction can often be hard to sustain. But, most commonly, *stories* direct us to *what* is told, while *narratives* tell us *how* stories are told. I take stories to be the skeleton of 'who, what, where, when and why', of *what* we tell, and narratives to be the underlying ways we tell and communicate, *how* a story is deeply fashioned by apparatus of telling. So stories, the *what* we tell, put characters into plots, with beginnings, middles and ends: they set scenes, create tensions and find resolutions. All good stories are expected to do this, postmodern irregularities notwithstanding. Narratives, the *how* we do this, examine the acts, apparatus, mechanics and structures that make it all work: just *how* we tell tales, present news reports, make films, send tweets, tell our stories. All stories are narratives, but not all narratives are stories. Power features in both; and both can take on an infinite variety of forms and shapes as they persistently muddle and mingle together.[2]

Janus-faced Narratives: The Inner and Outer Worlds of Stories

Follow the story. Understand the narrative. We start with this. Follow the story both inwards to the dynamics of vulnerable personhood, and outwards, to the tragi-comedies of risky societies. Like the Roman god who looked perpetually in two directions, we have a fine balancing act to perform as stories and narratives lead us to both inner and outer worlds. Look one way and, thanks to Freud and others, we now know much about the story of the inner life; looking the other social way, we find we know much less. Indeed, it is one controversy of stories that they frequently lead us into thinking psychologically when stories also lead us to the traumas and troubles of society. This study does some re-balancing by thinking of stories as social, and indeed political. Behind every story there is a social – often political – story waiting to be unpacked.

While many of our troubles get told as stories couched in individual terms, as 'personal troubles', they often have their roots in much larger structural traumas that are not immediately visible: traumas of human social isolation and community breakdown, housing and homelessness, poverty and unemployment, discrimination and exclusion, dislocation and migration, violence and war. Ultimately, our sufferings may be structural. And as we come to tell our tales, we may come to share these with others: we come to dwell in *communities of narratives*.[3]

Six opening stories

All sorrows can be borne if you put them into a story or tell a story about them.
Karen Blixen (interview in the *New York Times Review of Books*,
3 November 1957)

I am interested in reality stories and human stories, with tales of documentary reality and tales of human suffering. Such stories bring with
them the possibility of understanding the deep troubles of the world
and sometimes the hope of making things better. Both are evoked in
the opening quote from Karen Blixen (1885–1962), a Danish author
who often wrote under the name of Isak Dinesen.[4] To get us going,
this scene-setting overture invites you to consider six short, grounded
stories of narrative suffering at the start of the twenty-first century.
There is much to learn from them.

Malala Yousafzai: Injustice Icon

*I tell my story not because it is unique but because it is the story of many girls
. . . One child, one pen, one teacher, one book can change our world.*[5]
https://www.malala.org

I start with the contemporary tale of Malala Yousafzai (2014): an
iconic narrative memoir much discussed in the news, press and
media, becoming a bestselling book, a documentary film, a YouTube
hip hop video and even a choral piece for International Women's
Day in 2017. Malala's story is a modern 'celebrity story', a contemporary 'narrative icon', an already classic 'story of a girl who changed
the world'. The plot tells the first-hand account of a 15-year-old girl
shot in the head at point-blank range by the Taliban while travelling
back from a remote school in the Swat Valley of Pakistan with her
friends on the local bus. The date was Tuesday, 9 October 2012;
it was widely reported across the world. She was flown in a critical
condition to Birmingham in the United Kingdom for treatment at
Queen Elizabeth Hospital; recovered, she left ultimately in January
2013, by which time she had been joined by her family in the UK and
was settling into a new life in England. Ultimately, she has become
a global symbol of both peaceful protest and the importance of edu-
cating girls, addressing the United Nations Youth Assembly on her
sixteenth birthday (12 July 2013). She is the youngest-ever winner
of the Nobel Peace Prize (in 2014) and the co-founder of the Malala

Fund, an organization to empower girls through education in developing countries. In the autumn of 2017, she started a course of study at Oxford University.

Her story illustrates many key ideas of narrative power. She displays iconic power, the potential for counter-narratives, and the media clash over global stories. Coming to assume celebrity power, she becomes what the sociologist Thomas Olesen (2015, 2016) calls a 'global injustice symbol', or an *injustice icon* – here, a carrier of Western humanitarian values. This in turn raises the issue of how her story might be read across cultures. For the stories told by the British media were not the same as those told in the Pakistani media (Thomas and Shukul, 2015). The idea of *narrative states* (chapter 6) will start to suggest ways different countries handle stories and how they travel across borders. So, while it is true that much of the mainstream media in Pakistan reported Malala by citing the Western press, there was also a very clear development of a rival narrative too. While the Western media highlighted Malala as a victim of terrorism and a female activist for educational rights, the alternative media were very critical of this Western intervention, raising the issue of bias in contrasting global accounts. There is a danger in using one story to represent all of Muslim girls' experiences. For Malala's story actually feeds comfortably into Western binary (and maybe imperialistic) narrative structures that allow the West to ignore their own involvements and reinforce the idea of the dangerous Other outside of the West. In any event, her story was in some ways an unusual case – her parents had long been involved with education and were campaigners for education in Pakistan. Stories always need contextualizing.

Malala's story can be seen as setting the scene for thinking about the nature of power. She experiences the power of the Taliban *over* her body when she is attacked; but she also comes to know about her own power *to* act when she decides to help the world's women, empowering herself and gaining identity and solidarity. Engaging in what I will be calling narrative actions, she illustrates two contrasting kinds of *grounded ubiquitous power*: the 'power to' and the 'power over'. Here is what we might see as the distinction between ubiquitous power and *governmental power*. Malala faces ubiquitous power (a power found widely in society), *patriarchal power* (the power of men over women), governmental power (the power of states to intervene) and *global power* (in this case, the power of the United Nations). Ultimately, Malala's story draws attention to the locational symbolic violence against girls, their global inequality and their need for education. According to UNESCO, there are some 32 million primary-school-aged girls out of school, and 98 million more missing out on secondary schooling. Malala's story is part of a wider canopy of narrative about the violence against girls (see Kristof and WuDunn, 2010). Her story is also sent round the world through media and social networks: narrative power is also *mediated power*.

The Weight of the World: Parisians in a World of Class

You really feel you're nothing at all. That you are doing a job – a shitty job – . . . you've almost beaten yourself to death for nothing.
                    Teacher (Bourdieu et al., [1993] 1999, p. 468)

Pierre Bourdieu's remarkable sociological study *La Misère du monde* (1993), published in English in 1999 as the 650-page *The Weight of the World: Social Suffering in Contemporary Society*, provides us with a series of sociological interview stories from some seventy Parisians suffering on the edge of modern society. They confide 'their lives and the difficulties they have living those lives'. The study makes for very dark but gripping reading as you experience the varieties of pains people confront in the modern world and sense the traps their lives have fallen into, traps that are really not of their own making. Here are multiple stories of inequality, marginality and the moral devaluation of people: an official who is depressed by her own life, trying to help other people and finding her work and life plagued by contradictions; a teacher confronted with urban violence; a steel worker laid off and struggling to live on benefits; a trade unionist undermined. All are stories of everyday human suffering, but the truth of the tale does not simply lie within the story. The interview goes deeper and wider than usual to sense the tensions and contradictions in the social order that even the interviewed person can begin to glimpse, if not fully articulate. Sufferings are social, not simply personal. But this is not the typical way of seeing human sufferings, which focuses on the psychological. To take one example: here is Pierre C., a wine dealer. Like his father, he has worked in the industry all his life. He runs a small shop too – but it is all in serious decline. He was once an important figure in his community and a rich retailer well known for his local wines; now the supermarket and the big wine merchants have taken over and he has fallen sharply down the social scale. He is virtually bankrupt. Very disillusioned, even bitter, he locates the problems he faces in the way the economy and the government work.

Each interview like Pierre's is told through a transcript, but is also linked to a commentary from the interviewer: an attempt to bridge the storyteller and the coaxer of stories and to see the story as relational. Bourdieu, one of the twentieth century's most important and influential sociologists, took very seriously the idea of listening to the stories of people who were suffering the deep and disruptive troubles created for them by a profoundly unequal capitalist society. But he was scathing of standard media *vox populi*, and of social science questionnaires, opinion polls, surveys and other ways of accessing the voices of ordinary people – the mass. The true sociological interview has to go much further and look very deeply behind the surface to tap into the underlying structural forces that create and organize their problems. In the same ways that doctors look deeply behind their patients' surface complaints, so sociologists need to look deeply behind the stories told. Stories are both individual *and* social, personal and political.

We can take these stories as good introductions to *narratives of everyday human suffering, exclusion and inequalities*. Such stories are widespread in the world. It is the story of the 99 per cent versus the 1 per cent statistically documented so vividly in works like Thomas Piketty's *Capitalism in the Twenty-First Century* (2014), Joseph Stiglitz's *The Price of Inequality* (2012) or Angus Deaton's *The Great Escape* (2013). These are the disadvantaged of the richer industrial world: people at the bottom of the heap, whose stories do not usually get heard or told – indeed, with whom politics is rarely really concerned.

I will return regularly to the issue of narrative inequality, and ultimately to the possibility of the *democratization of narratives*: is it possible for all people to have their voice heard? Some claim, for example, that we might now be seeing contemporary media and digital change – celebrities, reality TV, blogging – as a 'demotic turn' whereby, more and more, the people can be found in the public spaces of the media (Turner, 2010, 2014).

Animal's People: A Fictional Memoir of Environmental Injustice

I used to be human once. So I'm told. I don't remember it myself, but people who knew me when I was small say I walked on two feet, just like a human being.

Sinha, 2007, p. 1

Our third story is a contemporary novel that mirrors the catastrophic man-made Bhopal Gas Disaster of 1984 in India. Animal, our picaro, is a 19-year-old boy with a spine 'twisted like a hairpin' – so twisted that he has walked on all fours ever since he could recall. He is a kind of disability freak, living his life from the dirt of the ground level, with his dog Jar, seeing (and smelling) life destroyed by the world's worst chemical explosion. He says:

> My story you wanted, said you'd put it in a book. I did not want to talk about it. I said it is a big deal, to have my story in a book? I said, I am a small person not even human, what difference will my story make? You told me that sometimes the stories of small people in this world can achieve big things, this is the way you buggers always talk. (p. 3)

The book takes the form of twenty-three tape-recorded interviews for a foreign reporter ('Jarnaliss'), who he accuses of coming to Khaufpur 'to suck our stories from us, so strangers in far-off countries can marvel there's so much pain in the world'. This story is set twenty years after Animal was born, confronting a catastrophe inflicted by an American chemical 'Kampani' ('corporation') upon his home town Khaufpur ('the city of fear'), which has had to live with the disastrous effects ever since. The Kampani, never named, was Union Carbide India, the town is Bhopal in central India, and the catastrophe is the world's biggest chemical explosion: the 1984 gas leak, which killed at least 3,500 people and left 500,000 injured.

Animal's People is a work of fiction that blurs the boundaries of fact and fiction, raising a problem that will haunt all our stories: confronting a reality puzzle, they live in a flow of reality–imagination. The book is even linked to a fictional website at www.khaufpur.com that makes this problem apparent. The problem of mimesis asks of all narrative: How does it imitate reality (Auerbach, [1953] 2003)? How does a story create a bridge between fact, fiction and fantasy? There have been life stories and documentaries about Bhopal (e.g. Bhopal Survivors' Movement, 2009), but this is a fictional tale. All the characters are invented, even as they may match people in real life. Animal's story folds into the genre of fiction, but it represents and signifies the facts of a powerful and destructive real-life event, the political scandal that surrounded it, the failures and advances of activism. So why invent a story when it is already a documentary told for real? What can literature offer us that documentary does not? The literary critic James Wood offers a suggestion – it brings us 'serious noticing': 'Literature differs from life in that life is amorphously full of detail, and rarely directs us toward it, whereas literature teaches us to notice. Literature makes us better noticers of life; we get to practice on life itself; which in turn makes us better readers of detail in literature; which in turn makes us better readers of life.' Fiction gives us detail, particulars, character and inner voices that are usually missing (Wood, 2009, pp. 43-4).

Animal's story is a story of the Anthropocene generation (Scranton, 2015). It jolts us into an awareness of the 'Great Derangement' of the world and how an 'environmentalism of the poor' degrades vast continents. A unique picaresque tale of environmental damage, it helps us to sense imaginatively how the lives of the many (often silenced, hidden and racialized) are being dramatically degraded and dehumanized through the slow violence of environmental catastrophes around the world – nuclear damage, war destruction, transport pollution, deforestation, land degradation, waste dumping, wildlife loss – and to think of the garbage workers who spend lives living off such waste. Animal becomes a synecdoche and an allegory for much global suffering: a unique tale that reflects much wider concerns. How can such global stories come to be told and made to count? Rob Nixon, in his vital study of many such world occurrences, speaks of slow violence: 'a violence that occurs gradually and out of sight, a violence of delayed destruction that is dispersed across time and space, an attritional violence that is typically not seen as violence at all . . . [they are] calamities that are slow and long lasting' (Nixon, 2011, pp. 2–6).[6] And so the stories of the damaged, dispossessed and disabled get lost, silenced. Animal says: 'I was born a few days before that night, which no one wants to remember but nobody can forget' (p. 1)

The environment ultimately suggests an epistemology of blindness, of worlds hidden from view (Medina, 2013). It poses a storytelling paradox: how can there be so much narrative talk about environmental toxicity – so many books, conferences, films, documentaries about the damaging of our planet – while those who are most affected – the poor, the racialized, the silenced, the dispossessed – are also ultimately ignored? Stories become all talk and little action. A few stories change the world a little, but so much more is needed. *Animal* gives us a sense of the need for a narrative humanity to help us see what science cannot.

The story is one of everyday lived consequences – the slow violence of perpetual lived environmental damage. Animal's story is a *body story* and a *disability story* that re-imagines the lives of millions of people in the world today. It also assembles a *binary narrative*: of the way the bodies of the world's poor children and adults have been poisoned, degraded, ignored and marked off from the normal. They become the people of the 'shit holes' of the world.[7] It ultimately asks, as much good storytelling does: what does it mean to be human?

Tweets from Tahrir: Quasi-digital Narratives?

Gsquare86 Gigi Ibrahim
The Tunisian Revolution is being twitterized . . . history is being written by
the people! #sidibouzid #Tunisia

Idle and Nunns, 2011, p. 28

Here comes another story. This is a social movement tale of political conflict in Tahrir Square ('Martyr Square') in Cairo in 2011. It is a story told by many in tweets, a story linked to small, direct exuberant political actions. It is a digital story, part of the emerging digital cultures that simultaneously draw on skills of the past while inventing new ones (Gere, 2008). Almost certainly we see a new dominant narrative mode of the future in the making. It is part of the now well-documented story of the 'Arab Spring' (some now call it the 'Arab Winter' because of its ultimate overall lack of success), a wave of young grassroots revolutionary activities that sprang up in Tunisia in December 2010, spreading though Egypt in January 2011 for eighteen days. There were civil wars in Iraq, Libya, Syria, Yemen; major protests in Algeria, Iran, Lebanon, Jordan and Kuwait. In Egypt, this revolution of the 'twitterati' – young, urban, radical, political, highly motivated – was hailed initially as a great success, and this was often attributed to the use of social media – a digital revolution. Its serving President of thirty years, Hosni Mubarak, was overthrown, resigned and was ultimately convicted of corruption in May 2015, and given a prison sentence.

Social movements have long played a role in telling stories to bring about change. But now we have new digital movements. In Tahrir Square, as people used mobile phones to tweet, blog and network, an exciting new politics was widely celebrated. These new narratives demonstrate the key role social media platforms now perform across the world, giving new momentum for collective action and reshaping politics.

Tweets from Tahrir (Idle and Nunns, 2011) is a book of these tweets. Looking through the texts and messages of the time shows a new kind of political narrative. Such spontaneous texts can have short lives and are notoriously difficult to analyse a long time after the events; but in this case a few insightful researchers managed to assemble a good sprinkling of them in this speedily published book, later presented as a film (2012). The book shows how (street by street, minute by minute) thousands of young people documented their 'revolution' through their tweets on their mobile phones at every stage of the uprising. The book simply reproduces a flow of tweets day by day (complete with avatars of the senders), organized into themes like 'The Day of Revolt', 'The Day of Rage' and 'The Friday of the Martyrs'.

These tweets are important. As more and more of our future political stories become digital, there are questions to be asked about their character and the new social movements that generate them. How prominent might these emerging everyday narrative forms become in political life? Are these short digital messages really stories? Tweets of 140 characters do not have the obvious classical features of stories (like plots, characters, etc.); they are hardly of the same order as many of the grand stories told in the past: the *Odyssey, Romance of the Three Kingdoms, Middlemarch, War and Peace* they are not. When they are put together, they can be made to look like stories (*Tweets from Tahrir* is framed with an opening 'The Spark' and ends the twenty chapters with 'The Cleanup'). But is each tweet a story? Maybe a new term is needed to capture these partial stories when contrasted with traditional ones: for the time being, the *quasi-narrative* might be a good approximation. These harbour the possibilities of new identifiable narratives. We will have a lot to say about digital narrative later as there is a wide raft of new kinds of digital storytellings: tweets, of course, but also blogs and blog stories, podcasts, e-mails, 'visuals', Instagrams and YouTube clips, hypertext archives, logarithms, big data, live data, interactive storytelling, mobile stories (with locative practices), selfies, self-measuring (and the quantified self), Wikipedia, crowdsourcing, flash mobbing and the rest! But right now the Tahrir story alerts us to a world of new narratives that did not exist at the turn of the twentieth century. Indeed, as I write, the President of the United States has chosen tweeting as his major method of political communication with millions of people and has become the most tweeted person in the world: these are certainly very powerful quasi-stories! And so *Tweets from Tahrir* leaves us with new questions for our times: How are narratives taking new forms with digitalism; how are new digital movements arising; and how might all this be changing the flow of power?

Luz Arce and the Chilean Truth Commission: New Testimonials

He pressed me down into the tub. The water kept rising almost covering my cheeks. I was frantic and I closed my mouth. Water started going down my nose . . . Suddenly he took me out of the water, held me and started to kiss my thighs. I tried to speak, to reason, but I couldn't.

Lazzara, 2011, p. 27; Arce, [1993] 2004, ch. 7

My next example is that of another life enmeshed in narrative power: the testimonial of Luz Arce Sandoval, a young Chilean woman. A member of Salvador Allende's Personal Guards (GAP) and working with the Socialist Party (Popular Unity Government) between 1971 and 1973, she was detained and tortured, along with thousands of others, when the oppositional military junta of Augusto Pinochet came to power in 1973. She was abused, raped and tortured by DINA (the National Intelligence Directorate), Chile's military service. Eventually the torture was too much and she finally gave in, becoming a traitor, betraying names, and ultimately working with DINA. This is part of what has come to be seen as Latin America's own holocaust, a 'cruel modernity' (Franco, 2013).

During Chile's post-Pinochet return to democracy, several commissions were established to investigate deaths, disappearances and human rights violations (including torture) under Pinochet (the Rettig Report (1990-1) and the Valech Commission (2004-5)). Luz Arce gave her harrowing testimonial of the horrors of the regime that she experienced and witnessed in the detention camps. But hers is also a story of her betrayals and, under torture, her collaboration with the state, a connection that resulted in the deaths of at least four people she knew. She subsequently has turned this testimonial into a book, *El infierno*, published in Chile in 1993, with an English translation, *The Inferno*, in 2004. As well as provoking interviews and public interest, it has led to a film and novel, both disguised. More researchers have now documented thousands of cases from the regime in many volumes of memory books (e.g. Stern, 2004–10). In all this, she becomes a controversial public political character. This is not just because of her betrayals, but also because she finds a deep spiritual renewal with the Dominicans. Her story has been revisited many times, and most significantly in Michael J. Lazzara's (2011) *Luz Arce and Pinochet's Chile: Testimony in the Aftermath of State Violence*.

In all of this, we can see a life story engaging with power in a number of ways. Power and narrative are in dialogue. Indeed, since the 1980s, there have been some forty Truth Commissions in diverse countries. They appeared in the wake of the 'Nuremberg trials' seeking some sense of justice for past atrocities. And now there are a multiplicity of Commissions serving a multiplicity of purposes gathering a multiplicity of stories telling multiple versions of truth. These are critical modern human interventions in political storytelling: as we attempt to make states accountable for their atrocities in the past, people assemble their memories and stories. Ultimately, they are about global social justice and raise issues of recognition, remembrance, revenge, reconciliation, reparation and redemption. This seems to me to be the first time in history that states themselves are starting to be held accountable for their actions through acts of collective storytelling. We will return to these Commissions later.[8]

9/11 and the New York Twin Towers: Global Icon

Every nation, in every region, now has a decision to make. Either you are with us, or you are with the terrorists.
US President George W. Bush after 9/11 at the start of the 'war against terrorism'

My final story is one that manifestly changed the world: the attacks on the World Trade Center on 11 September 2001. Not only did it change the course of 21st-century history: it generated major new narratives for our times about what a narrative could and should look like. As two 'terrorist' planes crashed into the Twin Towers in New York (and elsewhere) killing some 3,000 people, millions of people from all round the world looked on aghast live through their media, even as they photographed it and sent text messages to friends. A sociology friend of mine in hospital in the UK, drowsy it is true, thought he was watching a Hollywood movie! A major and shocking act of global power was subsequently followed by a major narrative event in which stories and memories were told from multitudes of angles in swathes of media in many hybrid forms across the globe: press, photos, TV, mobile phones, exhibitions, films, drama, opera, museums, catalogues, conferences and so on . . . How can we make sense of this frenzied mega-narrative event?

Raising a smorgasbord of issues, it links to *classical story themes* of sufferings, wars, contests, journeys. It speedily and famously created classic heroes and villains alongside dominant *binaries* of them and us (Bush said: 'You're either with us, or against us'), rapidly setting them into motion and establishing world conflicts and wars. But it also invents a distinctive modern media story: a new *language* of atrocity, violence, terrorism, securitization, and a politics of the exceptional state (with many TV series and box sets to follow!). It generated heightened emotions: a new world of *narrative affect* emerges where stories evoke strong feelings of anxiety, anger, grief. More: it is clearly a *global and international* narrative, moving swiftly, simultaneously across the world – even the moving plane captures this. It also gives us a plenitude of digital narratives – new stories for a twenty-first century of ubiquitous mobile messages of love and disaster sent by its victims and survivors (many died on their phones and you can hear their anguished voices daily in the National September 11 Memorial and Museum). More: it is a *visual narrative* – throughout history, narratives and stories have featured prominently in the world in the visual (think of the iconography of pyramids, cathedrals and power). Here a challenging new aesthetic is defined by its spectacular moment of origin, with television images flung instantaneously round the world and photographed by many, and yet then defined by its absences – as it became an image that could not be seen and understood.

All this starts to raise issues of *memory and remembrance*. In the years it took to open the Memorials in New York, there were endless contestations and conflicts as to how to represent the event (the Memorial finally opened in September 2011; the Museum in May 2014). It became *a self-consciously contested troubled global narrative*. Ultimately, it can stand as iconic for the hundreds of parallel incidents that have happened in its wake (and in it we can also detect a much longer history and genealogy: it did not arrive out of the blue). Almost twenty years later, for a new generation it is a narrative taught in schools and a narrative site visited on holidays to New York City. For many, it has already been forgotten – raising major problems of how we remember or fail to remember even the most recent striking events.[9]

Composing motifs

These opening stories bring many motifs that will re-appear in this book. To start with, they suggest a major diversity both in content and in form: a *narrative plurality*. Here we see narratives drawn from fiction, life stories, interviews, testimonials, the digital – and we will meet many more. Most look like personal tales but it seems clear they can never be understood simply as personal tales: they are also *Janus faced* and lead us to wider structural, often historical, issues. Nowhere is this clearer than with the interviews by Bourdieu, a sociologist who uses life stories to reveal the working of social structure. All of our stories are also lodged in worlds of narrative inequality: Malala in gender and ethnic violence, Animal in both disability and environmental injustice, and Luc Arce in Pinochet's rule of torture.

All of my chosen stories also come through a *mediated narrative*: books, news, Truth Commission, video, camera, tweet. They suggest the contemporary power of the media these days in storytelling: a mediated power. The tweeting at Tahrir Square, the media coverage of Malala, the media explosion around 9/11 – all these show the rising importance of digital narrative. And all my stories also reveal what I will be calling 'ubiquitous power': not simply governmental or state power as commonly defined, but power that moves into everyday life, in the home, the school, the prison, the media, the Instagram. We will have to consider the wide and ambiguous nature of just what this power is. Part of it will indeed involve the clash of narrative states: Pakistan, India, Chile.

All the examples start to illustrate a central idea: narrative actions. Each story is brought alive through human actions: without people doing things, the stories will not work. Human beings come to assemble a narrative reality, a narrative labyrinth. With them, we see new things happening: *narrative emergence*. We ask: Just what do people do with their stories? And we start to sense too that these stories have a dynamic of their own: there are *stories of stories*, with beginnings, middles and maybe ends. The stories are told at different points of *narrative time*: (a) retrospectively, (b) 'in the moment', and (c) looking ahead – suggesting that stories themselves have stories to tell. They move along.

All of the stories help us to sense that the world we live in harbours a reality puzzle of two realities: a narrative reality (a world mediated to us through the situated stories we tell about it, and the solidarities, communities and collectivities we create around them) and an ontological/true reality (an ever-changing, complex, maybe even contradictory 'true', real world we may ultimately never know but which does exist). Such a contrast immediately raises significant problems about truth and fiction, fact and imagination or mimesis – the representation of reality – that will haunt our pages (Auerbach, [1953] 2003). The ideas of Post-Truth and Fake News are naïve at best: since Plato and Aristotle at least, we have always lived with a reality puzzle. How, if at all, can we sense the truth behind all this talk? More: might these stories slowly come to suggest a kind of worldly wisdom that we can learn from as we hope to build a better world for all?

And here we see how narratives encode human values. Stories can bring good news and bad news. They may be our good companions, but they can also be our enemies. And bad stories may drive out good stories. As has often been said, we must be careful about the stories we tell, for they may become true. Once again we return to the reality puzzle, of narrative life and real life: there is suffering and misery to be found in both. And this is a subtext of this book: the fragility of narratives and the politics of a suffering humanity. All my selected stories push us towards *narratives of suffering*: they speak of human troubles and often give us clues as to ways to move ahead. Asking how people suffer is a hard, existential question. And so we turn to stories and narrative asking how people bring their sufferings into narrative form, tell their stories of troubled lives. How might they succumb to dominant narratives and how might they come to display resilience, resistance and rebellion? These stories are ultimately stories of human value, speaking of things that matter to people – often ethical or political issues. Politics becomes a struggle over human values. All this leads to a key political issue, a range of problems about human insensitivity towards others. Here is the inability to hear and listen to other people's stories and a world of narrative injustice. How does politics grow around such issues? And, ultimately, can such questions generate a more humane and progressive global politics?

Welcome, then, to a land of challenges and puzzlements around narrative power.

Act 1

Setting Scenes: Narrative Power as a Way of Seeing

Stories cannot live alone;
They cry out for action.
Action dwell in worlds of power.
Stories shape power;
Power shapes stories.

2

Narrative Actions of Power

I have hated the words and I have loved them, and I hope I have made them right.

Marcus Zusak, *The Book Thief*

The Book Thief, written by an Australian author Marcus Zusak (2007), tells the story of a young girl, Liesel Meminger, who lives bereft on the edge of Fascism while discovering the power of reading and writing as she writes her own life story. This power of words is reflected in the last line she writes in her book, quoted above. The narrator of the book is Death, who walks by her side, observing humanity and its failures. And he is there when the 6-year-old girl buries her little brother on the way to foster-parents in a small town near Munich. He is there when she steals her first book, and he is there when she rescues a book from the rubble of a book-burning bonfire. This is the time of Hitler, Nazism and the stench of mass death. Written primarily for the so-called 'youth market' in the early 2000s, *The Book Thief* soon became an international bestseller, a school text and a successful film. In the book, we see what happens when we bring together reading, story and power to create a dialogue. There is cruelty and control; there is love and liberation. Liesel discovers first the power of reading, then the power of writing, then the power of finding a voice. She comes to steal books to read in secret even as the Nazis publicly burn them. Narrative shapes power: Liesl and others get strength and imagination from reading and writing. But power also shapes narrative: the Nazis have power to control the stories and can burn books with the wrong stories. And Liesl can steal books from a rich employer's library to empower herself.

The Book Thief raises wide issues about how narratives link to power. Here is domination: the power *over*; and empowerment: the power *to*. Narratives routinely play contrasting roles: they can foster imagination, emancipate and give us hope; but they can also regulate, exploit and damage us. And, most importantly, stories only work when people act in relation to them; stories have absolutely no life on their own. Through narrative actions, they become social events. Throughout, I ask not just how people might act to get the power to find their own strengths through storytelling, but also how the power of others can damage. How do we both shape and become shaped by narratives? Human life here becomes an ongoing dialogue between the actions of power and the actions of narrative.

This chapter provides a background. It suggests nine orienting theses to guide our thinking about narrative power. These are:

Nine Theses of Narrative Power
1 Narratives make us human
2 Narratives live through human actions
3 We dwell in narrative realities
4 Narrative actions of power are produced ubiquitously in everyday living
5 Deep infrastructures shape narrative power
6 Narratives encode the struggle for human value
7 Narrative power is animated through drama
8 Narrative power is dialogic, contentious and fragile
9 Narratives have limits.

Here I look at the foundations of narrative thinking, show how people make stories work in their lives, and highlight the troubles and significance of power in all this. While I have looked directly at told stories in the first chapter, here I develop an imagery, a sensitizing language and a way of seeing and thinking about narrative power.[1] Although far from being comprehensive, it will serve to get us going. And as the great literary critic Kenneth Burke once remarked, 'every way of seeing is a way of not seeing'. So I end with some cautions. The more abstract language necessarily used in this chapter helps lay the groundwork for the rest of the book.

Narratives make us human

Telling stories is what makes us human: we are the thinking animal, and ours is a narrative humanity.[2] As Yuval Noah Harari sweeps through the whole of humanity's history, he boldly tells us that 'stories serve as the pillars and foundations of human societies' (2016, p. 178). Likewise, the leading sociologist of narrative, Arthur W. Frank, dramatically proclaims: 'Stories animate human life: that is their work' (2010, p. 3). Both mirror the writer Joan Didion's well-known provocative pronouncement that: 'We tell ourselves stories in order to live' (1979, p. 11). And, most recently, the writer Jonathan Gottschalk (2012) has written a book called *The Storytelling Animal*, in which he claims that stories can be seen as the key to what 'makes us human'. To all this, I simply add: stories are also always about value and power, and they are not all good news – they can also damage and dehumanize us. Bad stories can drive out good stories. For we are also the political animal: our capacity to dominate and subordinate others, to repress and emancipate, is also ubiquitous. This political narrative humanity is founded on differences and bound into language. It forces us to confront mimesis – the abyss of what a real world just might look like. And it is ultimately shaped by our vulnerability and the search for values and meaning.

Human difference, then, is our starting conundrum. Appreciating human differences has to enhance our humanity, while a failure to do so will dehumanize. As Hannah Arendt once claimed: 'Nobody is ever the same as anyone else who ever lived, lives or will live . . . We all act in uniquely different ways from each other and dwell in uniquely different narratives.'[3] And humans can acquire an awareness of this uniqueness and the troubles it might get us into. Arendt's own writings confront the issue of what it means to be agents of human difference in the period immediately during and after the Holocaust, when the significance of the differences of being a Jew (but also a homosexual, a gypsy, a disabled person) brought human catastrophe, trauma, evil. Human differences can congeal into monstrous systems of hierarchy, inequalities and dehumanization. Moved by power and domination, stories become markers of this.

Intimately connected with this is the power of *complex language,* widely claimed to be another major hallmark of our human condition. Stories dwell in language. Whatever its origins may be, genetic or constitutive (Taylor, 2016), language emerges in the history of early human life, manifesting itself in cave drawings and writings (see chapter 5). Of course, many animals have languages and can communicate – but none has the enormous complexity of ours. We dwell in a vast linguistic labyrinth, the only animal capable of complex and multiple layers of inner consciousness and dialogic selves, of thinking and memories, of speech acts and performance, of argumentation and rhetoric, of fictionalizing the world. We are the animal with the ability to create stories to pass down generations through speech, writing, art, music and now digital communication. As far as we know, no other life form can do this, except in the most rudimentary way (although the creation of artificial intelligence does raise a spectre of new forms of superior robots and singularities). With this comes our ability to invent fiction: to imagine other worlds, transmit valued cultures, adapt. What marks us off from other animals, then, is our ability to assemble complex, reflective, abstract and even fictional language.

And this means we live perpetually on a narrative edge – of what is reality and what is not. We daily revisit Plato's Cave of shadows. This suggests that, even as language helps us to live in a constructed flow of reality–imagination, a shared linguistic storied world, so we are driven to ask whether there is a world beyond that. Is there something beyond language, more material, more real, a deeper truth? We seem to live simultaneously in narrative worlds and real worlds. We speak our lives through stories that may not be real: we face the puzzle of reality and imitation, of *Narrative Truth*, of *Narrative Mimesis*.[4] Human beings throughout history have confronted this problem of mimesis – of the relationships between a reality and the fictional worlds imagined and constructed. And it creates a perpetual tension.

And so a fourth element appears: the puzzle of human vulnerability and the struggle for human value. Our lives are vulnerable in many ways: because of our bodies, our relationships, our environment and more (see Plummer, 2015b: 151-2). Even though we are precarious animals, we can partially repair this through our stories: they can act as a bridge over troubled waters. They can, sometimes, help us to make some sense of our lives and the world around us. Ultimately, stories are important in creating and sustaining value systems. Fragile as our grounded narratives may be, they are the harbingers of moral, ethical and political worlds.

Narratives live through human actions

A narrative cannot have a life unless it is brought into being by human actions. Indeed, at the heart of our lives is what philosophers call 'centered human agency' (C. Smith, 2003, 2010). Acting in the world shows the potential we all have to bring about new things (or, as Arendt calls it, 'natality'); it is another key to what makes us human. People may act creatively or passively, positively or negatively, but act they usually must. Narrative actions are, quite simply, those actions that orientate us towards story and narrative. And the stories we tell provide opportunities (or affordances[5]) for further actions. Life can then be seen as a relentless flow of recurrent narrative actions as people tell, hear, see, feel and perpetually act on stories. We ask: What do human beings do with their stories in the world? Often these actions are political; increasingly, they are digital.

Any narrative text that is not acted upon lies inert and without consequence. Action will create it and action will make it live. So a film without an audience, a book unopened, a tweet unread is of no consequence: texts call out for acts and action, and at that moment they start to come alive. There is a creative and new response to the story as it is told, as a dialogue with the text is set in motion. Without this active, agentic dialogue, a story has no life in the social world; stories on their own do nothing: they have to be animated and brought to life. Simply: ask not what a narrative says, but ask what people do with it. Ask how people listen to stories. Ask how people bring the full richness of their embodied, emotional senses to them. And ask how people interact with others through them. With this idea, many critical processes soon start to come into view: narrative empathy, narrative listening, narrative dialogue, narrative identification, narrative relationships and even a narrative self and narrative personhood. More will be said about these as we move on.[6]

Two key examples might help to clarify matters. First, our narrative actions are involved in *embodied empathic dialogues*.[7] Humans do not act alone in merely rational worlds (as so much social science would like us to believe) but move with feeling bodies in ambivalent relationships and conversations with precarious others. As we tell stories, we enable others to build a partial sense of our lives and worlds; they enable conversation to be concrete and they ultimately may provide sympathy and even compassion – but sometimes anger and hostility. Conversing, reading novels, watching films or tweeting are all major modes of narrative human action that can widen the spheres of human sympathy. In life, we cannot function with a story that stands alone: we need dialogue, not brute monologue. Stories themselves are at their best when relational, containing plots and characters that enable us to sense – and build empathy towards – a range of characters and different points of view. Narratives generate a sense of our differences;

dialogues make us see them; and empathy helps us to appreciate their importance. Embodied dialogic acts and empathetic acts are always important issues in grasping narrative actions.

Second, the narrative self flows out of the human capacity for self-reflexivity. As we necessarily come to learn to 'take the role of others' and 'dwell in the minds of others', we start becoming an animal that can provide 'an account of ourselves' as we see ourselves 'through the eyes of others'. Our telling of this self becomes sensitive to the presence of a circle of (different) others (significant others, generalized others, mediated others, digital others, feared others). We are shaped by and become dependent upon these others, whose own stories create wider potentials for broadening and shaping a sense of who we are. We start to *identify* with some stories, to *value* some of them, to *develop* moral awareness, and to create the possibility of *narrative othering:* of turning this other into an enemy.[8]

This raises questions about our emotions, our moral psychology, our unique personhood, and the ability we have to speak with our own seemingly singular narrative voice in the midst of others in the world. This self cannot really function without a narrative; we are not just the animal that tells stories but the animal who tells stories of who we are: our self. No other animal seems to have this potentiality to acquire a dialogically aware, historically informed and morally conscious self with a distinctive awareness of others, an inter-subjectivity. This narrating human assembles a phenomenology of the self and experiences a struggle for understanding – a hermeneutics.[9] It is one foundation of what came to be known in the 1970s as a Politics of Identity.

Narratives on their own mean nothing: they require human agency, action, empathy and performance to bring them to life. Yet, as narratives and their actions develop, so we can find them coming to have a life of their own: regulated, reproduced and ritualized into powerful narrative realities.

We dwell in narrative realities

No one arrives in a world without stories. Every day we tumble into a deep labyrinth of *narrative realities*. So while people certainly can make their own stories, they rarely do so under conditions of their own choosing. However important narrative actions are, the world we arrive in is preformed and stuffed full of language, characters, plots and rhetoric that have become ritualized. Social scientists call these 'social facts', 'the objective reality of narratives', a world of public dominant narratives, or, most directly, narrative realities.[10] Narratives become social facts that exist independently of us, stand over and above us, and exert a definite powerfully coercive force on our lives. There is no easy wishing them away: we have to confront these stories of the world as the solid frames and realities of our existences. And such powerful narrative structures often reach back deeply into long-standing (even archetypal) forms and histories. We can rarely, if ever, live in narratives entirely of our own making.

Narrative reality inhabits narrative worlds: communities, networks, crowds, social movements, assemblages, narrative labyrinths. All are worlds of complexity that stand independently over and above us, both regulating and supporting us. Here is an ecology of narrative worlds, a carving-out of kinds of 'safe' homes where stories can live and flourish. Typically, this will bring a communication *technology* as a means for telling stories; a communicative *culture* of value worlds and memories; the emergence of narrative *standpoints*, along with a narrative *habitus* displaying the rituals, routines and repetition of stories; and a narrative *self* that belongs and interacts with all this. Narrative worlds provide structures to give voice to people (Couldry, 2010). Ultimately, narrative actions construct narrative realities that in turn define our standpoints in the world.

Living Mediated Narrative Power

To take the case of technology and narrative reality – these days, the technology of our narrative realities has become increasingly digital and electronic As communications media develop over time, from cave arts through print worlds to digitalism, so we face differing forms of listening, storytelling and potential power. In the early twenty-first century, we have come to dwell in five modes of communicative production: speech, writing, print, electronic media and digital technology. The rise of mass media (the mechanical and electronic media) in the nineteenth century has now merged with and been overtaken by the arrival of digital media in the early twenty-first century (Web 1.0, 2.0 and 3.0). There has been an opening up of transformative new and hybrid possibilities for rethinking of both contemporary narratives and power. Communications power becomes a central source of power in modern societies, exerting extensive influence over our lives. All this suggests a profound reworking of both personal life and narrative life – a 'deep mediatization' of human life is taking place (Couldry and Hepp, 2017).

Most modern stories now have a media life, and they function within what have been called *media logics* and *logics of connective action* (Altheide and Snow, 1979; Bennett and Segerberg, 2013). The study of narrative has increasingly become the study of *mediated lives*. We now talk about (and study) *Mediating Migration* (Hegde, 2016), *Mass-Mediated Terrorism* (Nacos, 2016), *Mediated Youth Cultures* (Bennett and Robards, 2014) and 'mediated marketplaces' (Leiss, 2005). Media now constitute the major sense of a public sphere, of a world 'out there'.

The Public Labyrinth as Hubs of Engagement

The classical world of stories lived in a public sphere, but this has long been in a state of continuous transformation. When Habermas wrote his influential *The Structural Transformation of the Public Sphere* in 1962, he could designate a public sphere of 'events and occasions "public" when they are open to all, in contrast to closed or exclusive affairs' ([1962] 1989, p. 1). He could also see that the rise of the media and commercial interests were leading to its demise. This old space where citizens could get to talk freely about public affairs and engage in 'deliberative reasoning' was changing. Hugely influential and widely discussed, his work has now had to be modified over the past half-century in many ways. Since he wrote his major statement, the world has dramatically undergone change (as Habermas himself recognizes)[11] and the old distinctions of public and private are being replaced by a wide array of *hubs of engagement*. Taken together, we now have multiple *public labyrinths of narratives* – the new spaces where narratives work. Public labyrinths blur and muddle the old private/public distinctions, as they become multiple, proliferating fragmented hybrids of interconnecting, heterogeneous spaces – sometimes converging, sometimes diverging. The world of public and private is now itself partially visible, partially invisible and often so vertiginous in complexity that is hard to navigate or even conceptualize. The deeply inner life finds it harder to escape being made public, even as the public world is increasingly invaded by the personal. The issue now becomes how stories are to be negotiated in this dense connected labyrinth. Contemporary stories have to nestle in, and wrestle with, this much more complex space, suggested by table 2.1.

Table 2.1 Hubs of engagement in the public labyrinths of narrative realities

The rise of diverse ...	Creating their own storied public worlds –
Social movements	e.g. a Black Public, a Woman's Public, a Queer Public, a Right-wing Public (Warner, 2002)
Electronic media	Giving us new forms of public debate, e.g. the reality show and celebrity culture (Turner, 2010)
Commercial media	Spreading a pervasive promotional culture, e.g. advertising, consumption and markets (Davis, 2013)
Digital networks	Blurring public/private lines, e.g. Twitter, Facebook, YouTube breaking down old boundaries (Karatzogianni et al., 2016)
Hashtag networking	Creating new 'bubbles' of audiences focused on multiple publics (Rambukkana, 2015)
Global networks	Generating transnational and digital global public spheres (Volkmer, 2014)
Art worlds	Creating public spaces for theatre, museums, festivals, intellectuals, mega-universities (Barrett, 2012)
Religious cultures	Revitalizing public spaces: while old religions stay, new ones are grafted on (Butler et al., 2011)

Narrative actions of power are produced ubiquitously in everyday living

Where does power fit with this? Like narrative, power is a very human thing with a very long history as a contested idea. It follows many divides, requires many distinctions, and takes many forms. One prominent thinker, Steven Lukes, claims: 'how we think about power is controversial ... there are endless debates ... with no sign of imminent resolution' ([1974] 2005, p. 62). He is surely right: I have detected hundreds of accounts of power ranging from the claim it is 'an empty term' and 'should be abandoned' (Latour, 1986, p. 278) to the exhortation that 'Power is the most fundamental process in society' (Castells, 2009, p. 10).[12]

Knowing the idea of power will always be contested, I use this term broadly and in a much wider way than is often found in political science courses. I see power as ubiquitous social action and certainly not to be simply restricted to the narrow, though vital, case of state and governance. It flows through all aspects of society and at its core is a relation of asymmetry and a process of influence. Some key characteristics of these political actions include being:

- *Possessed of potentiality*: this suggests the classic distinction between *power to* (potentia) and *power over* (potestas). These can both empower and dominate. Hence, narrative actions can empower us, but also come to dominate us.
- *Relational*: this suggests an asymmetrical social relationship between identities of dominance and subordination. Hence, narratives live on hierarchical relations of domination and subordination.
- *Constitutive*: this suggests an energy that assembles or causes things to happen. Hence, power assembles narrative even as narrative assembles power.
- *Ubiquitous and processual*: this suggests a flow throughout all aspects of society and relations. At its core is a process of influence.[13] Hence, there is a perpetual flow of narrative power.
- *Contentious, agonistic values*: this suggests people draw on their power to make value claims, often falling into conflicts with each other over such claims.[14] Hence, there is a ceaseless potential for conflict over narratives. But there can be cooperation.
- *Embodied, intersubjective and everyday*: this suggests power is not simply out there but enters the corporeal body and feeling worlds of everyday life. We experience power through our bodies and others. Hence, narratives become intersubjective and embodied too; together we come to experience daily the power of everyday narrative life.
- *Dramaturgical*: this suggests power is densely dramatic, highlighting performance and performativity. Hence, narrative needs this performance to come alive and to make things matter.
- *Cultural and material*: this suggests how power is both symbolic and also always grounded in material organization – narratives are grounded in economies, embodiments and environments (increasingly, it is *digital*).
- *Structural*: while power has many sources, at the broadest level it is found in structured institutions such as the government, the economy, violence and culture – religion, education, media, digital. Narrative power is embedded in such structures.

Narrative power is a relational and dialogic process oscillating and undulating throughout the social world and working to pattern the degree of control people experience and have over their own lives and the lives of others. We can speak of narrative power relations as domination and regulation. Produced ubiquitously in everyday living, narrative power sensitizes us to the ways lives are asymmetrical and can be dominated, shaped and influenced (sometimes damaged and exploited) by stories; how, in turn, people resist and sometimes empower themselves through new stories. To talk of narratives as empowering is to engage in a language of liberation and the capacity to do things; to talk of narratives as dominant is to suggest a language of control and regulation, of a stable overruling of others – and it raises the issue of how people will comply with this. Stories flow into lives making some abundant in capacity (empowered, actualized) and others diminished (inferiorized, marginalized, weak, victimized.

Stories shape the lives of others. There is *a continuum of influence and coercion*: at one end, there are the gentle ways in which we influence each other in our everyday lives through stories, and at the other lies the more brutal coercion, torture and violence of hard power – while many narratives are willingly consented to, others are much more visibly controlling, regulative and forceful. Some narratives will be authoritative and legitimate; others will not.

Narrative actions are processual. Narratives flow into power situations, making some open, flexible and participatory, and others closed, rigid and limiting. Narrative power flows into dialogues through the habitual networks of social activity, making some alive with possibilities (democratic, participatory, enhanced) and others infused with oppression and dominance (hierarchic, authoritarian, degraded). Power makes narrative claims and generates narrative conflicts, leading to a contentious politics. And, ultimately, narrative actions and narrative power are animated through the dramaturgy of performance and performativity as it flows through the whole global negotiated networked social order – controlling and empowering, closing and opening, making some things possible and others impossible. Narrative power can ultimately congeal into negotiated narrative assemblages. The power to tell or not tell a story under the conditions of one's own choosing is part of the wide social and political process.

Deep infrastructures shape narrative power

Where does this power of our narrative realities come from? What are the sources of power?[15] Most directly, narrative power is grounded in dominance–subordination relations. It is to be found in asymmetrical narrative actions as people live their lives in wider historically structured social worlds. Table 2.2 suggests narrative power is generated through and enmeshed in: (1) social institutions, (2) communications, (3) social location, and (4) everyday life.

Table 2.2 The infrastructure of dialogic narrative power: four sources

Sources of dialogic narrative power	Examples	Infrastructure focus on
1 Institutional	Stories of power: economic, political, cultural, violence, etc.	Social institutions such as economy, government, religion
2 Communicative	The language, writing, print, media and digitalism of stories	Communicative worlds Media worlds Digital worlds
3 Locational	Stories situated at the intersections of class, gender, ethnicity, age, disability, sexuality, nation, etc.	Social divisions Inequalities Social movements Intersectionalities
4 Everyday	The lived stories of everyday life: at home, prison, work, in the street, etc.	Situations and encounters

By *institutions*, I mean the big things, such as the state, violence, the economy or culture and religion (Mann, 1986–2013).[16] By *communications*, I mean media and digital: in the twenty-first century, this has become so pre-eminent that it must be seen as a major source of power in its own right. Stories are generated through the power of media and digital worlds, contain powerful messages, and then in turn exert enormous power over our lives (Castells, 2009; Thompson, 1995). By social *locations*, I raise at least ten positional dimensions: from our economic standing, gender, ethnicity, age, religion and sexuality, to our health, community, nation, and on to our wider links with the environment. These all shape power in the human world and will be found in the stories we tell: our class stories, our stories of nation, our race stories. They connect to each other through processes often now called intersectionality (Collins and Bilge, 2016).

And, finally, by *everyday*, I mean the stories that arise through the power of the social situation of everyday life: in face-to-face encounters, in families, communities, crowds and audiences, school, refugee camps, prisons. Ultimately, all power rises up from everyday life: it is what makes power happen throughout history; and increasingly it is the digital everyday that is becoming more and more prominent (Bratsis, 2007; Highfield, 2016). The stories we tell get shaped through our asymmetrical encounters with others: embodied, emotional selves serve as the locus of action; our daily situations establish the routine practices and strategies we deploy; and, within this, there are key issues of resources available (or not available) to people (economic, social, cultural, embodied, etc.). For example, living in a prison, a concentration camp or a refugee tent circumscribes relations in an almost total way. Universities also dictate the kinds of actions and stories that can and cannot be told, as do newsrooms, social movements, shops, texting and committee meetings. While much storytelling is mundane, it is always embedded in political relations.

Understanding narrative power will always keep bringing us back to these. They can be seen as an infrastructure of narrative power. It is not an abstraction: it is lived and breathed in the situated actions and the selves of everyday life within wider social and mediated structures. Power flows through human actions as they are played out. And, again, it turns out we cannot usually choose any old stories that we like: they are structured through power relations. This is narrative power.

Narratives encode the struggle for human value

Stories are all about human values.[17] And values are central to human life. Some – religious parables, ethical exemplars, moral tales, political propaganda – are apparent because they are very explicit about this. Likewise, the vast advertising, celebrity and promotional industry is centrally a peddler of stories about consumption and material and monetary values. Children's stories have a long lineage of being moral fables, suggesting issues of goodness and naughtiness. News is essentially a parade of moral and political stories. And documentaries usually have not-so-hidden value agendas. Role models of values are embedded in many of these tales. It will be hard to find any narrative that is not ultimately about the rich varieties of human values.

But valuative work, assembled over the millennia via religion, lawmakers, philosophy and everyday life wisdoms, are always lodged in ambivalence and antinomy. Ethical, moral and political issues may be central to being human, but they are always plural and in tension. They do not make life easy. Ultimately, politics itself is always a struggle over these differing human values. And across different groups around the world, stories have taken different genealogical pathways to their different value stances. They bring with them not just a sense of the good, but also a sense of the bad, and the righteous.

Stories highlight the ways in which humans face their everyday

problems – their 'slings and arrows of outrageous fortune' – in practical ways: often as (unstated) dilemmas (or binaries). Philosophers
usually speak about such problems very abstractly, but stories help
ground them in the details of ambiguous, often emotional, everyday
living. Wayne Booth (1988) has indeed claimed that reading can be
an ethical act and that reading good stories brings the power to make
us good or better people. Recently a new field – narrative ethics – has
emerged to deal with all this. Here the feminist philosopher Hilde
Lindemann Nelson tells us just how much of our ethical life could
come from stories:

> Narrativists have claimed, among other things, that stories of one
> kind or another are required: (1) to teach us our duties, (2) to guide
> morally good action, (3) to motivate morally good action, (4) to justify
> action on moral grounds, (5) to cultivate our moral sensibilities, (6) to
> enhance our moral perception, (7) to make actions of persons morally
> intelligible, and (8) to reinvent ourselves as better persons. (Nelson
> 2001, p. 36)

In looking at a narrative humanity, we see that our stories harbour
what I have previously called 'the grounded moralities of everyday
life' (Plummer, 2003, ch. 7). From birth to death, I see stories as
a spiralling circle of values from our innermost vulnerabilities out
to the widest cosmos (see table 2.3). Starting with our own human
vulnerabilities arising from body, environment and relationships, we
begin by trying to make sense of our frailty in the world (*stories of
existential values*). We are helped in this (or not) through direct relations with close others: through human relationships and how to deal
with these from birth onwards. Here we start to learn how to be cared
for by others and also how to care for ourselves: to be kind towards
others; to develop compassion towards, and ultimately recognize,
both their and our own vulnerability and right to dignity. This is what
every mother is likely to know about her baby and it is the broadest
ethical background to life and story (*stories of relational (attachment)
values*). And as we move outwards, in what has been called a circle
of sympathy, so we acquire broader values. We start to ask questions about what it might mean to live in a fair and better society
for all. Here, issues of autonomy (freedom) and authority (power
and dominance) appear. along with issues of social justice, rights,
equity and fairness (*stories of social justice values*). This may eventually
lead to very broad questions – we ask: How we can live a virtuous
life in this world? This is as Paul Ricoeur (1992, p. 172) succinctly

Table 2.3 The struggle for human value in life and story: antinomies and ambivalences of narrative

Source	Questions	Possible value antinomies[18]
(1) Existential Being human: our unique differences, agency, capabilities, vulnerabilities and value	At birth we are surrounded by problems posed by the human condition: of being, body, relationships, environment and living. How best to exist in the world?	Ways of being-in-the-world *agency – passivity* *autonomy – constraint* *creativity – destructiveness* *resilience – weakness* *dignity – dehumanization*
(2) Relationships and attachments Living with self, others and community	From birth to death we live, connect and relate with other people. How best to live with others in the world?	Ways of relating in the world *altruism – selfishness* *empathy/compassion – indifference* *care – neglect* *kindness – cruelty* *love – hate* *belonging – isolation*
(3) Social justice How the state, economy and society work	We live in a society. What is a good society, and good governance? How might this be achieved?	The good society is built on: *reciprocity v. narcissism* *social justice v. injustice* *social equality v. inequality* *democracy v. authoritarianism* *social rights and obligations*
(4) Virtues and human flourishing Living the best we can in life and society	How to do the best during one's time on earth? What is this best – this 'good'? The problem of virtue (and virtue ethics)	Seeking human virtue *beauty – ugliness* *knowledge – ignorance* *truth – falsehood* *… and 'multiple virtues'*
(5) World– universe Living with other cultures and world – being in the pluriverse	How to live with others across human variety, cultures and nations? How should we live in the cosmos?	At peace in the cosmos *cosmopolitanism – parochialism* *sustainability – neglect* *peace – war* *cosmic – local* *hope – despair*

puts it, 'aiming for the "good life" with and for others in just institutions'. Here are issues of what has long been called 'virtue ethics' (*stories of virtuous and flourishing values*). We may think about the injunction that we should 'Proclaim the natural dignity and inherent equality of all human beings in all places and in all circumstances' (Tremblay, 2009, p. 17). And, ultimately, we have to find our place across cultures and in the cosmos. Little human beings can think big things (*stories of world–universe values*). A certain cosmopolitanism also becomes necessary.

Narrative power is animated through drama

To change the world, to set narrative power fully to work, a story needs to become dynamically alive. And to bring narrative alive, we need drama: the drama within the text and the drama of actions around it. If story gives us the plot and narrative the mechanisms, then drama is the mode that can really bring it all alive. And we have long known that human social life itself is dramaturgical. From Aeschylus, Sophocles and Euripides, through Shakespeare and Pirandello, to today's street theatre, political dance, rap music and protest performance, the theatrical qualities of everyday life can hardly be missed. Any introduction to drama education will tell us all this, and a lot more besides. Table 2.4 suggests some of the key elements of drama.

All this seems quite straightforward: we can see drama at work on stage, television, radio, in film, video, music, spectacle, sport and, increasingly, through digital media. More: we do not need to go to the theatre to see drama – we can find it in everyday life. In *Daniel Deronda*, talking about politics, George Eliot remarks that 'there is no action possible without a little acting'. We can find drama in the power of religion, the stock exchange, celebrity or the election speech. Indeed, in the earliest work of Erving Goffman (1922–82), *The Presentation of Self in Everyday Life* ([1956] 1966), this dramaturgical metaphor is put right at the heart of understanding how everyday human life works. It shows how all of us become key presenters and managers of the impressions we give of our selves – through language, dress and prose – as we move across scenes and settings using our various poses and props. And to turn this round fully: politics itself is dramaturgical, a 'theatocracy'. Both Aristotle (1991, 1996) and Cicero (2004) long ago showed the skills of political oratory, and the power of dramatic rituals that often accompany politics.

Once set out like this, then, it is not hard to see how so much power, in all its forms, functions with drama in politics. Stories are energized into power relations through drama and performance. Scripted staging, acting and audiences are present in political elections, political campaigning, parliamentary and congressional speeches, ceremonial events, news reporting, social movements and pressure groups. We can trace it throughout history: in corona-

Table 2.4 Storytelling and the key elements of narrative dramaturgy

Scripting	The story (with its characters, plots, tensions, themes, etc.) now becomes a dramatic script (either closed or improvisational) to be enacted.
Staging	A creative or production team comes together to produce the drama. A producer will bring the whole event together. A director will orchestrate all the key elements. Matters of design, costume and dress, background and scene setting, movement and choreography, voice, sound, etc., will then have to be attended to so the production will be staged well.
Actors	A script is cast, often with the help of a casting agency: there will be lead actors, supporting actors and often an ensemble too.
Roles	Roles form scripts, guide expectations and will be coordinated and performed.
Performance and performativity	The languages of scripts anticipate what is to be done: the presentation of the production is assembled though body, emotions, words and deeds.
Audience, spectators	The story is presented to audiences who read, watch, listen and appreciate the drama.
Aesthetics	The human dimensions of rhetorical skill, embodiment, engagements, feelings, cognition and thoughts, stylistics, 'poetics of representation', appreciation, etc., can then bring it all together into a stylistic whole.

tions, revolutions, pageantry. These days, we can even speak of the narrative nation and the performing state. We can sense a deep connection between power, narrative and drama, and many political events of recent times have been so analysed. It is there in the theatricalities of the Hong Kong Umbrella Movement. We see it in the Polish post-1989 Solidarity as it stages freedom in a 'theatrics of the round table' - 'a masterpiece of performative democracy'. We find the debates over climate change are social drama. Obama's presidential victory is a performance victory; the Egyptian 'revolution' is *performative*, and the entirety of life in North Korea is seen as engulfed in scripting and stagecraft.[19]

Two key ideas to guide us here are performance and performativity. *Performance* is quite easy to see and grasp – we can all see (and often 'do') drama – while *performativity*, by contrast, is a little more complex. Drawing from the philosopher Austin, the idea suggests how words can anticipate actions, how words have consequences, effects and affects. Performativity puts narratives into actions, making stories come alive by naming them and recognizing them, ultimately creating a kind of self-validating, self-fulfilling linguistic prophecy.

So performance is an action, performativity is an effect of language, and both are important in dramaturgy. Narrative power brings together both performance and performativity.

Narrative power is dialogic, contentious and fragile

Manuel Castells once said: 'wherever there is power, there is counter power' (Castells, 2012, p. 5). We might add to this that wherever there is narrative, there is counter-narrative. Wherever there are human values, there are counter-values. There is at best a dialogue, at worst a war over such matters. People dialogue; stories clash; politics adjudicates. Narrative life is continually contested; political life is perpetually contentious.

Stories themselves reveal this: there is the basic and probably universal plot of situation, tension and resolution. A good story will always frame a tension – usually a conflict – that ideally leads to a resolution. Without tension, a story cannot work well. And power too will always imply dominance and a dominated – agonistics and conflict, contest, cooperation. So both story and power live in perpetual tension. Narrative life, being bound up with variety, vulnerability and the search for meaning, dwells in a fragile landscape.

This imagery of narrative power I have been creating must suggest just how fragile, complex and unstable its workings are. We dwell with human differences, language variety, unique vulnerabilities, mimesis and labyrinth realities, along with the multiplicities of actions, conflicts, empathies, dialogues, embodiments and performativities. Wow! This is a lot to deal with. All these things suggest that narratives can never be simple and straightforward. More, they live in a constantly changing world: media mutate, people change, societies transform, and governments totter from one contested crisis to another. Time and story wait for nobody. They move on: complex, contingent and emergent. Finding the truth about a story, as we will see later, will never be easy.

This leads me to sense a world of narrative fragility generating major puzzles. We can start with *the puzzles of plurality* so central to the thinking of William James, Hannah Arendt and others. We live in a world of multiplicities and plurals: finding the singular is rare, probably impossible – and if found, it can be dangerous. People may like the singular – it feels safer – but it is rarely possible. Then, in seeming

contradiction, there are *the puzzles of phenomenological uniqueness* dem-
onstrated in the works of authors as varied as Proust, Virginia Woolf,
Sigmund Freud and many others. Any tale told is but a gloss on the
rich and sometimes dark streams of consciousness and lived angst
of any life. Chekhov writes about the complexities of a kiss, while
Proust dwells on the multiple memories created by a madeleine![20]
Thirdly, there are always *the puzzles of contingent time–space*: no story
is fixed outside of a flow of ever-changing moments and locations
that perpetually shape them. Stories have their own stories as they
shift and change moving through time and space, from birth to death
to afterlife. Stories do not, and cannot, stay fixed. Some stories show
potentials for permanence (for telling us some grand truths about
our lives and humanity), but, ultimately, they all dwell in worlds of
perpetual change. Narrative is hence never-ending, always facing *the
puzzles of emergence*. Narrative, being dialogic, cannot suggest simple
direct causal links between power and story, or inevitable outcomes.
That would bring a crude and unnecessary determinism and closure.
Instead, and more gently, it reveals a never-ending, two-way narrative
process which fosters uneven and perpetual change: power, narrative
and story feed on each other and move the world on, for good or bad.
There is always more to narrative than power – just as there is always
more to power than narrative. But when they engage in human dialogues, the consequences can be striking. Storytelling opens up doors
providing opportunities for many things. There is a perpetual human
open-endedness, change and indeterminacy to social life.

Narratives have limits

We have travelled far: but now for a major caution. On a bad day,
I start to doubt some of the arguments I am making. Indeed, this is
what being critical partially means: thinking, arguing, pondering and
raising doubts against yourself. So I act: get up, make a coffee and
read the news narratives on the media. Syria is in ruins; more terrorist attacks; refugees are drowning; another famine is announced;
Korea tests yet more nuclear missiles; there are even more corruption
stories; another government topples; more women abused; human
cruelty abounds. All these are the stories of the day and they disturb
me greatly – a visceral angst and anger ascends. Why do I read
this every day? What disturbs me too is that these are indeed just
stories: I am not there with the action, with what is going on. But
then again, even if I was there, what I would find would be agonized

narrative actions painfully emerging out of trauma. But they would still be stories told. I am reduced by story and narrative to the role of bystander. How do we get to real humanity? Do our stories ultimately reduce our humanity? *Where does this storytelling end and the real life begin?*

Stories are widespread in social life and can do many things. But they are no panacea and have very serious limits. I want to understand the working of stories and to ask how we may do them a little better. Indeed, I turn at the end of many chapters, and in the final chapter, to consider how we can enhance stories and build upon them to help lives flourish: to build a politics of narrative humanity. But obviously doing this can be no solution to all the world's ills. And so I have a few somewhat ironic cautionary comments to hang above my desk to remind me that, even as I take stories seriously, I must always also simultaneously be thinking beyond them.

- *Beware that a narrative reality is never actual reality.* I find the relation between the two is highly problematic and so a major issue to keep returning to is the reality puzzle. How can we distinguish between the fictional reality, narrative reality, narrative truth and *the really real reality*? Indeed, is there a true reality behind the story? In chapter 7, I turn to the ideas of narrative wisdom to help us continue in making sense of this.
- *Beware of overstressing the word and the text.* It so easy to focus too much on texts and ignore the real embodied, emotional human interactions around them. This is *the overtextualization of the world*. Much literary theory and academic writing does this. Hence, I have introduced the key idea of narrative actions (and interactions and relationships), and return to embodied, emotional human beings all the time, which I see as ways of moving beyond the important but limited text. Stories on their own say nothing: we need to see what people do with stories in their everyday worlds.
- *Beware of individualizing.* Very often, I find narratives become only personal stories and lack a concern with the underlying causes of structure, history and power embedded within them. Hence, I stress the fact that narratives are Janus-faced: it is usually easy to see the personal face of stories and that people matter, but we need also to counterbalance this by learning to think about the social, history and power. Stories take us not only deep down into the psyche but also deep down into the social structure. The truth rarely lives in the individual surface story.
- *Beware of abstractions.* And finally, too often I find myself wander-

ing into a dense and almost incomprehensible world of concepts, abstractions, theory, leaving behind real people (as I have in this chapter!). Theory is important but always limited: the devil lies in the detail. Always return to the detail of the story.

All of which is to suggest a profound irony of this book. While we need to take our stories very seriously, we will always need to think and move beyond them.

3

Narrative Power as a Struggle
for Human Value

Do we want to live in a controlled society or do we want to live in a free society?

Edward Snowden, *Citizen Four*

The story of whistleblower Edward Snowden is another story of our times. In 2015, the two-hour film *Citizen Four* won the Academy Award for best documentary. Shot in real time, it told the story of former Central Intelligence Agency (CIA) employee Edward Snowden as he leaked classified information from the US National Security Agency (NSA) in 2013, exposing their work to the media through the investigative journalist Glenn Greenwald and the *Guardian* reporter Ewen MacAskill. Most of the film is shot live by controversial filmmaker Laura Poitras, mainly in a hotel room in Hong Kong where Snowden is in hiding. It ends with his departure to Moscow for safety. Filmed every step of the way, it is slow but thrilling. The film shows how the NSA has been gathering information about its citizens and how it turns Snowden into a criminal on the run. It takes us to a Brave New Global Digital World where our private stories are now seen to be under the surveillance of the state; it shows us the significance of hacking and it reveals how our narratives are now of global interest to the state. Snowden is another iconic story in search of a better world.

To add layers of complexity, the Hollywood director Oliver Stone made another film of *Snowden* in 2016 – which mirrors the documentary in a number of ways. (It was not funded in the United States and was not a success there.) So now we have reality, documentary and movie. And more: there are other films, many books and even games that have resulted in what has been called 'The Snowden Effect' – whereby the story has led to an increased public concern about security and surveillance. Snowden challenges us: 'Do we want to live in a controlled society or do we want to live in a free society? That's the fundamental question' (Snowden, 2014; Greenwald, 2015; Harding, 2016).

Here is a story of power, making explicit the role of the state in surveillance. But it also shows the power of the story – a 'Snowden Effect' that may bring about social change. And here too is life working to make sense of it all: a struggle for cosmopolitan or world human value. The idea of narrative power leads us to ask: *How does narrative shape power; and, conversely, how does power shape narrative?* The focus ultimately is always dual: there is a power within the story (we tell stories of power) but the story can also generate power – the power *of* narrative. Human social life can be seen as an agonistic struggle over human value, with stories as the harbingers of such values. As we confront *stories of power*, so the *power of stories* nudges our lives along. We inhabit a narrative reality where stories have the power to shape our values. And this is the basic distinction on which this chapter spins: the narratives of power and the power of narratives.

In the first part of this chapter, I simply illustrate a few of the many dominant meta-narratives in which we dwell, highlighting the way they create a canopy of human values. In a second part, I sketch out some of the ways these stories shape our lives: personally, relationally and culturally. The scene set, we will be then ready for the plot.

The stories of power: canopies of world human values

The stories of Malala, Luz Arce and the Tahrir protest can all be seen as struggles over what it means to be human. They speak to human vulnerability, relationships developed, fairness pursued, a good life and a better world. Throughout the ages, people have tried to make sense of a very wide range of stories, often locating underlying forms or patterns. Very commonly, such stories are built into a morphology, a simple classification claiming our stories speak to: (a) journeys/voyages/quests; (b) sufferings/troubles; (c) conflicts/battles; (d) consummations / finding the light; and (e) coming home.[1] It is not hard here to sense a key organizing story trope of human differences, sufferings, conflicts and consummations (maybe even redemption). Indeed, there is almost a master story that starts with the brute fact of humanly unique differences and vulnerabilities that almost inevitably generate tensions and conflicts over values that in turn needs some kind of resolution. This is the very stuff of stories, the basic plot of *narratives of human endeavours and suffering*: it is there with Edward Snowden, as well as the *Iliad, Middlemarch* and *Harry Potter*.

While there do seem to be basic plots to stories, my concern here is not simply with the story but with narrative actions. Previously, we have seen the key sources of the infrastructure of narrative power. Here they are mirrored in stories. In what follows, I sketch a few instances of the way stories are about power – the narrative reality of power stories. Table 3.1 suggests a wider listing, but here I can only deal with a few examples.

Narrative Values of Governance Power

I start with a most apparent story. In his study of *Narrative Politics*, Frederick Mayer says: 'Storytelling is the lifeblood of politics . . . it is what politicians do, what organizers do, what lobbyists do, what joiners and voters and protesters do. That stories matter is not news to those who practice politics' (2014, p. viii).

Politics is stuffed full of stories performed though language in 'political spectacles' (Edelman, 1977, 1988). Here are narrative

Table 3.1 Some meta-narratives of power and their stories

1 Institutional	Stories of politics and governance (democracy stories, state stories, social movement stories, cosmopolitan stories); stories of economics (work stories, business stories, finance stories, money stories); stories of cultural institutions – religion, education, science, media; stories of violence (war stories).
2 Communicative (mediated/digital)	Stories of news, stories of celebrities, stories of advertising, promotional stories, stories of entertainment, stories of sport. All digital stories – Facebook tales, tweets, Snapshot images, YouTube.
3 Locational	Stories of class, stories of work, stories of gender, stories of ethnicity, stories of age, stories of religion, stories of family, stories of health, stories of disability, stories of sexualities, stories of community, stories of nation, stories of environment, stories of the cosmos.
4 Everyday	Stories of our daily interactions – the practices and strategies we deploy; stories of an embodied, emotional self as a locus of action; stories of the resources available to people (economic, social, cultural, embodied, etc.); stories of organizations

actions of power galore. Elections generate dramatic stories from competing sides; social movements and trade unions generate new stories of protest; blogs and tweets tell political stories. They become the bread and butter of the news media. We find stories in election manifestos, political memoirs, news coverage, commissions, tribunals, personal testimony, celebrity stories, activist art, protest movements, blog activism, political tweets – as well as in documentary film production, music making, poetic vision and art across the world: all those media which tell us daily of a politically failing world we need to change. And popular culture is simply rife with political stories, from *All the President's Men, The Lives of Others* and *Malcolm X* to *The West Wing, House of Cards, Game of Thrones.* (See, for examples, Alexander, 2011a, 2017; Butler, 2005; Couldry, 2010; Davis, 2002; Poletta, 2006; Selbin, 2010; Solinger et al., 2008.)

I write this book against a perpetually changing background of dramatic political storytelling. Here are the tales of Trump and Obama, Putin and Xi Jinping – and all the kings and queens, chieftains and presidents that have come before them. The history of United States presidents has been looked at as a history of stories: Evan Cornog's *The Power and the Story* (2004) looks at the multiple presidential narratives from George Washington to George W. Bush, and claims that 'Presidential life stories are the most important tools of persuasion in American political life.' As I am writing, we witness the departure of Obama and the arrival of Trump: the narrative contrasts could not be greater. The world of Obama's elegant speeches drawing from full-blown rhetorical artifice and a wide knowledge of principles of democratic governance, and the short, angry, almost ugly tweets of Trump, are two wildly contrasting visions of political narrative reality. It is not just that their content is oppositional, so too are their modes of storytelling and the ways they present their political selves. Much has been said about this. What these examples show, as we have seen before, is the artifice, rhetoric, binary nature, drama and narrative of politics (Alexander, 2012b; Fuchs, 2018).

Likewise, in the UK, the Brexit referendum consumes UK politics with a flood of stories: over twenty books have been published with titles like *Unleashing Demons: The Inside Story of Brexit, The Brexit Club: The Inside Story* and *Alice in Brexitland.* There is nothing new about this. Leading UK political scientists Anthony King and Ivor Crewe have examined a very wide range of 'blunder-related horror stories' involving the UK governments (King and Crewe, 2013, p. xi). But such stories can be found with all governments. And they are usually hushed-up stories kept in silence.[2]

Narrative Values of Religious Power

The history of narrative power could readily be written as the history of the narrative actions of religions. Religions are always about more than religion: they are about 'ways of life', 'world building' and crafting 'sacred sites' that become inseparable from issues of values and power (Berger, 1967, p. 3; Laine, 2014; MacGregor, 2018). Simply to visit the spectacular religious buildings and artefacts of the past, and their vast activities of narrative production, is to sense how people living in the time would have been overwhelmed by the sheer magnitude of the drama of the temples in which they worshipped, and how overflowing with stories those sacred sites were (and still are) (Barkan and Barclay, 2017). Most people ask the big questions about how the world was created, how people should live, what happens after we die, what the meaning of life is. And they get stories as answers: through parables, rituals, songs, art, poetics, architecture, festivals and pilgrimages. The Romans, for example, built their temples to their multiple gods. Many of the earliest writings and printings were religious stories.

And they take on an important aura as they dramatize their stories with great ritual passion. This religious/spiritual body is largely a performance body. The Hindus tell their tales and enact performances around multiple gods and goddesses in the mythical narratives of the *Vedas*, the *Mahabharata*, the *Ramayana*; Judaism gives us the *Tanakh*, the *Talmud*, the *Midrash*; Christianity gives us the Bible, Old and New Testaments, full of parables and stories. The Qur'an is the word of Allah revealed to Muhammad during the last years of his life: most Muslims try to learn to read it in the original Arabic, read part of it every day and perform daily ceremonies related to it. Buddha's words – the *dharma* – were passed on by word of mouth, as most religions were originally. Hundreds of thousands of smaller religions also tell stories, making their stories sacred. And religious narratives become deeply embedded in ritual, and performative enactments: in chants, confessions, music, prayer, dance, pilgrimages, festivals, sacraments, daily routines, icons, buildings – even wars. Throughout time, as today, religious stories exert extraordinary special powers over their peoples. Neil MacGregor has documented all of this in his exhibition, radio programmes and book, *Living with the Gods* (2018).

This is no less true today than it was in the past. The contemporary crisis of world religions and fundamentalism is a crisis of storytelling, as modernity and secularism create new challenges. Religion is widely performed and becomes increasingly digital with the arrival of the electronic church, online worship, religious identity games and even digital jihadism. The power of religious narrative is ubiquitous and constantly renewing itself throughout the world (Campbell, 2012; Chambers et al., 2013).

Narrative Values of Economic Power

Never neutral realities, economies are always a major source of power. And *economic narratives* display the power of how economies work, providing us with myths and languages to make sense of them. There is a grand human cast of economic storytellers from Adam Smith and Karl Marx to Friedrich Hayek and on (see Butler-Brown, 2017). They have brought us economic stories galore of *Homo economicus* with sweeping meta-narratives, embracing all in their wake: the grand narratives of capitalism, socialism, liberalism and the rest, captured in the writings of economic historians and the tales of bubbles, crashes and crises.[3]

Currently, they provide the elaborate ideological machinery of neo-liberalism that attempts to make us think that economy, wealth and GDP are the most important features of a society. Here is a landslide of narrative actions around markets and freedom, money and financing, work and consumerism, brands and branding, promotional cultures, poverty and deprivations, crisis and corruptions. Such stories are rarely out of the news, and they sit at the heart of our everyday passionate stories about how we should work, make money, shop, sell, find a home, make profits, be poor, be greedy and be generous. These are the dominant stories of our time; but this has not always been so. We hear (and tell) stories that derive from money, markets, finance institutions and public relations.

They also provide popular culture with some fine novels such as Robert Tressell's *The Ragged-Trousered Philanthropists* and John Steinbeck's *The Grapes of Wrath*, which show us how the economy can bedevil the poor. Philip Mirowski and Dieter Plehwe (2015) tell the tale of *The Road from Mont Pelerin* about the people who made the neo-liberal world and their politics. By contrast, the films of Michael Moore's *Capitalism: A Love Story* (2009) and Charles Ferguson's *Inside Job* (2010) show the corruptions and failures of neo-liberal economies. GDP has been graced as a 'Great Invention' and has its own story (Pilling, 2018). Meanwhile, Chrystia Freeland's *Plutocrats* (2012) takes us into the world of the global super-rich. Economics is a storytelling activity bound up with the very economic system itself.[4]

Those who doubt that the idea of the story is really relevant to economics should look no further than the world of advertising and public relations. In a telling study, Christian Salmon ([2007] 2017) locates 'the narrative world of brands', and shows how 'the invention of storytelling management' creates a 'propaganda empire'. Here we are witness to the rise of *a promotional narrative culture*. Business has taken on a strong storytelling strategy through the narrative actions of branding and creating logos. To sell their commodities, every major brand has to sell its story: to watch their advertising is potentially to be trapped in their narrative. We do not have to look far to discover a major industry of courses, training and books such as *The Leader's Guide to Storytelling: Mastering the Art and Discipline of Business Narratives* (2011) and *Business Storytelling for Dummies* (2014). As we move through the branding and logos of fashion (the stories of top-end Louis Vuitton, Prada and Tiffany to lower-end Primark, Lidl, T. K. Maxx), of digitalism (Apple, Microsoft, Amazon, Facebook, YouTube, Twitter), and other major brands (Coca-Cola, McDonald's, Shell, Mitsubishi, Toyota, Walt Disney), we see the latest manifestations of what Adorno called the culture industry: 'The entire practice of the culture industry transfers the profit motive naked into cultural forms' (Adorno, 1944] 1991, p. 99). It is now also a promotional culture – and one that has gone global too.[5]

Consider too one major counter-example to all this: the writings of the Canadian author Naomi Klein, who is one of a very large group of activist storytellers. Across several key bestsellers, she tells stories that show the wrong workings of big capitalism, big governments and big globalization – and the human and environmental damage they do. Her first major work, *No Logo* (1999), told the story of the rise of Branding and the Superbrand: the Swoosh (Nike), the Shell (Shell Oil), the Arches (McDonald's) and countless others. In detailed tales, we hear how the brand targets certain audiences, creates an image and a story, and works to conceal some of its working practices (mega- profits and poor work relations). In her most recent book, *No Is Not Enough* (2017) she examines 'how Trump won by becoming the ultimate brand'. There is economic narrative power at work across the world.

Narrative Values of Violent Power

War is the most extreme case of political violence and humanity's struggle over value. Since 3600 BCE, it has been estimated that some 14,500 major wars have been waged, killing some 4 billion people. In 2015, about a fifth of the world was in conflict (there were some thirty wars being conducted). Throughout history, wars have always been one of the major ongoing narratives (and activities) of human life: from Homer's *Iliad* and Virgil's *Aeneid* through Shakespeare's *Henry V* to Tolstoy's *War and Peace* and on to computer games like *World of Warcraft*. The history of human life is the history of competing narratives at war with each other. There is a tragic vision of humanity here. Simply: people will not agree. But ultimately it reveals a key dilemma for all of human life: that of conflict or cooperation? For we can also find societies and groups coming together to share stories and narratives and find ways of cooperating with each other, despite their human differences. So, along with friction, there may also be co-operation.

For the sociologist Philip Smith (2005), *every war has its roots in the ways we tell and interpret stories*. He asks why we wage wars – 'How do we bring ourselves to believe that the sacrifice of our troops is acceptable?' – and examines the modern cases of the Suez Crisis of 1956, the Gulf War of 1991, and the War in Iraq of 2003. He shows how cultural structures and narratives shape our understandings, providing us with stories of national identities and tales of war and anti-war rationales. Comparing these stories generated about war between different cultures, he suggests that conflicts are not over real worlds but interpretive schemes. In my terms, they are about the struggle over values. At the heart of all this, he suggests, there are 'binary codes' and contests that have to be negotiated around various themes.

The power of narratives: the value of stories in life

So, we live daily with a multiplicity of stories of power. As we encounter stories of power (religion, economy, violence, etc.) and their values out there in the world of narrative reality, so we act towards them in our everyday lives. Ultimately, we can take them into our being – our personhoods. We do not just make narratives of power, they also make us. There is a flow and dynamism to this narrative power that works on three levels: the public, the relational and the personal. Stories are crafted and layered between our outer (public) worlds and our most inner (personal) life. As we move between the public and private, new stories can emerge in the spaces between them: in embodied human relationships and narrative actions. These three-layered worlds are in constant dialogue with each other.

And this will bring both good news and bad news. Our stories might work to stimulate imagination, make life safe and secure, generate new ways of seeing, bring emancipation, But they may also work to narrow horizons, render life fearful and threatening, and regulate, restrict and repress us. Table 3.2 outlines some of the major functions of stories.

Stories as Personhood: The Personal Role

Personal or inner-world stories are the stories we tell ourselves, the stories we listen to, the stories in our minds. This suggests a psychology and psychodynamics of self and story: making bridges between

Table 3.2 The power of stories: how we make stories work for us

The power of the ...	The work of stories to ...
Personal	Create autobiography – how a life holds together: continuity and coherence
	Make cognition and meaning – how a person thinks and makes sense of life
	Express emotion – the affective: how a person is moved and feels
	Do embodiment – how a person comes to be a body
	Assemble self and identity – how a person comes to be a person
	Make valuations – how humans struggle for truth, ethics, aesthetics, good societies
Social and cultural	Make social worlds – how a society builds itself through storytelling practices
	Educate – how a society informs, represents, knows and imagines itself
	Regulate and mark boundaries – how a society creates order, holds itself together, controls
	Inspire – how a society dreams, plays and imagines
	Valuate – how a society struggles for values: truth, ethics, aesthetics, good societies
	Transform – how a society can change itself
Relational and interactive	Create bridges, connect selves – how society and culture connect with the personal
	Create dialogues and empathy – how human interaction generates understandings
	Facilitate bonding and belonging – how communities and groups connect
	Engage in 'othering' – how outsiders and enemies are created
	Make valuations – how values, ethics, aesthetics, truths emerge out of actions

the unconscious and the body, feelings and the self. Freudians may seek the Oedipal tales within; Jungians may seek the mythic archetypes that guide our storytelling; cognitivists may seek the story genie in the brain; and psychologists may locate the stories we live by. We simply breathe stories into our lives, letting them infuse their way into our thoughts, senses, feelings and bodies, encouraging the development of subjectivities, selves, our personhood and very being. And we may hardly know we are even doing it. Consider four ways we do this: through self, cognition, emotions and embodiment.

At the most basic level, stories provide part of the tool kit for narrating the 'self we live by': 'my story defines who I am: we each seek to provide our scattered and often confusing experiences with a sense of coherence by arranging the episodes of our lives into stories' (McAdams, 1993: 11). The prominent neurologist Oliver Sachs (1993-2015) opens his book of essays on brain disorders, *The Man Who Mistook His Wife for a Hat* (1985), with this celebrated observation: '"We have each of us, a life story, an inner narrative – whose continuity, whose sense is our lives . . . A man needs such a narrative, a continuous inner narrative to maintain his identity.' Likewise, though from a very different viewpoint, Judith Butler (2005) speaks of 'Giving an account of oneself'.[6]

Crucial to this sense of narrative personhood is the idea that stories give our lives *meaning, value* and *cognitive power*: they make us pay attention, process and organize information, structure our interests, foster our values, map out our knowledge. When this fails, they can limit and cripple us. For the humanist psychologist Donald Polkinghorne, narrative is 'the primary form by which human experience is made meaningful' (Polkinghorne, 1988, p. 1). It gives us the power to create meaning for our moments, document our daily doings, and ultimately build a potential canopy of human life values: a life, a shelter, a coherence. They can sediment to become our memories, good and bad.

Stories are powerfully connected to all our senses; as we perform them, they help shape our moods, generating affect and engorging us with emotional narrative power. They can be sensual: they can make us feel passion, structure our sentimental life and feelings. We are moved by stories. Stories have the power to affect love and hate, guilt and shame, sadness and grief: they shudder through our bodies, triggering how we see, feel, listen, touch, smell and, indeed, breathe and live in the world. They can create moods of sympathy, love and compassion – as well as moods of suffering, frustration, despair. Stories produce emotional responses and narrative affect.[7]

Finally, this emotion runs in parallel with our bodies: stories help give us embodied narrative power, or narrative embodiment, helping us not only to make sense of our sensual bodies, but also to shape them. Feminist stories of the body deal, for example, with such issues as eating disorders, reproduction, violence and abuse. Stories of sickness bodies (illness stories) can relay the full panoply of illnesses. (e.g. Frank, 1995; Kleinman, 1988; Plummer, 2012). I recall clearly how framing stories of my own illness helped me deal with many aspects of my ill health. As stories become embodied, so they give us plans and animations for moving our bodies around the world – often in 'fear and loathing', lust and longing, anger and rage. At their worst, our bodies will not listen to stories at all: they become split, cut off, damaged.

Stories as Culture: The Public Role

So far, I have spoken about the personal power of stories, and this is how we see them most commonly. But stories are Janus-faced – and so also look outwards to wider issues of relationships, history and culture. While we may not typically experience stories like this – they seem personal rather than cultural – stories do exert a very definite cultural power: they are central mechanisms of social control, dehumanization and regulation, working both positively and negatively.

Positively, stories can *facilitate connections and belonging*: creating a 'we group'. They can build notions of community, including nations and states, facilitating a sense of peoplehood, 'national identity' and, ultimately, what has been called 'the performance state'. A good story is always needed for group cohesion – a story of who we are and why things are as they are. They can *establish trust*: good stories work in symbolic ways to make people feel secure in the world. More: stories can *foster imagination, innovation and creativity*: it is through stories that people can be inspired, dream impossible dreams, invent new ideas, make new worlds, and sometimes face nightmares. Stories live in science, music, art. They also *provide history and social memory*, serving a significant historical function. The very word 'history' links to story. Stories can tells us stories of our past, becoming our memories, giving shape to our lives. They can memorialize our lives in our families, our schools, our works, our loves, our communities; they speak out from photograph albums, the music we hear and love, and the books we read and cherish. But they can, of course, also fail to do this. Stories can also act as *safety valves* enabling us to escape from life's burdens: for entertainment, carnival, leisure, ritual, diversion and play. Stories also *provide guidelines and memories, maps and scripts for locating our human actions in past, present and future:* it is through stories that people can generate a sense of how they are situated in the wider human world. They can for example, spread the idea of human rights. But not all these maps and memories are for the good: some can suggest trauma and harm.

So, more negatively, stories can also bring intense conflicts between groups with different ethnic, religious, tribal stories. They can bring narrative othering whereby stories display enemies. Conflicts between states are actually a conflict over stories (see Casanova, 2007; R. M. Smith, 2003). They can be the basis for war (e.g. C. Smith, 2003).[8] They can also *regulate and dehumanize lives*: stories can become rule-books and technologies that order what to do, how to behave, and what to believe. They can become part of generating the *Technologies of the Self* (Foucault, 1988). Stories also work to *sustain inequalities*: all cultures tell stories to maintain the power of the dominant groups and reproduce stories that work to justify inequalities, division, social exclusion (Bourdieu, 1984). Stories can also *create and spread cultures of fear*: crime stories, abuse stories, terrorist stories make people feel lives are at risk. Stories can also *generate greed*: market and promotional cultures persistently tell stories of material profit-making.

Just these few examples show that there are very big and important tasks for our little stories to do. Exerting cultural power that can be both emancipatory and regulatory, stories have an almost unbelievable amount of work to do. And in all of this, the problem of mimesis – of representation, of life copying art or art copying life – is never far away.

Stories as Relationships: The Interactional Role

Finally, bridging the public and personal – in the middle, so to speak – is the dynamic that makes them work: what might be called the sphere of *interactive, dramatic, relational stories*. Stories make us connect with people. They create bridges between the public and the personal: between the outer worlds of culture and community and the inner worlds of personhood and body. These are the stories that emerge in our worlds of everyday face-to-face power encounters, the stories we tell to each other in groups, in schools, in hospitals, on street corners – the stories of everyday life.

A striking example of this is the rise of celebrity narratives and power, which bring into focus another form of power: *affective power*. Affective power suggests the 'emotional attachments that audiences have towards celebrities' (Marshall, [1997] 2014, p. xxv). From Valentino to Diana, George Michael to David Bowie, 'a new public intimacy' has been created. These new connections with the media are one-sided and involve a lot of emotional investment from audiences without any obvious reciprocal relationship: they become parasocial relationships bringing one-sided affairs with media narratives that have the illusion of being face-to-face engagements (Rojek, 2015; Zenor, 2014).

It is the narrative self that is crucial in making this bridge: the self leads us to 'the other' – we are not alone. The narrating self gives stories their lived, dynamic, Janus-faced character (inward- and outward-looking), and enables the active 'internalization of reality' (Berger and Luckmann, 1967). Simply put, real breathing and emotional people act towards stories through others: they draw upon the stories given them in the wider culture; they listen to them, make sense of them, and use these ideas in their social life. Stories are, in part, conversations with the self. At the broadest level, as Arthur Frank suggests (2010), they serve as companions: sheltering us from the storms, throughout our lives we recall tales of our birth and childhood, our youth and adulthood, our ageing and dying.

There are many ways in which this can happen, and social psychologists have been helpful in providing accounts of some of these processes.[9] Stories come alive through relationships – through narrative acts, empathy, dialogue and memory, all of which connect us to others. These processes hang together. Stories depend on the processes of role-taking and empathy: we have to be able to take the role of characters in the plots, make sense of them and often empathize with them. The notion of role-taking implies we can, reflexively and reflectively, enter the mind of another and see the world from their point of view. In the classic formulation, the story or text comes to act as a looking-glass self, reflecting the world around it. This is so essential in watching a film, reading a book or sending a text message. Thus, 'Who are the others?' becomes a key question. Harbouring multiple others, positions and characters, stories require, however briefly, that we make mental mappings of the world from others' views. They can enable us to dialogue with others as we converse through stories. This basic understanding underpins Bakhtin's accounts of the necessity of dialoguing.[10]

We have come full circle, back to the powerful idea of narrative empathy. By helping us appreciate a very wide variety of ways of being human, stories help us appreciate human diversities and conflicts through our communications and conversations. Narrative identification is the process by which we come to identify with the stories and interpolate or introject through them to build our identities, collective and individual. Stories breathe humanity into people by helping them recognize the difference of other lives and cultures (Keen, 2007).[11]

Once again, we must be clear: they can also bring horror stories, *narrative trauma*, that can regulate – even destroy – our lives. Each one of the key processes I have named above brings its own darker version: to be unable to take roles, to fail to dialogue, to lack empathy, to fail to identify and attach with others, to 'other' and dehumanize.

Ultimately, good stories can become our good friends, our best friends, trusted and true. Bad stories can become our traumas, our problems, our fears. Stories can make life easier; but they can make it harder too. Little stories can grow into big stories; and big stories can fade into minor ones. Critically, bad stories can drive out good stories, just as good stories can drive out bad stories. There can be *self-fulfilling narrative prophecies*. Stories matter. Stories are indeed the Wealth of Nations.

The practical power of story crafting

It turns out that stories may just be among the most useful little things that human beings have ever created. While our large human brains certainly encourage abstraction, philosophy and 'blue-sky thinking', ultimately, like all animals, we are practical animals, much happier with the down-to-earth. Stories are pragmatic: played out in practice. They are the centrepieces of most *religious narratives*: told in parables and pictures in holy books, on stained-glass windows, in liturgy and scriptures. They are the basis of complex *legal narrative* systems. Developed in advocacy, told in court cases, and written up as case studies, stories become the basis of much of the practice of law. There is a *Storytelling for Lawyers* (Meyers, 2014). Lawyers have to be able to construct 'the right' narratives in court for the right audiences, and the training of lawyers might be seen as a training in the skills of good (or even devious) storytelling. There is even now a new development in Narrative Criminology (Presser and Sandberg, 2015). Stories are also a key to much medical work, as doctors and nurses seek to understand the patient's story. Indeed, this insight has led to a growing interest in 'illness narratives' (Frank, 1995; Kleinman, 1988) and *narrative medicine* (Charon, 2006). And good storytelling has also become central to doing good business. In public relations, advertising and promotional culture, we find narrative branding as the hallmark of successful business. Indeed, in neoliberal capitalism, storytelling has become big business (Salmon, [2007] 2017). Human activities persistently generate stories across all spheres of life.

The moral and regulative order of narratives: the problem of others

So here are the stories of power and the power of stories. They hang together and shape the values we live by. Sketching just a few of the wide-ranging stories of our narrative canopy helps us gain an underlying sense of the ways in which a connected world narrative reality is made, which can give us key characters (archetypes, role models, celebrities, icons), plots (templates), themes (practices) and values (ethics) that will guide, change and regulate our lives. We find ourselves in a public labyrinth cluttered with stories of economy, religion, power, celebrities and the rest, that are external to us yet exert a very definite pressure on our lives. And such narrative realities play their role in social life, both positively and negatively. Positively, stories can guide, inspire, even empower; negatively, they can control, dehumanize, regulate. Societies are always both *moral and regulative* orders. Christian Smith argues that humans, us, 'persons', are 'moral believing animals', and that 'human culture is always a moral order'. He writes: 'Human cultures are everywhere moral orders. Human persons are nearly inescapably moral agents. Human actions are necessarily morally constituted and propelled practices. And human institutions are inevitably morally infused configurations of rules and resources' (C. Smith, 2003, p. 7).

And yet, from another more critical angle, this moral order is also a regulative order. Norms, values, discourses and stories reach out into people's lives to exert a very definite control or governance over them. This was a key contribution of Foucault (1988) – to make us appreciate what he called 'the technologies of self'. These moral–regulative orders and their narratives can be found everywhere. For example, as Molly Andrews (2007) has shown us so clearly, they were busy at work in South Africa both in the dehumanizing stories of apartheid and in the stories that were generated after its collapse, as well as in the subsequent deep search for Truth and Reconciliation through narrative reconstruction. Stories also had a key role to play in the bitter East/West divide of the Berlin Wall, its fall in 1989, and the subsequent transformations of national identity surrounding it. They were there in the reworking of gay communities in the aftermath of the AIDS crisis; in the conflicts in Northern Ireland; in the struggles to recognize Indigenous Human Rights in Australia; in the conflicts of Tiananmen Square; in the Arab Spring; in the persistent contemporary struggles over child sexual abuse. Here, there, and almost everywhere, narrative is at work in a moral–regulative order.[12]

This moral–regulative narrative order acts as a classificatory grid, a binary net. It was Emile Durkheim who classically suggested this binary problem of moral order in his celebrated analysis of the normal and the pathological (Durkheim, [1895] 1964). For him, these are the twin processes bound up with the very conditions for social life: they provide basic classifications of the normal order while marking out moral boundaries, unifying people against common enemies, clarifying that there is a 'we' and a 'them', the 'other'. It is hard to find societies that do not do this. And it has been shown to work in many instances: from witchcraft trials and purification rituals to community scapegoating and moral panics around drugs.[13]

Some take this basic classifying urge to an extreme. John Steinbeck in *East of Eden* memorably suggests there is only one story, or rather one basic divide: between good and evil. He suggests a binary tension that we will see again. I quote:

> I believe that there is one story in the world, and only one. . . . Humans are caught – in their lives, in their thoughts, in their hungers and ambitions, in their avarice and cruelty, and in their kindness and generosity too – *in a net of good and evil*. . . . *There is no other story.* A man, after he has brushed off the dust and chips of his life, will have left only the hard, clean questions: Was it good or was it evil? Have I done well – or ill? (Steinbeck, [1952] 2017, p. 34, my italics)

Steinbeck suggests only one story, or rather one basic divide: between good and evil. And we can find this everywhere. This example of the 'narrative binary' is one of the most basic features of storytelling, and indeed social life. People, it seems, love a good binary; and both life and stories deploy them everywhere.

The sociologist Jeffrey Alexander (2006) is one of many who have developed analyses of culture as a series of binaries. He finds it in many areas of social life: the binary structures of motives, relationships, institutions, civil society, revolutions, East–West. In every society, our narratives can be read through binaries.[14] For example, he suggests the following binary structure of relationships as:

Open	Secretive
Trusting	Suspicious
Critical	Deferential
Honourable	Self-interested
Altruistic	Greedy
Truthful	Deceitful
Straightforward	Calculating
Deliberative	Conspiratorial
Friendly	Antagonistic (2006, p. 58)

Most of these binaries do not usually work very well if pushed too far: they are ideal types and heuristic tools. But they do sensitize us to unmistakably dramatically different narratives and how these can be very useful starting points to understanding a very wide and deep process of what we have already seen as narrative othering. The personal problems of self and other now become mirrored in the public world. So, as stories mark out binary boundary codes – of the 'good' and 'evil' – they also do their work of humanizing and dehumanizing people. One group 'belongs', the other is excluded: a world of who 'we' are can be contrasted with a world of 'the others'. There is a social process of othering, or alterity, whereby we see 'the categorization of enemies' (Edelman, 1977, p. 32), in which 'Enemy stereotypes empower' (Beck, 1997, p. 82).

Conclusion: The power of stories to change the world

'You just have to look. People are telling stories everywhere to change the world.' So say Ricki Solinger and her colleagues[15] as they introduce a collection of stories drawn from grassroots community movements across the world. From Uganda to Darfur, China to Afghanistan, Cuba to South Africa, we hear voices and communities facing problems and trauma – and dealing with them through storytelling. Here are confrontations with the environmental crisis; with the loss of traditional culture by Indigenous peoples; with living with the Holocaust and genocide; with prison degradation; with refugees, community decline, health problems including AIDS, violence against women, genocide, religious intolerance and more. In every case, the story becomes a major strategy to move beyond trouble. And these stories are told in many ways: in folk drama, oral history, recordings and memory books. All over the world, people, it seems, are dealing with their problems by getting together to build new communities and tell stories in diverse ways. Narratives give us stories of power just as power shapes the narratives we live by.

For sure, stories can damage and regulate: but they also bring a potential to inform, inspire, influence. They are the beating heart of social movements, therapeutic culture, educational reform, humanitarian aid and Truth and Reconciliation commissions. Stories can provide the power of transformation at personal, practical and social levels. As we interact with others and share stories, so we may change the world. This is a persistent theme and hope of this book: stories can remould lives and social structures, raising political challenges, provoking change and setting new political agendas. We can start to sense a politics of narrative humanity.

Act 2

Locating Tensions:
The Fragility of Narrative

Narratives are never settled.
Haunted by memory
And troubled by reality,
Ruptured by injustice
And disturbed by governance,
Distorted by medias
And saturated by the digital,
We dwell in the fragility
Of our Narrative Labyrinths.

4

Narrative Inequalities

> I have found that to make a contented slave, it is necessary to make a thoughtless one. It is necessary to darken his moral and mental vision, and . . . to annihilate the power of reason. . . . He must be made to feel that slavery is right; and he can be brought to that only when he ceases to be a man.
>
> Douglass, *Narrative of the Life of An American Slave*
> ([1884] 1997)

In 1884, Frederick Douglass published his *Narrative of the Life of Frederick Douglass, An American Slave, Written by Himself,* a short and straightforward classic 'slave narrative'. Published by the Anti-Slavery Office and priced at 50 cents (soon with European editions, and 30,000 copies available in five years), it is only eighty pages long. He was later to write further stories and soon secured a rising reputation. Indeed, he moved rapidly from being a fugitive slave to being a lifelong reformer, activist and, ultimately, statesman.

Douglass's story is one of thousands: it set a pattern of story-telling about the dehumanization, inequality and atrocity of racism and slavery that continues to this day. Slavery is one of the sharpest visions of what dehumanization means: a 'removing the human-ness'.[1] And over the past century and a half, the slave narrative has evolved into a major genre of writing.[2] By the 1930s, the New Deal's Federal Writing Project published *The American Slave: A Composite Autobiography* (Rawick and Rawick, 1972) in forty-one volumes. A more popular (now paperback) version is *Lay My Burden Down: A Folk History of Slaves* (Botkin, 1992). It asked: 'What does it mean to be a slave? What does it mean to be free? And, even more, how does it feel?' The whole project became a leading HBO documentary,

Unchained Memories: The Slave Narratives, which consolidated an accompanying iconography of slavery. It was but a short step from this to Alex Haley's monumentally influential *Roots* in 1977 (re-made as a four-part film in 2016), the story of Kunta Kinte, a 17-year-old sold in Gambia as a slave, and the seven generations that followed him in the USA.

Over time, a major new genre of fiction emerged that reconstructed slavery experiences and championed the civil rights of Blacks: William Styron's *The Confessions of Nat Turner,* 1967; Ernest Gaines's *The Autobiography of Miss Jane Pittman,* 1971; and Ishmael Reed's *Flight to Canada,* 1976. This writing often took a specific form, 'neo slave narratives', in which the fictional novel came to 'assume the form, adopt the conventions, and take on the first-person voice of the antebellum slave narrative'.[3] Increasingly, the complexities of locational power – of gender, class and race oppressions – came to be recognized. Likewise, Toni Morrison's hugely successful 1987 novel *Beloved* brought out the deep repression of and violence towards women slaves and revealed the interplay between who speaks, who defines, and what stories are listened to. All this work sets up patterns, genres and sensitivities that helped shape a Black public sphere.

But it is only recently that museums of slavery have been established. Only in 2002 was the Museum of Slavery, 'Lest We Forget', founded in Philadelphia. In 2014, the Whitney Plantation opened its doors to the public for the first time in its 262-year history, as the only plantation museum in Louisiana with a focus on slavery.[4] Now there is a constant flow of cultural memory events. In 2013, the top film was *12 Years A Slave* (gaining three Oscars, including Best Film); in 2016, *The Underground Railroad,* telling the story of Cora, a slave on a cotton plantation, became a bestseller (Whitehead, 2016); and, as I write, James Baldwin's *I Am Not Your Negro* was nominated for an Oscar. The latest manifestation of the struggle against Black subordination has been the #BlackLivesMatter movement: these stories have now moved online. George Zimmerman's 2013 acquittal of the murder of Trayvon Martin led three radical Black organizers (Alicia Garza, Patrisse Cullors and Opal Tometi) to create a Black-centred movement. There is a deep irony here. Racialized violence defines US history, yet the silenced slave's voice constantly returns to shout. Subordinated voices do often rise up, but change is painfully slow. A deep structure of oppression does not die just because stories are told. As one historian, Ibram Kendi, says, there is a deep long-term racism 'Stamped in America' from the beginning.[5]

All human stories are potentially lodged in deep, durable, damaging and dehumanizing infrastructures of powerful historical inequalities (Tilly, 1999).[6] And people strain against them. Slavery is a prime example: it was established as a seemingly 'legitimated' human form millennia ago. But it is far from alone.[7] I call the multiplicity of these voices the *subordinated standpoint*. Born out of dominance, a silenced story struggles to be told: the Abject and the Abused, the Disabled and the Dispossessed, the Minority and the Marginal, the Serf and the Subaltern. And as some of these stories gradually get to be told, so we learn of how, at the heart of human differences, there is a process that structures lives into a deep inequality and exclusion that in turn generates human suffering: materially, symbolically, politically and physically. Stories of *material inequality* speak to the ways people suffer economic, environmental and embodied injustice: through poor work, poor health, poor wealth and income, poor living conditions. *Symbolic inequality* reveals injustice through dehumanization: people are robbed of their humanity and meaning, and face suffering exclusion, narrative othering, subordination and narrative injustice. *Political inequality* leaves people powerless, disenfranchised, without voice or agency. And *physical inequality* shows power breaking down into violence.

My concern here is with the infrastructures of *locational power* and *everyday power*. I ask how, throughout history, people have come to be dominated, and how oppressed people come to *re-imagine their existence*. How do they find voice, handle brute injustices, assemble subterranean standpoints? Here is an ecology of stratified storytelling that suggests four key moments: domination, exclusion, resistance and empowerment. In doing this, I visualize a cruel reality brushing up against a creative imagination. And I start to envision a politics of narrative humanity.

Narrative domination

Our stories do not float in from the imaginary heavens but are grounded in worlds of domination and subordination: people have to live with them and find their own ways around them.[8] So, while the human world is always awash in stories, they are certainly not all told, witnessed, seen, heard or believed equally. And they never have been. While, every day, almost every one of the earth's 7½ billion people, the narrative masses, will be busy telling, and listening to, their unique tales in their multitudes across little groups and families up and down every land, few will ever be heard beyond these very small circles. How do some stories come to dominate?

I start with the view that societies and groups develop a hierarchy of narratives structured through the power of institutions (e.g. governance, economy, religion), culture (e.g media and digital), location (class, race, gender, etc.) and everyday situations (workplaces, families). This is the infrastructure of narrative power. Imagine initially a ragged pyramidal structure. In these worlds, a few at the top have extensive and pervasive dominant narrative power (the master elites, the narrative privileged – usually men – a narratocracy, perhaps); there is a middling range of those who can sometimes be heard; and very large numbers gravitating towards the bottom with little or no voice: the subordinated standpoint (giving us, for example, the 'slave narrative' or the 'disabled narrative', as we will see). This is true of all countries around the world. There is *a hierarchy of credibility*, with dominant voices at the top given high legitimacy and credibility, while those below are given low or zero credibility. And as Toni Morrison ([1987] 2004) says: 'Definitions belong to the definers, not the defined.' Power structures resources, and this includes narratives. And in the contemporary world, capitalism is its modus operandi.[9]

We find this in major ways in the interconnecting webs of caste, slavery, global poverty, racism, heterosexism and patriarchy that structure unequal stories into habitual institutional forms. Governance, economy, religion and media power shape these forms. But there are other forms of power. Locational power structures narrative through hierarchies of class, gender, ethnicity, sexuality, health, age and nation; and they in turn generate social exclusions. And, ultimately, they are experienced through everyday power in daily embodied, emotional, negotiated actions. All human stories live in this damaged and damaging system of indisputable powerful historical inequalities.

The broadest facts of this global hierarchy of human inequality are very well documented.[10] For example, a major report claims that the top 1 per cent have more wealth than the remaining 99 per cent of people, and that the 62 richest people in the world have as much wealth as the poorest half of the global population. Most people own nothing. And their stories are also taken as nothing. There is also plenty of research on how concentrated global media networks running the world's media have become. This is a major part of the infrastructure of narrative power. Comcast, AT&T / Time Warner, Disney, 21st Century Fox and National Amusements (Viacom and CBS) are now said to run 90 per cent of the US media. Half the world is disconnected from the digital world, even as just a handful of people own and run it. In 2018, ten of the world's top twenty billionaires run digital media, with key figures being Jeff Bezos (1st, Amazon, $112 billion), Bill Gates (2nd, Microsoft, $90 billion), Mark Zuckerberg (5th, Facebook, $73 billion), Larry Page (12th, Alphabet/Google, $52.5 billion), Sergey Brin (13th, Google, $47.5 billion). Here is a new world of the Silicon Valley super-rich. A complex widespread world documentation shows just how much the media are monopolized by a few large companies, some major governments (such as those of the USA, China and Russia) and a few super-rich people. There are usually strong racial and gender features to all this. And, recently, there are strong claims that these inequalities are growing.[11]

The big stories of power   A key puzzle here is just how this dominant narrative elite consolidates and routinizes their narrative power? How do their stories come to get accepted and shaped into mass narratives? Where does this consolidated big power come from? Over the millennia, there have been many answers to this question. One answer tells this story of big power lying in the hands of rulers, states and governments: Leviathan. In a democracy where the people elect the leaders, the power might then ultimately lie in the hands of the people. These generate *governmental and state narratives*. A second answer tilts towards the economy, where power lies in the hands of the rich, the wealthy, the plutocrats and those who own the means of production and communication: power flows from a ruling class or an economic power elite. These generate *economic narratives*. This was the powerful story of Karl Marx. A third sweeps out even further to suggest that power is ultimately propagated through cultural means, notably throughout history by religions, ideology and so-called 'soft power'. So that, even though rulers and the rich play key roles, it is the ways in which cultures work upon our lives that ultimately puts power into play. This has been variously called *cultural power, linguistic power, symbolic power*: power is embedded in the very language and media we use. Finally, some see power as residing in brute force: in the power of the military, the armed forces, wars and violence. This is the ultimate act of power, or, for some, what happens when power breaks down. It generates *narratives of violence*.

There are swathes of writings on all these themes, and much to be said for all these arguments: these questions are interconnected sources of power. There is real power in the institutions of economy, power, religion and violence. Each has a role to play, often at different key moments in different histories and cultures (Mann, 1986–2013).

A major strand of contemporary thinking highlights cultural hegemony. The idea of the hegemon goes back to ancient Greek states and suggests how dominant orders are maintained by ideology (stories, language, narrative, etc.) that is handed on, perpetuated as a kind of belief. When this breaks down, orders have ultimately to be maintained by violence. World histories can be written as histories of changing hegemonic orders – and the very stories we tell help to maintain the silence of other stories.

The stories of little power   But hegemonic narratives render reality too unitary and homogeneous: looking simply at dominant institutional narratives can make us see the world too simply. One way of fracturing this is by approaching narrative actions through the multiple divisions of *locational and intersectional power*. Class, gender, ethnicity, sexualities, age and generation, disability and health, and nationhood – all have their role to play, and run through the hegemon from top to bottom, puncturing any pyramidal view of dominance and inequalities by stratifying it with further key social divisions.

Narrative exclusion

Ralph Ellison begins his classic, *Invisible Man*:

> I am an invisible man. No I am not a spook like those who haunted Edgar Allen Poe: Nor am I one of your Hollywood movie ectoplasms. I am a man of substance, of flesh and bone, fiber and liquids – and I might even be said to possess a mind. I am invisible, understand, simply because people refuse to see me. Like the bodiless heads you see sometimes in circus sideshows, it is as though I have been surrounded by mirrors of hard, distorting glass. When they approach me, they see only my surroundings, themselves or figments of their imagination, indeed, everything and anything except me. ([1952] 2015, opening lines)

Here a Black life is being rendered invisible. A dominant story frames the strategies that work to exclude: to silence and shame, discriminate and displace, stigmatize and scapegoat. Symbolic violence is committed. Stories can be sent away: to the ghetto, the refugee camp, the extermination camp. And real violence can be used as a last resort. Here we also have narrative exclusion and three major recent works have alerted us to its ongoing significance. The Italian philosopher Giorgio Agamben speaks of *Bare Life* (1995), the Polish-English sociologist Zygmunt Bauman speaks of *Wasted Lives* (2003), and the North American sociologist Saskia Sassen speaks of *Expulsions* (2014). They all suggest deep structural processes at work, and here I draw from them all.

Thus, when Agamben re-alerted us to 'bare life', he returned us to a classic Greek (Aristotelian) distinction between the quality of a life and the mere biological functioning of it.[12] The idea of 'bare life' returns us to a conception of life in which the sheer biological fact of life is given priority over the way a life is lived. And this means the life is not given the distinctive features we accord to humanity. We become dehumanized. The extreme case of this is the concentration camp, but we can see it also in the contemporary experience of the refugee, the abject poor and the prisoner. And when Bauman spoke of wasted lives, he alerted us to large numbers of people in the world today whose lives have become seriously damaged by strategies of exclusion and assimilation, working side by side. Some people's lives are literally lived on rubbish dumps. While some people are sucked into the social order, others are vomited out. Destroyed by violence, brutalization and extermination, they live lives outside of society. Finally, when Sassen suggests seeing a new world order in the making which cuts across countries and nations, she reveals how large numbers of people are being ejected from the mainstream of the world, often gathered in large, damaging dumping waste-lands and institutions. Visually, this is well illustrated in Ai Weiwei's *Human Flow* (2018), a major film about the refugee and environmental crisis. These groups have many stories to tell, but they will rarely be heard.

Several processes shape this narrative expulsion. *Economic expulsion* brings large numbers who have no wealth or property, and little or no work. They have stories of work degradation, austerity, unemployment, poverty and harsh lives to tell – but they are rarely heard. *Environmental expulsion* brings large numbers who experience environmental crisis, often illness, and are rendered homeless. They have stories of living through climate crisis and environmental injustice, but they are rarely heard. *Political expulsion* brings large numbers who are ejected by their state through war and conflict. Here are the stories of the displaced people, migrants, refugees and dispossessed, often silenced. There were over 65 million 'displaced' people in 2016. *Media expulsion* brings large numbers who are without modern media communications and hence live outside the modern narrative world (about 4 billion live without the internet). *Incarcerating expulsion* brings large numbers (some 9 million) who are physically cut off from the world through incarceration in prisons, refugee camps, etc.

They live in the most dehumanized and degrading situations, cut off from visibility. The stories of their damaged lives are rarely heard.

To help us grasp all this narrative exclusion, we need to be clearer about the idea of locational power, which asks questions about our social positioning in the world. It asks just who we are in the scheme of things, how we are to be identified, how we are valued – or not. The questions become: *Who am I? Who are you? And where do we stand together in the world?* A sense of valuations, hierarchies, intersections, privileges unfold, whereby we can place ourselves in a pecking order, raising the possibilities of narrative debasement and empowerment. It may even lead us to ask: *What is the purpose of my life here on this earth?* Such narrative power through location can be found everywhere. *How do oppressed people imagine and re-imagine their existence?* Drawing from ecological theory,[13] we look at the conditions under which multiple voices grow into different worlds, where some, the subordinated, are rendered unheard, given no space to speak and no credibility if they do. They are devalued as speakers, and their stories are silenced.

Entering this land of the subordinated narrative self, we see how stories work their ways to categorize, label and sometimes stigmatize us. You are designated a Woman rather than a Man; a Black rather than a White; French rather than Algerian; Straight rather than Gay; Poor rather than Rich; Disabled rather than Normal; Muslim rather than Jew; Outsider rather than Belonging. All these simple designations and situations bring complex different stories and shape different opportunities for people to face. And, sometimes, power and its stories do not work well for us. We can soon find a very wide range of narrative standpoints – of nationhood, class, gender, ethnicity, sexuality, health, age and more – growing out of power relations in our lives that can have a major influence on who we are. And, more than this, they will reach deeply back into our historical pasts and become intersected with each other (Collins and Bilge, 2016). Table 4.1 charts the dimensions and some of the issues around living with locational power.

Living with Locational Power: Vulnerable Selves, Standpoints and Narrative Othering

To help understand what is at stake, consider my earlier arguments about the importance of self-reflexivity for being human. The narrative self writes itself through an awareness of others. As we see ourselves through the eyes of both self and a circle of others, so we are

Table 4.1 Living with locational power and narrative standpoints: modes of excluding stories?

Location: Who am I?	Exclusion and binary othering: Who is other?	Emergent subordinated narrative standpoints and their movements
1 Economic	Poor/Rich	E.g. work narratives, class narratives, trade union narratives, slave narratives, caste narratives
2 Gender	Male/Female	E.g. women's narratives, gender narratives, transgender narratives
3 Ethnicity	Black/White	E.g. ethnic narratives: Blacks and others
4 Age/ generation	Young/Old	E.g. generational narratives – stories told historically by different age cohorts. Also: narratives of youth, old age, etc., and their social movements
5 Sexuality	Straight/Queer	E.g. LGBTQI, etc.; Queer politics and its stories. The rise of Trans. and their social movements
6 Religion	Religious/Secular Jew/Muslim	Religious stories of all kinds, and their movements, including fundamentalist narratives
7 Health/ disability	Sick/Healthy Abled/Disabled	E.g. disabled/crip stories; health stories – AIDS movements, cancer stories, etc. (and their health movements)
8 Family and community	Local/Outsider	Stories of belonging to 'my primary group' and their social movements
9 Nation	Citizen/Immigrant	E.g. nationalism and its social movements; war narratives; post-colonial narratives; Indigenous narratives
10 Environment and universe	Nature/Technology	E.g. stories of nature v. technology; narratives of sustainability and humanity and their social movements

influenced by them. It is this connection with others that is central to locating ourselves as being human. At the simplest level, then, as we ponder *Who am I?*, we become engaged with locating ourselves in worlds of definitional 'others' who help create (usually binary) boundaries, borders and labels. Stories have cultural power and they work both positively and negatively. Positively, stories can facilitate connections and belonging: creating a 'we group'. But negatively, stories can also generate 'out-groups' fostering hostilities and hatreds. So here are two major narrative processes developing: of narrative standpoints and of narrative othering.

The idea of narrative standpoint has a long history, claiming that domination generates new forms of embodied consciousness. The classic idea comes from Hegel ([1807] 1977, ch. 4). Here is the Slave–Master narrative, in which a master clearly has power over a slave. Hegel also sees that, out of this relationship, the slave develops a new self-consciousness – a response which in turn helps create a new negotiated space which the master has to deal with. Building on this, Marx wrote classically of the formation of 'class consciousness' (and hence, ultimately, the importance of narrative in generating class awareness). And this shift in consciousness can be found across a wide range of modern movements. Thus, Paulo Freire ([1970] 2017) influentially spoke about a 'pedagogy of the oppressed' as he examined colonized racism. Frantz Fanon ([1961] 2001) called for 'conscientization' in outcast postcolonial groups, advocating violence as a key way out from subordination – his work also became a manual for revolutionary groups and change. Gayatri Spivak (1988) spoke of the stories of postcolonial repression as 'the subaltern'. Susan Harding (1986) and Nancy Hartsock (1998) developed 'feminist standpoints' as women developed a new awareness of their oppressed situations. Queer activists developed a queer consciousness arising to challenge the dominance of heteronormativity (Sedgwick, [1990] 2008). And the disability movement generated Crip theory; Robert McRuer (2006) articulates the central concerns of Crip theory and considers how such a critical perspective might impact cultural and historical inquiry in the humanities. Out of deep conditions of domination and exclusion, people create their own insights, understandings, knowledge and narratives.

Closely allied with this is the process of narrative othering. As we have seen, this key process of narrative othering can turn the 'out-group' and 'outsider' into 'the other' and then 'the enemy'. Stories come to mark out binary boundary codes of the 'good' and 'evil', the included and the excluded: others come to be defined as different, alien and not like us. An almost inevitable human friction arises from this presence of others – and, out of this, change emerges. A core paradox starts to appear: as we bond with our in-groups, so others in the out-group strengthen their bonding too. And so we see the 'inventing of enemies' (Eco, 2013). A double-bind of mutual hostility is created (Appiah, 2018; Kapuściński, 2006; Morrison, 2017).

Narrative resistance

Everywhere in the world, people have to confront dominant, hegemonic worlds: they have to deal with institutional, media, locational and everyday power. They face the exploitations of work and class, the discriminations of race, the abuses of gender, the tensions of age and generation, the ritual oppressions of religion, the heterosexisms of sexualities, the tyranny of sovereignty and nationalisms, the postcolonialisms of states, the prejudices of all kinds of differences. This is the site of everyday power where people bring their embodied, emotional selves to try and deal with their potential exclusion and dehumanization. Responding in very different ways, they engage in narrative actions that help them resist or rebel, accommodate or assimilate to dominating tales. Out of their subordinated situations arise *subterranean narrative perspectives and standpoints* that respond to all this. It is one of life's major challenges. And as Rebecca Solnit ([2004] 2016, p. xiv) says: 'Every conflict is in part a battle over the story we tell, or who tells and who is heard.'

This is abstract, so an example will help. I have been aware of Ken Loach's films all my life: from *Cathy Come Home* (1966) and *Kes* (1969) to *Bread and Roses* (2000) and *Jimmy's Hall* (2014). Always controversial, he is one of the UK's leading filmmakers. (Indeed, he has warranted a documentary on his own life and work: *Versus*, 2016.) In his fifty-year career, he has perpetually told the stories of those suffering the domination of others – not in abstract ways, as I do here, but through the telling and dramatization of their stories. His work persistently shows just what people do when they are put down by other people, suffer from it and yet somehow deal with it. He has made over fifty films on this theme.[14]

Three snapshots. In one of his earliest and most influential films, *Kes*, he shows how a working-class boy becomes estranged from school and family yet finds solace with the love of a kestrel. In a middle-period film, *Bread and Roses*, he portrays the invisibility and dehumanization of Latino cleaners as they work for the Los Angeles rich; their low pay makes them resist by going on strike. And in a more recent film, *I, Daniel Blake*, he gives us a tale of poverty in the UK. Ill, bereaved and workless, Daniel Blake confronts the new UK benefit system and the authorities who treat him abysmally throughout. The wider story is that of a mean-minded conservative government implementing a new austerity policy, showing its dire impact on human lives: the welfare system is crumbling under policies that display carelessness, uncaring and cruelty. At every juncture, Daniel Blake meets officials and bureaucracy that show little kindness or understanding. But at the same time, he does meet ordinary people who display a common humanity in myriad ways – some people can still give you hope even as others let you down badly. The horrors of life unfold for Daniel Blake. We see him being humiliated by officials but being cared for in a food bank; we see him being put on hold on the phone (for nearly two hours) and the brutal indifference of a welfare system devised both to save money (ostensibly) and to cut back on welfare scroungers. It is a welfare system that feeds on the binaries of good and bad people. But he meets other desperate people along the way where kindness prevails in little lives. Ken Loach's voice is just one of many that reveal both narrative power and narrative inequality.

His films show a small part of a massive worldwide extravaganza of human cruelty being met with resistance. Over the millennia, people speak out, shout, protest, write and now film and digitalize their grievances. They document their experiences of subordination and exclusion. In great literature, art, poetry, autobiography, history, film, social science and a myriad of ways, we know this universal story of how people negotiate their oppressive worlds. Looking back over history, we find an extraordinary parade of people whose narratives have been marginalized, silenced and inferiorized. Here are the billions living largely invisible, insecure lives, frequently brutalized, shamed, dishonoured and dehumanized. Here are stories that could not initially be told but that gradually struggle to find ways to do so: often in politics and poetics, arts and research. Here are the multitudes of moving and often elegantly told stories of how people react to the force of extreme situations of brute power. Here are the subordinated standpoints of:

The Crippled and Disabled (McRuer, 2006); the Colonized (Fanon, [1961] 2001); the Dalit (Bagul, 2018); the Queers (Sedgwick, [1990] 2008); the Indigenous Peoples (Samson and Gigoux, 2017); the Inmates (Goffman, 1961a); the Peasants (Scott, 1985, 1990); the Poor (Sainath, 1996); the Prisoners (Sykes, 2007); the Refugees, Immigrants and Displaced (Nguyen, 2018; Sayad, 2004); the Slaves (Botkin, 1992; Douglass, [1884] 1997); the Survivors – of the Holocaust (Levi, 1988), the Gulag (Solzhenitsyn, 2003), Stalin's Russia (Figes, 2008); the Welfare Claimants (Tyler, 2013); the Women (De Beauvoir, [1949] 2015) – veiled (Abu-Lughod, 1986), raped (Brownmiller, 1975), abused (Woodiwiss, 2009; Woodiwiss et al., 2017); the Working Class (Bourdieu, [1993] 1999); the Young (Skeggs, 1997; Willis, [1978]

2018); all those living with the everyday racism around the world (Lamont et al., 2016). And the many others.

Here are the struggling-to-be-heard stories of locational and every-day power dwelling in infrastructures of domination and oppression. They may emerge harshly through physical violence: as people get tortured, are hung on trees, sent to Gulags and gas chambers. They may emerge more softly: as a persistent and damaging downgrading of the self, an inferiorization of being, an abject and insidious moral devaluation. Over time, symbolic violence is done. And what arises here is a kind of worldwide subterranean under-life developing beneath the surface of dominant worlds – a seething multiplicity of complex responses. People may well go along with the dominant world on the surface, whilst simultaneously creating a heaving, massive discontented world of grumblings, fantasizing, posing, denials, mockeries, everyday protests and resistances. Here is a world of acting, often masking real feelings, as skills or weapons are developed to handle dominance. As people come to experience the ever-present potential for the exclusion of their life along with its moral devaluation, a sense that people 'should know their place', the anxiety of facing an honour code with which they need to conform, so we find a full repertoire of dramatic stagecraft emerging: real life and drama interconnect. Some people will be overwhelmed and engulfed by this dominant order, acquiescing and fully embracing it, performing respectability. Some may 'pass', pretending to be something they are not. Others may artfully learn to play along with it while mocking it inwardly. Some will distance themselves from it: 'this is not my culture'. They may improvise, building humour out of it. Some may engage in denial. They may withdraw mentally from it. For others, it may, literally, make them sick. Some may resist. They may rebel against it. And they may get violent – sometimes very violent. These days, they will use social media to create alternatives. And much more. There are a lot of possibilities.

Narrative empowerment

What we find here then is a vast world of infra politics: a world of adjustments, tinkering skills and 'resistances through ritual' that allow people to live in the dominant world while not believing in it.[15] Though there could never be one pattern or essential trajectory for all, a spectrum of narrative responses can be teased out, from complete acquiescence to bloody revolution, from brokenness to resilience. In the Preface to Fanon's *The Wretched of the Earth*, Jean-Paul Sartre claims that: 'We only become what we are by the radical deep-seated refusal of that which others have made of us' ([1961] 2001, p. 15). Here are some of the ways we become what we are:

I Collaborative Narratives: staying with dominant stories
>   1 *Hyper-conformist narratives*: exaggerates acceptance; often self-loathing; the HyperNormal.
>   2 *Conformist narratives*: deferential, colonized.

II Negotiated Narratives: living under dominance but developing weapons to resist while not challenging the existing order
>   3 *Innovation narratives*: develops new creative story, but not threatening of dominant stories (e.g., crime, corruption).
>   4 *Retreatist narratives*: withdraws from the dominant narrative into own world (e.g., isolation, illness, mental illness, religion, drug use, denial, 'dropping out', indifference, despair, etc.).
>   5 *Ritualist narratives:* resists dominant stories through repertoires of rituals (e.g. humour, mockery, games, distancing, posing. etc.).
>   6 *Reformist/rehabilitation narratives:* Looking for ways of changing within the system (e.g. campaigning, therapy).

III Counter-Narratives: not accepting dominant stories, seeking change
>   7 *Resistance and rebellious narratives*: challenging, arguing against, finding ways to reject the dominant story.
>   8 *Radical and revolutionary narratives:* rejecting and seeking change. Possible violence.

A portrait is emerging of great narrative complexities around worlds of inequality, exclusion and dehumanization. There are many who engage in *collaborative narratives*: who stay with the dominant stories. At one extreme, there is the complete identification of the subject with the dominant narrative. Primo Levi, living in a concentration camp, observed a 'gray zone' where this kind of story can even be found within some inmates of the concentration camp:

> the harsher the oppression, the more widespread among the oppressed is the willingness, with all its infinite nuances and motivations, to collaborate: terror, ideological seduction, servile imitation of the victor,

myopic desire for any power whatsoever, even though ridiculously circumscribed in space and time, cowardice, and, finally, lucid calculation aimed at eluding the imposed orders and order. All these motives, singly or combined, have come into play in the creation of this gray zone. (Levi, 1988, p. 28)

This response is also found in the stories of right-wing women, the working-class Tories, the self-loathing queer, the right-wing populist movement. The character of Sambo, for example, described controversially by Stanley Elkins in his classic work on *Slavery* ([1959] 1976, pp. 81-139), shows a slave so completely subjugated in body and spirit and under absolute control that he becomes 'dependent, docile and childlike'. Here the subordinated accepts the status quo of inequality, actively supporting it and embracing it. These stories celebrate this ultra-conformity and the value of the existing order. They become 'HyperNormalized', enduring role engulfment and often overwhelmed by it.[16]

Resistance narrative actions are another cluster of responses, suggesting narrative actions that seem to stay with the dominant narrative while actually not really being part of it: they live under dominance while developing weapons to resist this order. Here people engage with rituals, retreat, innovate, reform. They resist the dominant tales in many ways. These people create and perform embodied narratives that help them mock and mimic, resist and innovate, withdraw and retreat from the dominant narratives that surround them. Some become (i) *ritualists* resisting dominant stories through repertoires of rituals of humour, mockery, games, distancing, posing, etc. They engage in everyday grumblings about the ways their worlds are run by others. Others (ii) *retreat* and withdraw from the dominant world into their own worlds of isolation, illness, mental illness, religion, drug use, crime denial, 'dropping out', indifference, despair, etc. Some (iii) *innovate*, developing a new creative story, perhaps finding solace in looking after their home, playing music and sport, or even developing criminal activities. They find a way to live in a culture that is not hospitable to them. Still others might tinker with change and become (iv) *reformists*: they look for ways of changing things within the system.

Ultimately, there are *rebellious narrative actions* that argue against, and find ways to reject, dominant stories. Just as there many who conform, so at the other end of the spectrum lies a cluster of more overtly political responses of radicalism, rebellion, revolution. These stories generate oppositional counter-narratives and reject dominant

orders: of capitalism, racialism, patriarchy, institutional regime, heterosexism, environmental damage. They can come from right or
left – or, more correctly, from those who look back to a better past
('Regressionists/Traditionalists') and those who look forwards to a
changed better future ('Progressivists'). They are protest stories and
can become full- blown counter-narratives, not accepting dominant
stories, seeking change. Social protest movements have a long history
and we can see them everywhere across the contemporary world.
They are central to modern politics – a key part of civic society,
working democracies and effective social change. Initially linked to
poor people's movements, they are now widespread in every area
of social life, from AIDS ACT UP in the 1980s to the Hong Kong
Umbrella Movement in 2014 (Lee and Chan, 2018). (See Crawshaw
and Jackson, 2010, and Weibel, 2014, for wide-ranging stories of
activism and change in the face of great injustices.)[17]

Social movements are ubiquitous in 21st-century life. They tell
passionate stories. People come to tell stories of their grievances and
sufferings. They tell angry stories of their enemies and wrongdoings.
They tell visionary stories of better fortunes. They retrospectively
tell inspirational stories of their victories. They archive their successes. Increasingly organized through media – or against it – they tell
their tales in mediated forms. And they do this most concentratedly
through the collective actions of social movements.

Progressive politics of the twenty-first century?

And so, over the past two centuries we have become more and more
aware of the power of narrative in social movements, especially in the
battles over inequality, social division and global injustice. And gradually a new politics has been developing, with new stories to tell. The
old stories of left and right have been somewhat re-worked. While
the political polarity between the forces of traditional hierarchy and
of progressive egalitarianism remain, new political stances abound.
With varying emphases and disagreements, all this has led to a very
wide-ranging emerging set of new stories and political goals. So, in
this chapter, I have been drawing not just from the classic politics of
inequality and redistribution but also from a range of emerging progressive politics, some of which can be seen in table 4.2.

This rich complexity makes contemporary politics lush with wider
hopes and dreams. In contrasting ways, all these new accounts
provide a critique of those worldwide national and local politics that

Table 4.2 Progressive politics of the twenty-first century?

The politics of	Purpose: a society fit for humanity
1 Difference (Young,1990)	Living well with human variety
2 Division (Fraser,1997)	Redistributing wealth, recognizing others and reducing inequalities
3 Belonging and othering (Yuval Davis, 2011)	Expanding belonging in the circle of others; weakening othering
4 Agonistic democracy (Mouffe, 2013; Wenman, 2013)	Recognizing the likelihood of conflicts and learning to live well with them
5 Knowledge, ignorance and representation (Connell, 2007; Fricker, 2007; Hartsock, 1998; Medina, 2013; Santos, 2014)	Recognizing standpoints; looking for truth
6 Dialogue (Bakhtin, 1981; Koczanowicz, 2014	Talking through differences; finding common grounds
7 Rights (Turner, 2006)	Creating equal dignity for all
8 Care (Engster, 2007; Tronto, 2013)	Looking after self, each other and the environment
9 Compassion (Armstrong, 2011; Ure and Frost, 2014)	Understanding and caring for others; looking after the disadvantaged
10 Cosmopolitanism (Appiah, 2006; Van Hooft, 2009)	Being open to others and their diverse cultures

remain cruelly insensitive to the varieties of global human suffering, difference, inequality and complexity in the human world. They are critical of not just governments, but also religions, businesses and many other dominant groups that negate the powers of human differences and of human voice and are blind to human suffering. And they are usually aware of how knowledge, ideas, stories and narratives are the means through which these sufferings are both sustained and transformed.

Ultimately, the new progressive politics senses the importance of listening to and learning from multiple voices, developing ways of appreciating them while learning to live together with them as we negotiate a better human world. They recognize that stories and narrative are a key tool for doing this. Once again, we find the elements of a new politics of narrative humanity: a new world just might be in the making.

5

Narrative Digitalism

Does the Internet dream of itself?
Werner Herzog, 2016 documentary *Lo and Behold*

Werner Herzog is one of the world's great storytelling filmmakers. In two magnificent films, Herzog spans 30,000 years of changing storytelling. In *Cave of Forgotten Dreams* (2010) he takes us on an exploration of the Chauvet-Pont-Arc Cave in France. Some thirty millennia old and protected by a landslide that sealed it off hermetically, the cave was not discovered until 1994. In the film, we move tentatively, slowly and cautiously around it, smelling the ancient darkness. A glorious vista of cave art awaits us. Mainly drawings of animals – mammoths, cave lions, bears – they are often in action and movement. They seem to be telling us stories from a past and Herzog suggests to us that they could be made to move in shadows, possibly telling us some of the first ever stories of humanity. We will never know for certain. But they do raise questions now of our past humanities and their links with us today.

Cut to six years on and he shifts tack. In *Lo and Behold: Reveries of the Connected World* (2016) he ruminates on ten tales of the internet – one of humanity's greatest revolutions. Here is the story of the scientists discovering and building the internet; of those whose lives have been severely damaged by it; of hermits who have to live outside of the electronic magnetic field of mobile phones; of those who see it as a way of escaping the earth as our planet increasingly fails. And he poses a question to many of his storytellers: does the internet dream of itself?

Communicating narrative power through the millennia

At least 30,000 years separate these two stories of human narrative actions. In this chapter, and living with the weight of history, I start to chart some ways narrative power has changed. How have our narrative eras of the past been transformed into a 21st-century mediated and digital age? Thanks to much research work, we now know quite a lot about the extraordinarily complex history of communication. Sometimes we can find a kind of technological determinism suggesting technology drives communication – in the well-known ideas of Harold Innis and Marshall McLuhan particularly, the motto becomes 'the media is the message'. But here I want to be more flexible: the idea of *narrative mediations* merely suggests bridges between changing institutional media structures and transforming texts, stories, narratives. Tracing transformations in the infrastructures of media forms, each wave of change brings cumulative shifts in both power and the ways we narrate. At present, we have come to dwell in a hybrid of five infrastructural modes of communications power: speech, writing, print, electronic media and now the pervasive world of digital technology. To this might also be added the visual, which has a history of its own. As we will see, each mode generates and shifts the workings of power, making today's world of communicative narrative a very dense and complex hybrid structure.

Across eras, different technologies of narrative have highlighted different kinds of narrative power. Oral cultures, for example, revealed the power of early imaginations in cave art and brought epic stories as harbingers of memory; writing and manuscripts brought elites and religious stories; printing brought journalism, novels, autobiographies, extending stories to a wider range of 'mass' readers and deepening the story into inner psychic worlds. And in the very short and recent modern period, there have been two waves in quick succession: the electronic revolution of mass and mechanical reproductions, and digitalism arriving in the last seconds of recorded human history. These bring us 'audiences' and the new fragmented texts of our times. Throughout all this, there have been striking shifts in power. Early stages of writing were fundamentally elite, as were early stages of printing; but print fairly rapidly became the great democratizer, as well as – some say – the definer of the modern nation state. And some now claim that digitalism is the true equalizer, even as others suggest it is heralding a new era of robotic rule.

Marshall Poe's *History of Communications* (2011) assesses these transformations over the millennia, asking how improvements and new forms of communications have enhanced our well-being. He answers ambivalently. For each of these shifts in modes of communications is cumulative: the old ones do not die out, but are simply added on to the new forms, making both narrative and power richer but more complex. Today, we live in a world of sedimented layers of many ways of narrating. As we have incrementally moved away from early oral and visual cultures to writing, print, reading, and on to 'the age of mechanical reproduction', the electronic and, ultimately, digital era, so we have moved to an ever-increasing complexity. Here, now, in the twenty-first century, we are experiencing a radical transformation as all forms of narrative work together and infuse simultaneously into our mediated, political and narrated lives. And we cannot as yet predict where all this is going to lead us, despite numerous attempts to do so.

The Power of Speaking Stories

I jump ahead: let's start at the beginning. First, and for most of human history (*Homo sapiens* appeared around 200,000 years ago), life was lived in small groups, sometimes roaming, gradually becoming sedentary, and ultimately settling. Storytelling was direct and face-to-face, and power was local. This first era – commonly called 'preliterate' (and sometimes 'tribal') – has lasted for the longest period of human history by far, and poses two critical questions: (1) How did human gestures, signs and language emerge?; and (2) How did early oral narratives organize early literacy work?

Explanations of the origins and workings of human languages are usually split between those that the philosopher Charles Taylor (2016) has distinguished as the Designative (enframing) and the Constitutive (constructing). One looks for a frame that arises outside of language; the other sees language as 'making possible new purpose, new levels of behaviour, new meanings'. For our purposes, we need not take sides. What seems clear is that a basic model has emerged from many researchers that recognizes language as an evolutionary collective invention. Genes play their role, biological capacities are established, but language also becomes a cultural tool arising out of early communicative, cooperative adaptations, constantly modifying as it evolves over history. Language arises to 'solve the twin problems of communication and social cohesion' (Everett, 2012, p. 6). We also see this history of storytelling and narrative as changing, even if it has evolutionary roots.[1]

Stories were important in this preliterate period, and we know more and more about them. Ruth Finnegan's *Oral Literature in Africa* (1970) traced the history of storytelling across the continent of Africa; Walter Ong's *Orality and Literacy* (1982) introduced the idea of primary and secondary orality; and, more recently, Lynn Kelly's *Knowledge and Power in Prehistoric Societies: Orality, Memory and the Transmission of Culture* (2015) examined the archaeological record of three sites, Chaco Canyon, Poverty Point and Stonehenge, to reveal the material mnemonic devices used in oral cultures that can facilitate the holding of a vast array of pragmatic knowledge (such as plant properties, navigation, astronomy, genealogies, laws and trade agreements).

From studies like these, we know many things about oral stories: (1) They stay 'close to the human life world', being local, situational and participatory, rather than abstract and distant. Oral cultures are not very good at elaborations or abstracted thought. (2) 'Verbal memory is understandably valued in oral cultures.' Research on archaeological sites shows that they display features that are best understood as tools to help aid memories: there are standard set expressions, mnemonics, formulas. (3) Oral stories stay practical: 'They use stories of human action to store, organize and communicate much of what they know.' (4) Often oral stories get 'structured in proverbs'. There are no records or writing facilities to aid memory, so oral stories, serving as memory aids, are needed. (5) They are traditional and depend on sounds. It was a very different world of narrative power from today.[2]

The Power of Writing Stories

In a famous article, Jack Goody and Ian Watt once remarked that 'Man's biological evolution shades into prehistory when he becomes a language-using animal; add writing and history proper begins' (Goody and Watt, 1968).[3] This phase of so-called 'history proper' began with larger, more stable forms of human territorial settlements, and flourishes between roughly 3500 BCE and 1450 CE. And so, after a very long early verbal period about which we know little, the history of power, communications and stories starts to become much better documented. Although marking and drawing can be dated back to the Cave Age, the first written records are about 6,000 years old, and the first empires appeared about 5,500 years ago in the Middle East. We can take as a landmark *The Epic of Gilgamesh*, an epic poem from ancient Mesopotamia (George, 2003). It suggests the power of a very different world and symbolic order.[4] The

writing and 'manuscript era' emerged in the ancient civilizations of
China, Egypt and Mesopotamia, and continued until around 1450
CE, when print arrived. In this manuscript era, only a few people
could read or write (Poe, 2011, p. 73).

Writing is indeed one of the great inventions of humanity: it gives it
a new power by restructuring consciousness. Walter Ong (1912–93),
the great scholar of orality and literacy, once remarked that: 'Literacy
opens possibilities to the world and to human existence unimaginable
without writing' (Ong, 1982, p. 175). Writing creates the possibility
of storing stories and dividing the story world between people who
can write and people who cannot. It makes possible the manuscript,
the letter, the poetic and the earliest autobiographies – along with the
rise of debates on the skills of calligraphy and writing forms. It sees
the start of an individualism of authors, and an interest in the idea
of an author of the text, as well as the construction of 'the reader'.
Initially, only a few very specialized groups were able to become
literate, and we see its development in specialist/elite sites such as
monasteries and early universities. Often it was linked with elaborate ornamentation in single manuscript books. While the growth
of literacy cultures is significant, this is mainly so for special groups:
written stories are held in a few powerful hands and gather a distinct
aura. They can be seen as early harbingers of social inequalities, as
they usually excluded women, all lower orders (though slaves would
often write for their masters) and outsiders: they became a marker of
the standing of different groups, cultures and even whole societies.[5]
At the same time, scholars debate whether this was repressive or ultimately accelerated social change.

The Power of Printing Stories

While the origins of printing lie in China, in the West it is convention-
ally seen as developing since Gutenberg. By 1500, some 20,000,000
books had been printed (Anderson, [1983] 2006, p. 37). Print cultures, as they say, started to change the world.[6] In a famous and
much-celebrated account, the historian Benedict Anderson (1936-
2015) linked the rise of the modern absolutist nation state about 500
years ago to the emergence of the printing press under capitalism
('print-capitalism', as he calls it). By the eighteenth century, with
the growth of the news press, large numbers of people were brought
into the political arena as they 'imagined' nation states. Print cultures
brought a host of narrative innovations that have really shaped the
pre-digital modern world. Printing meant that stories could now be

reproduced, standardized, disseminated and preserved (Eisenstein, 1979–82, pp. 978-92). As reproduced stories became more widespread, they encouraged greater literacy, creating a new literary 'reading public' and making the divide between the literate and the illiterate more significant. And the nature of the stories themselves started to change. New modes emerged, such as novels, autobiographies and 'serials', that brought a new sensibility to others, heightened an awareness of the interior workings of the mind, and created a mode of personal and private reading. Indeed, it has been widely claimed that the novel accompanied the rise of individualism and extended the range of human sympathies and empathy. A sympathy with other characters very different from (or even very similar to) ourselves becomes a necessary feature in approaching these complex new narratives (see Bjorklund, 1998; Keen, 2007; Watt, 1967).

New political stories also started to become much more available. The political sociologist Charles Tilly (2004) shows the rise of political tracts and manifestos that could now be widely read, playing a critical role in the rise of modern social movements from the French Revolution onwards. None of this happened with ease; even with the French Revolution, there was great hostility to this new class of readers. And yet access to dangerous ideas became more possible for a wider range of groups. Slave narratives, for instance, showed the growing importance of becoming literate so that others could read and share stories of trouble – which were maybe ultimately to be acted upon. Here is enhanced access for marginalized groups: the working class and women can start to read the stories of others (e.g. Rose, 2001). Stories of the nation state also created the possibility of belonging – with the emergence both of national identities, and also of identities of people who do not fit (C. Smith, 2003).

The infrastructures of mediated narrative power in the twenty-first century

For most of humanity's history, our central narrative mode has been that of gesture, image, symbol, speech. Over the last two millennia, we witness the gradual introduction of narratives that involve, first, writing and literacy, and then new forms of technology: print, mechanical reproduction, electronic media. Ultimately, at an astonishing pace, our current fragile moment has brought us the internet and digitalism. This is no place for a detailed history of all this. But just consider a few landmark inventions and what they have done to stories.

From Mechanical to Electronic

The mechanical camera emerged around 1839, setting in train a new visual world of narrative reproduction never possible before and leading ultimately to the ubiquity of recorded images: from camcorders to digital photography to Snapchat. Photojournalism and family photography are but two new tales this brought. The telephone arrived around 1876, bridging remarkable distances and heralding the mobile phone and a dramatic reordering of human stories. New forms of non-face-to-face conversational stories were generated: the phonograph arrived around 1877, anticipating the Walkman and the iPod 100 years later: nowadays, iTunes and Spotify let us have music wherever we go – we live our lives against a backdrop of musical narratives! We have moved from the live, local musics of the largely silent past to a cacophony of lyrical narratives – from the Great American Songbook to contemporary rap. The 1890s saw film arriving in time to herald the twentieth century as 'the century of the film', generating new visual narrative screens that would eventually become streamed directly into our homes. So now we have photo, film, video, recorded music – new media forms to tell new stories. All this has seriously changed the world, introducing a wider and wider audience to more and more diversified storytelling practices.

The Arrival of the Internet and the Digital

Just what this most recent change means is caught pithily by Marshall Poe: 'Let's look at the internet', he says: 'It is *diffuse* – everyone can get it; *iconic* – messages can include words, pictures and sounds; *unconstrained* – messages can be long; *dialogic* – messages will move rapidly; and *mapped* – messages will be easy to find' (2011, p. 266, his italics). A dramatic new world is in the making: a radical transformation simultaneously of our media, political and narrative lives. We stand at the very beginning of these new 'media', becoming explorers who live on the edges of perpetual change and potential chaos and crisis.[7] And we cannot predict where this might lead us. But certain trends are detectable.

Critically, for much of the world, there has been *a growing, pervasive global integration of life with modern media*. The sociologists Nick Couldry and Andreas Hepp (2017) call this 'deep mediatization'. Life has always been integrated with story and talk, and, later, books and then television: but new media gadgets, computers, mobile phones and other technologies have now become embedded, even embodied, in our daily lives. Often integrated into or onto our bodies, we live with media technologies twenty-four hours a day. Within just fifty years, it has become inappropriate to separate out reality from media: as I write, about half the world lives life in a mediated digital everyday reality that engages perpetually in digital narrative actions; and as this rapidly expands, future generations may only know this digital life. Older notions of distinctive and separate public spheres start to break down as *heterogeneous global public mediated worlds* – a public labyrinth – appear. And this has led to a profound re-ordering of time–space relations in the world: the local meshes with the global and narratives become perpetual. We are never far away from a new story anywhere in the world. Our sense of home and belonging, our sense of time, and our very sense of the public and private get reordered. Narratives have simultaneously become wildly *diversified* and, at the same time, *converge* into a few basic media forms, becoming a kind of monster hybrid assemblage of systems (located on our Apple wristwatch, for example). Even as we find the media becoming more *participatory* (we become celebrities, host our own blogs, run our YouTubes, market ourselves, become reality programmes, develop citizens' news and hashtag ourselves silly), so we are also witness to the arrival of the *internet of things*, where gadgets and computers talk to each other, creating a new world of narratives living without people. And much of this new world sees a widespread *commercialization of media* across the world, with a heavy concentration of ownership and big business: owners of media are among the richest people in the world.

This new mediated narrative world lives in *perpetual innovative crisis*. New technologies are constantly being developed and redeveloped so that one new form rapidly succeeds another: from telegram to radio to television, from film to video, from phone to mobile phone, from Web 1.0 to Web 2.0 to Web 3.0. We never know just what will come next. This innovative crisis is one of the reasons why modern narratives and media become increasingly *risky and unstable.* And this instability goes deeper as modern media themselves facilitate the rapid dissemination of a very wide range of *disruptive narratives*: of cruelty and abuse, of criminal activities, of surveillance, of cyber-attacks. The new technologies bring with them a wide range of disruptions that can make life less safe and orderly – putting life, and narrative, at risk.

Human life has always been complex; but this new world has reached such layers of complexity that no one person can really understand its full working. What we find now are ever-increasing numbers of specialists with complex narratives who can provide little grasp of other parts, or indeed the working of the whole and its past. In this sense, we live in a world out of our control.

While some see this as a growing emancipation from distant and overarching power, fostering a higher level of engagement and participation of all, others see it as bringing a new dark age in which digital power has become concentrated in fewer and fewer hands. There has now begun a major debate about media, publics and their potential for democratization (Bridle, 2018).

A brave new world of narrative? Transforming stories digitally

As Chadwick ([2013] 2017, p. 68) tellingly says: 'All older media were once newer, and all newer media eventually get older. Media and media systems are always in the process of becoming.' The media are perpetually changing. That said, it does really start to look like a new era may be emerging for our storytelling. In its extreme form, this means our ancient narrative life increasingly nudges towards worlds of virtual reality, augmented reality, artificial intelligence, the internet of things, and even singularity and the post-human. There are many signs that we are now entering narrative worlds of virtual stories, robotic stories and transhuman stories. And so, as some recent researchers remarked, 'Before the Internet becomes too ubiquitous, researchers and policy makers need to seize the current moment to understand the profound political changes already under way' (Margetts et al., 2016, p. 226).

Take a quick glimpse at just some of the striking changes that are happening in story worlds. Some transformations enhance equal and participatory power; others create greater risk. Thus, *digital storytelling* assembles stories online: from mundane blogging (bestsellers like *Fifty Shades of Grey* often start online) to highly interactive story circles where authors write their stories collectively online (B. Alexander, 2011; Alleyne, 2015). The presence of hyperlinks within digital texts also makes new kinds of writing and reading possible: a *hypertext storytelling and reading*. The need for linear reading or writing of stories declines as people skim, scan and skip around, clicking on links that can now take them elsewhere. Challenging the power of close reading, it creates wider possibilities of access to complex consortiums of stories and inter-textual narratives (Hayles, 2012). More: as images are made, shared, stored and streamed, a new omnipresent *visual culture of storytelling* – YouTube, Instagram, Snapchat – emerges: a world of selfies, pop music, sextings, documentaries and images of all kinds (Kuntsman, 2017). New *stories of the quantified self*[8] also arrive: self-tracking brings a 'self-knowledge through numbers', often through wearable devices, helping us to know more and more about our beings and bodies. A new transforming story of our life can be documented from birth to death: eating, sleeping, walking, health, moods, social media status, etc. The website *The Quantified Self* lists over 500 tracking tools (e.g. Lupton, 2016, and the Quantified Self website)! And futuristic storytelling brings new open-ended kinds of stories with multiple possible endings and contingencies that shape different outcomes. Films like *Run Lola, Run* provide multiple stories simultaneously showing different outcomes and shapes: different contingent possibilities move into a range of potential outcomes. Open-ended stories are assembled through varying nodes and opportunities (Bode and Dietrich, 2013). Through all this, old communities reshape into new digital communities: every arena of social life – political, religious, familial, celebrities, etc. – now has its own blogosphere, tweets and hashtag cultures. Many new practices arise around this – *digital activism, digital journalism, digital fundraising, digital humanities* and *digital curating*, whereby all kinds of stories can be selected and archived, or linked to novels, communities, etc. Digital politics starts to change the shapes of democracy. And *digital gaming* becomes a widespread integrated part of new global media culture, often transcending conventional narrative with distinctively new playful forms. Then there is *Big Data* and *AI (robotic) storytelling*, in which the machine writes the narrative: the story is built from an algorithm, told without people. Ultimately, many of our new digital messages should perhaps not really be called stories at all: they are just digits, messages or algorithms. An algorithm is hardly a story. Maybe we should call them quasi-narratives. Or perhaps, more darkly, the end of the story? As we move from cave writing through books and film, we now reach a world of hybrid media narratives of growing complexity and uncertainty. What are our narrative futures?

Digital narrative worlds

In an extraordinarily short period, much of human life has precariously clicked itself into digital life: the written narrative has become the digital narrative.[9] For many everyday lives are now immersed in a pervasive (some say, addictive) digitalism – so much so that, a generation ahead, very few will even remember the existence of the non-digital. Mobile phones are our constant companions and we look at them every few minutes. On a typical day in 2017, there were some 3.5 billion Google searches. (Though, as I write, there are estimates this has already increased to 4.464 billion a day and 1.2 trillion per year worldwide.) There are some 5 billion YouTube videos watched every day, with users posting 300 hours of video for every minute of actual time.[10] This is a very different world from the one that existed a mere quarter of a century ago. We cannot be sure where this risky world is headed. A ubiquitous digitalism has reordered time, space and relationships – and it has met ubiquitous power. There is already little we can do in society that stands apart from this new growing digitalism. *Narrative life, its stories, imaginations and realities are transforming under the rule of digitalism.* As our wired selves make us four-dimensional (Scott, 2015), we face new complexities and risks. Trouble is apparent everywhere, even though it is often ignored.

To get some leverage on this complexity, I find it helps initially to think simultaneously of this sphere as being both: (a) micro – a massive surface enterprise of never-ending little digital narrative actions; and simultaneously (b) macro – a vast, deep moving system, a *digital/internet infrastructure* through which everything moves.

Clicking Culture and its Micro-Narrative Actions

From hypertext to selfies, a new world of digital stories has arrived: our new digital narrative actions have turned us into the Clicking Animal. Whether we are engaging with tweets, Facebook messages, e-mails, Instagrams, Google searches, Wikipedia searches, YouTube, or hashtagging, we are never far from a digital click. The puzzle is whether these lead us to narratives as we have known them in the past. *Are digital actions really narrative actions?* Is the digit and the logarithm taking over from the story, or are these just new forms? Are we starting to live in a world of quasi-narrative and story factoids? As we click away, a narrative metamorphosis is happening which is rendering our newer mediated stories increasingly:

- Fragmented – from tweets to soap operas, stories increasingly come to us in little bits; wider or deeper visions, 'whole stories' get lost …
- Formulaic – stories often follow established algorithms, memes and hashtags to fix patterns, logics and styles …
- Fast, speedy – stories come in rapid succession: there is little time to ever 'let stories breathe'.

- Overloaded, saturated – stories pile up and we can become overwhelmed with it all: there seems no end. There is 'a catastrophe of abundance' (Keen, 2015).
- Open-ended and never-ending – stories become less finite. Unlike classic novels, poems or films, there are no longer finite beginnings, middles and ends. They are often never-ending: soap operas roll on forever, box sets never end, when does a tweet cease? The classic linear form of narrative dies ...
- Connected and participatory – stories become less fixed and 'out there'. Through social media, the World Wide Web, hypertexting, etc., a new mode of connectivity and relating our stories to each other appears ...
- Segmented – stories come to live in 'bubbles' of multi-media, niche 'narrowcasting' geared to very specific audiences. More and more of the same things are followed by the same limited number of people. Oddly, this may force a decline of diversities ...

And with these comes a new shape of politics for the future: fragmented, formulaic, fast, connective, participatory, segmented. Ultimately, these transformative stories set up new challenges with new risks.

Deep Digitalism, Platform Capitalism and Its Macro-Narrative Actions

These seemingly isolated and free-floating 'digital clicks' are part of a global labyrinth of deeper and wider digital narratives: a deep infrastructure. It may provisionally help to use an old metaphor – that of the iceberg tip – but then to muddle it with the idea of labyrinths. While the global digital world works with only an iceberg tip visible (the usual hybrid storied content of chat, films, music, blogs, photos, video, games, shopping, news and the rest), heaving beneath are vast layers that are much harder to detect and understand. And these might be seen as digital narrative labyrinths, a really layered complex matrix of circuits and pathways. For the moment, just imagine four layers: visible iceberg tip, concealed surface, deep and dark, foundational. The iceberg tip is the daily multitude of basic narrative actions we engage in every day, from texting and tweeting to blogging and e-mailing. For many this is 'all ye know on earth and all ye need to know'. With a little work, though, we can soon find a whole system of rules, regulations and less apparent actions that are just a little step from the surface: our narratives are subject to all kinds of filters and algorithms, and rules. Behind this scene lurk the actions of networks of corporations, governments and criminals, watching and intervening. One click away from this is a 'Dark Web' where a world of potentially dangerous and damaging stories loiter and lurk. It is a world of dangerous, criminal digital stories (Bartlett, 2015). And ultimately underpinning all this is the vast digital infrastructure that is chaotically busy: (a) organizing processes, platforms and formats – a world of global connectivity and digital infrastructures at work; and (b) reading, and organizing the world's data profiles. In this world of deep data mining, we find visions of new narratives emerging – Big Data stories, surveillance stories, stories from the Dark Web, and the rest – that are ultimately economic, controlled by a few mega-companies. A new form of capitalism is in the making – called by some a 'platform capitalism'. And as digital expert Monica Horten says: 'Those who own the infrastructure have the ability to determine how things should be' (2016, p. 17). Corporations regulate this infra-structure, and ultimately the meta-narratives. A few digital compa-nies are among the biggest corporations in the world (Srnicek, 2016).

So here are two major tendencies: one is towards the chaos of a multiplicity of 'tiny acts of participation' creating a vast labyrinth of perpetually streaming new mini-narratives, hypertext narratives, quasi-narratives, and maybe non-narratives. By contrast, another moves into the flowing connectivity of the hybrid global digital sphere where these tiny acts cluster into a deep concentration of capitalist corporations and mega-states across the world, becoming Big Data, Big Narratives and Big Platforms. One remains a world of personal meaning, the other becomes a world of dehumanized macro-meaning and regulation where small everyday micro-narratives often grow into big macro-narratives. As one small clicking narrative of love, shopping or politics becomes a digital consumer profile, so new Big Narratives are being mined through huge capitalist and state organi-zations for the meta-narratives of our mass lives (Margetts et al., 2016; O'Neil, 2016; Owen, 2015).

Digital narrative risks: the limits of an over-mediated life

We are now able to sense a new world that digital narratives are taking us to. Are we facing a potential narrative metamorphosis?[11] Just how might our global digital narrative actions working in the global digital labyrinth put human life and narrative at risk? Is this all good news?

With less than a quarter-century of this rapid change behind us, parallels have been drawn here between our emerging digital and anthropogenic age and both the 'Wild West' and 'Piracy on the High Seas'. In both these earlier periods, developing a new world order (of markets and world navigation) was preceded by a chaotic wild lawlessness. Table 5.1 summarizes many of the critical problems that we are facing right now. They will take much time and energy to sort, and at many levels too: international, national, local and personal. One hopeful empirical study of 'networked teens' in the US by danah boyd (2014) points us to the very many problems that young people currently face through living immersed digital lives; and, while recognizing the difficulties and complexities, she nevertheless finds that the kids themselves are actually pragmatically finding ways of working out their problems and finding solutions. As they say: 'It's complicated!' So there is hope. Still others have suggested the idea of a digital citizenship, which is being explored in some countries to at least help to develop ways to handle new forms of digital etiquette and responsibility in education, health and personal life.[12]

Here we find rafts of new digital stories posing new risks. All bring the possibility of people being harmed or functioning less well in the world. Quite centrally, there has been the proliferation of new forms of *cruel stories* – tales calculated to bring hurt. Everywhere, it seems, we are telling stories that can damage others: cyber-bullying, grooming, revenge porn, cyber-stalking, trolling (inciting hatred online by posting abusive or inflammatory messages), baiting (humiliating by telling sexual stories about someone), spamming (directing vast quantities of unwanted messages), flaming (unwanted abuse, often in live chat forums) and computational propaganda (use of robotic accounts and automated bots to spread fake stories rapidly).[13] Much of this feeds from and nurtures a widespread narrative misogyny, narrative homophobia, narrative racism, narrative vigilantism and narrative violence (see Aiken, 2016). Timothy Garton Ash raises the problem of 'Trial by Twitter'. As we create indelible narratives – hard to erase – is there a right to be forgotten, or must our digital narratives live with us forever (which raises the issue of how we can (or cannot) remove our digital stories and narrative traces)?

Such cruelty also spreads out to the world of governance – political or ideological extremist groups, hacktivists, terrorists and transnational criminal organizations develop *cyber war stories* (including *cyber espionage* and *cyber terrorism stories*). Here, the security of the state's

Table 5.1 Digital risks in the early twenty-first century: nine issues

Digital risks	Problems to handle
Digital narrative cruelty, abuse, hate speech and crime	How do digital stories harm people: who harms, who gets harmed, how and why? And what is to be done? (Aiken, 2016)
Digital narrative surveillance and weaponization	Who knows what about our stories as the public and private are transformed? Is there an invasion of our freedom? How might our data be used against us? And what is to be done? (Lanier, 2018; Noble, 2018; O'Neil, 2016).
Digital narrative cyberwar	How do cyberwar narratives put society at risk, and how is our security breached? And what is to be done?
Digital narrative self	How is digitalism changing who we are? Is it transparent narcissism or does it bring a new awareness and politics? And what is to be done? (Storr, 2017)
Digital narrative transformations	What risks take shape as narratives take on new features? How do fragmentation, fastness and segmentation, etc., pose challenges? And what is to be done?
Digital narrative dehumanization	How ultimately might digitalism lead us to new worlds where we become 'less empathetic, more fearful, more isolated and more tribal' (Lanier, 2018)? Does it 'diminish and disorient us' (Carr, 2011)? Does real human life matter less and with this come the end of human storytelling? And what is to be done? (Keen, 2018)?
Digital narrative inequalities	Who has no access to the digital world? Whose stories are excluded? How might algorithms work to exclude (Noble, 2018)? How are narrative inequalities – the digital divide – being reshaped? And what is to be done? (Norris, 2010; Van Dijk, 2005).
Digital narrative control	Who owns the digital media and who has the power? Does digitalism lead to more democratic systems, more populist systems, or more authoritarian systems? Is the new capitalism a platform capitalism? Who regulates and dominates narratives? And what is to be done? (Bartlett, 2018)
Digital environmental damage	What damage does digital power do to the environment? And what is to be done? (Bridle, 2018).

computers is at risk. And closely linked to this is the rise of all kinds of *surveillance and control stories*, in which 'our every click is registered somewhere', so it may be being monitored by someone else. We see the weaponization of data, as many companies, governments and interest groups gain access to all our digital data. They can mine and monitor our lives for Big Data and secret data: George Orwell's fiction is now reality. And some of this we do to ourselves, becoming *self-surveillance stories*. As we monitor and document our intimate bodies and activities online in meticulous detail, the traditional narrative self becomes a quantified self (Lupton, 2016). Here are the *biometric narratives* (the tales of our scanned fingerprints, body, brain and eye, and health); *genetic screening narratives (*the Human Genome Project (HGP) suggests our very DNA harbours our stories); and *Geographic Information Systems (GIS) narratives* (the spatial tales of just where we are, through geo-location devices such as Radio Frequency Identification Tagging (RFID), the Global Positioning System (GPS), and satellite monitoring and drones). Our most personal details become lodged somewhere out there in the grand public labyrinth!

Another major set of digital risks, then, centre around *ontological stories*. How is digitalism changing the very nature of who we are? How is the narrative self – a bedrock of our historical humanity – becoming a digital self? Is digitalism shifting our very ways of existence, rewriting and rewiring *stories of a changing humanity*, bringing into being something very different from what we were? At the simplest level, the story of the self is changing: the selfie epitomizes this. For some, such as Will Storr, it flags a major self-absorption and the illusion of the search for perfect selves; but for others, it brings a new selfie citizenship with new narratives to challenge old ones (Kuntsman, 2017; Storr, 2017).

New narratives bring the potential for new ways of thinking. With *fragmentation, formulaic narratives, speedy narratives, saturated narratives, open-ended narratives, participatory narratives and segmented narratives*, new styles of narratives have rushed into the world and are reshaping the way we tell stories. Will the sheer velocity (speed), numbers and complexity of new narrative texts saturate and overwhelm us? Are we creating new forms of narrative that make us less thoughtful, critical, analytic and historically aware in our thinking? Is there a dumbing down, a move to the narrative surface? Might our brains even become rewired for this new mode of thinking? And this leads to another major risk: ultimately, the risk of *narrative dehumanization* becomes apparent.

And so we start to ask: How will the digital write our future stories? Can an algorithm write a story? What does an internet of things do to stories? What might a robotic narrative (*RoboNarrative*) look like? How might artificial intelligence (AI), robots and sensor networks take our narratives (and human life) beyond human control? How ultimately might digitalism lead us to new worlds where real human life will matter less, and with this *will we see the end of human storytelling?* Where people and their stories once were, so we now have technologies and their digits. Where people and their stories once lived, we now live with the internet of things weakening the charm of face-to-face storytelling and human communications. Is there a digital *takeover*? Is the new story the story of the singularity, the transhuman, the posthuman? And how will power now dialogue with the machine?

Democratic Fatigue and Digital Risk?

A final cluster of problems might be called *political stories* and make us confront issues of inequality, justice and democracy. Within a quarter of a century, digitalism has reorganized both politics and political storytelling, and, at this time, nobody can predict where this will take us. Digital narratives are leading to major transformations across the whole of human life: economy, education, health, sexuality, gender, religion and more. Unsurprisingly, they are also changing the landscape of our political narratives, shaping recent political events like Brexit in the UK, the election of Trump in the USA, and the seeming crisis in Western democracy. We are only starting to grasp how significant these changes might be.

Digitalism is creating many new styles and opportunities for shifting narrative power. Some claim it just may bring greater opportunity for being politically engaged than has ever been known before as 'ordinary people fed up with the mechanisms of representative politics build a 'connective politics' that may well replace representative democracy' (Tormey, 2015, pp. 123, 133). As a fluid, leaderless, participatory social network of activism arises spontaneously, so new narratives appear from the ground, often generating drama, turbulence and change. Much discussed is the way that, around the world, people have galvanized new grassroots activism through social media: the Occupy Movement, the Arab Spring in Egypt, the Umbrella Movement in Hong Kong, the Gezi Park Movement in Turkey, Indignados in Spain. Here are the *Networks of Outrage and Hope* (Castells, 2012): worlds of online activism, cyberprotest, liberation technology, digital rebellion and the People's Platform. Here are instant global narratives responding to key issues of politics, as a new 'networked advocacy' of horizontal, leaderless, 'swarms' mobilize on key issues (Gerbaudo, 2012). Indeed, Margetts et al. (2016) ask: Could people mobilize today without social media?

Contemporary politics is increasingly about how these new hybrid networked media work. The scandals around Brexit, Hilary Clinton and Trump, the wide rise of populism, Facebook, Cambridge Analytica are indicating political life is taking a different shape – and so might democracy be. At the simplest level, digital politics is transforming how political parties, social movements, public bureaucracies and global governance work. Capitalism itself is being modified through it: a new, parasitic platform capitalism is emerging, where Big Business goes in pursuit of new commodities and Big Profits through Big Data, as they become transformed into platforms, building international political blogospheres (Highfield, 2016; Srnicek, 2016). A plethora of new forms of political stories are emerging. Very apparent are the political blogosphere, petition signing, crowdfunding and the new digital journalism, but table 5.2 suggests some more of the new surface manifestations to look out for.

Many believe that this new digitalism will bring us a better new world. But there are also many critics who find a scary, dark side: not just a new incivility but the possibility that new digital narratives are weakening the chances for democracy. Indeed, so far, many new digital movements have regularly failed in their goals, made situations worse or left the same groups in power.

And as 'the people' become the makers of digital media, so the human and fabricated nature of media reality becomes apparent daily. The media itself become disbelieved, even an object of attack. We become aware of being stranded in a language of 'fake media'. There is a breakdown of trust – so vital to democracies. The world and its media can no longer be trusted. More: the segmented public spheres reduce the possibilities for dialogues across common ground. Niche narratives mean like only speak to like – differences are magnified. The hope for finding the democratic centre becomes weakened as groups become more and more polarized. Indeed, new media platforms, audiences and groups appear around these niches: people find their own. Hence the rise of regressive, right-wing and populist organizations promoting hate narratives – attacking class, race, gender, disability and sexuality groups. People may find their voices, but these may work against pluralism, debate and democracies.

For many, the quality of language in (political) narratives is also starting to decline. Incivility is becoming the new medium of communication. Dialogue declines. The tweeting of Donald Trump arguably moved the global political world towards tweeting as a major form of communication – with a manifest debasement of public

Table 5.2 Are these the new digital narratives of power?

Online activist stories	Real face-to-face live politics becomes rarer as politics moves to being increasingly a media event via Twitter, Facebook and the rest.
Hybrid mediated stories	Politics now happens across texts, images, videos, audio recordings and social media, and links all connected. It comes to us from many directions.
YouTube stories	Politics becomes increasingly a matter of images, slogans and icons. There is little room for engagement: politics is consumed rather than actively debated.
Niche or bubble stories	Politics comes to live in its own small segmented worlds, which become 'echo chambers' with their own audiences.
Selfie citizenship	Stories are told through selfies that protest and make political claims.
Demotic politics	Stories are told by ordinary people, which often can make them into celebrities and leaders outside of the conventional realm of politics.
Hashtag publics and their stories	Stories create temporary virtual communities that 'pop up, come out, provide support and taper off'.[14]
Automated bot stories	Stories can now be initiated and sent in multiple numbers by software robots to spiralling wide audiences. Claimed to be widely used in the Clinton–Trump election of 2016.
Fake stories	Within such an unregulated system, the potential for stories to involve lying, propaganda, fraudulence and damaged language becomes more widespread. Always an ever-present fear, it now escalates.
Chaotic stories	There is little control over many of these media, and so wild, chaotic stories can readily be told.

political language. (Even before his presidency, books appeared that documented and critiqued his tweeting (Fuchs, 2018)).

The struggle for value, again: towards a critical human digitalism

Digitalism can enhance narrative power in so many ways – along with AI, it is our future. At the same time, a nightmare scenario of multiple digital risks is developing that suggests possible catastrophic dangers and disenchantments for both humanity and our narrative life. While there are certainly many who sing in praise of the digital life, there are also now large numbers who are deeply critical and concerned about humanity's impending future (see Peters, 2013). Digital life is too important to be left in the hands of the digital experts. There is a need to ask persistently: *Just what is digitalism doing to our humanity?*

Here is a positive possibility: many of these documented digital risks posed by digitalism for narrative are not really new at all. We have been here before throughout human history – and, in the recent past, notably with the industrial revolution. Many are simply new developments – an escalation, perhaps – of older persistent human problems. Our humanity has long suffered variants of these dangers and risks. And it has also long tried to develop human values that can help us deal with them: call them the humanist values of dignity, justice, rights, empathy, care and the rest. Such values are multiple, contested and changing but, that said, a broad sense of what they stand for is emerging.

Taking such values seriously, how might we best confront this digital narrative crisis? One suggestion noted is that of a digital citizenship or a *critical human digitalism* based on shared cosmopolitan human values. Instead of seeking a digital humanity where we bend the human towards the digital, we seek instead a human digitalism where we bend the digital towards the human. Thus, the seemingly new problem of the *narrative digital divide* really just takes us straight back to the perpetual problem that Tilly names as deep durable inequalities: we are just witnessing the latest version of it. New forms of a damaging capitalism are emerging. We can perhaps move ahead on this through the continuing old humanist ideas of the struggle for social justice. Likewise, the seemingly new dire problem of *narrative cruelty* is really a centuries-old issue of humanity's inhumanity to humanity with its long history of violence. We move ahead on this by arguing for *care and kindness as central human values*. How are we to look after each other in a digital world? Likewise, narratives have always highlighted war from the *Iliad* onwards: so, that there is now *cyberwar* should come as no surprise. What we need is a very sophisticated Peace Studies to help us champion a better way here. *Surveillance* is really the old problems of the public and the private, of free speech and of the visibility of who knows what, and who regulates what? The problems of confidentiality were of a much smaller scale in the past. Now, for example, many governments have direct access to all this. We need clarification of freedom and free speech, of the public sphere. Regarding the accusation that the contemporary media have encouraged *narrative narcissism and individualism*: the preoccupation with the self can be at least dated back to the rise of the autobiography. And dehumanized narratives raise the centuries-old problems of dehumanization – and the need for developing strategies of *human dignity*.

Narrative power is about the perpetual struggle over human values. As the twenty-first century confronts major new problems about the future of narrative, it is forced to confront new digital infrastructures and new modes of digital politics. Thinking clearly about where this is heading becomes vital. The importance of human values in making sense of this newly emerging narrative reality will become ever more significant.

6

Narrative States

All the world's a stage,
And all the men and women merely players.
        Jacques in William Shakespeare's *As You Like It*

Violence is the most extreme form of power, and genocide is its most extreme form. Violence reveals the power of the narrative state in full throttle: the power to define, to story, and to exterminate the 'others' and their tales. The acts of narrative othering and narrative exclusion are here grossly magnified. The Nazi Holocaust that slaughtered some 6 million is modernity's darkest hour. But Rwanda is a case of continuing modern atrocity: between April and July 1994, members of the Hutu ethnic majority in the east-central African nation of Rwanda murdered as many as 800,000 people, mostly of the Tutsi minority, creating some 2 million refugees. Harrowing tales of this can be found in Jean Hatzfeld's *Life Laid Bare: The Survivors Speak* (2007) and Philip Gourevitch's *We Wish to Inform You That Tomorrow We Will Be Killed With Our Families*; and the films *Hotel Rwanda* (2004) and *Shake Hands with the Devil* (2007) visually dramatize the horrors. And, most recently, BBC 2 and Netflix have produced *Black Earth Rising* (2018), a major series about the international dramas of Rwanda. Power, story and reality meet once more.

As Rwanda generated so many deaths and disrupted lives, we have to ask how a society or state could ever come together again there? Ananda Breed's *Performing the Nation: Genocide, Justice and Reconciliation* (2014) shows how. In her ethnographic account of post-genocide Rwanda, she documents the ways a new political order was created through the drama of Gacaca courts and the fostering of a new unified Rwandan narrative identity. In 1999, a National Unity and Reconciliation Commission was set up to arrange for public debates around reconciliation, human rights and peace. And between 2005 and 2012, every citizen was required to attend on a weekly basis the traditional Gacaca civilian court systems. Here, the tribunal Gacaca courts were organized

> as a national performance to stage the power of the RPF [Rwanda Patriotic Front], the collective guilt of the Hutu population and to memorialize and commemorate the genocide through a weekly ritual of testimony, justice and reconciliation . . . A culture of music and dance . . . excavating memories of the genocide as a traumatic point of departure from which history is rewritten and Rwandacity is enacted, iterated and performed. (Breed, 2014, pp. 56-7)

Here, very visibly, the power of the narrative state works directly through everyday actions of story, drama and ritual. Actions of power are driving narrative, just as narrative actions are driving power.

Narrative governance: negotiating political structures

Stories are never told in isolation from wider power structures: ultimately they must be linked to the wider landscapes of belonging and the infrastructures of governance, states, civic culture and social movements.[1] Looking back to my six opening stories in search of a better world (see chapter 1), each of them suggests a broader landscape of longing to belong that situates the tale. With Malala, she confronted gender terrorism in Pakistan, the failures of the education system for girls, the rise of the Islamic state, and the creation of a worldwide humanitarian movement. Animal brings into focus the landscape of Bhopal, the death or injury of some half a million through an environmental catastrophe, the link with an American company, the ravaging of an environment needing help. Luz Arce tells changing stories of Pinochet's reign of terror. And the digital revolution in Tahrir was directly linked to the governance in Egypt of Mubarak. All the time, my Janus-faced stories totter between personal tales and wider public landscapes that connect to national and global issues. Narratives are always embedded in different kinds of political structures – territories, regimes, networks, assemblages, states, nations – and they generate different sensitivities to human value, belonging and storytelling. In this chapter, I start to suggest a much-needed broader view of narratives than is usually taken.

The Contested States of Stories: Narrative and Front-line Journalism

To get a striking sense of what is at stake here, consider the case of front-line journalism. At its best, this will always call power to account. Journalists who live on the front line of world states and their conflicts engage daily in narrative combat. They hear tales told of abused power and of lives under threat; they live with the narratives of suffering; they confront full-scale war and face narrative risk. And they also tell their stories: Kate Adie (2009) on the front line in Iraq or Anjan Sundaram (2017) battling for free speech in modern-day Rwanda. From the Crimean War to Vietnam, from the siege of Sarajevo to the fall of Baghdad, here are stories told under precarious regimes in danger zones, and high-risk stories of organized crime, corruption, religious conflict, land development, disputed sovereignty (in China, genuine autonomy for Tibet and the rights of ethnic Uighurs in Xinjiang are forbidden topics) and lèse-majesté where there are laws against insulting top officials (currently Turkish President Recep Tayyip Erdoğan and Egyptian President Abdel Fattah al-Sisi are examples). Let's be clear: 60-90 journalists are killed every year on the front line, and this is currently dramatically on the increase. Between 1996 and 2014, over 2,100 journalists died in the field (Cottle et al., 2016, p. 36).

Simon Cottle suggests two major kinds of dominant orders from which journalists face the most dangers and risk: (a) societies that are unstable because of national and international conflicts, e.g. Iraq, Syria, Libya, Egypt; and (b) societies that are uncivil because of corruption and crime, e.g. India, the Philippines, Colombia, Mexico, Brazil. In many such countries, the workings of free speech and the ability to tell stories falls away, and a key indicator of this is the freedom of the press. There are now several organizations that regularly map press freedom and journalistic danger zones. Reporters Without Borders, for example, was established in France in 1985 as an international non-profit NGO (Non-Governmental Organization) and now has a presence in at least 150 countries, with consultant status at the UN. It is based in Paris and publishes the *World Freedom Index*. (It is often seen to have a bias against third-world dictators and neglects the problems of the USA, Europe and the West.) Since 2001 it has also published *Predators of Press Freedom*, which lists key people to watch, and a *Press Freedom Barometer* which provides annual reports of journalists killed, imprisoned, kidnapped, arrested or forced to flee a country. Recent *Freedom of the Press Reports* claim that:

- Some 3.4 billion people in the world live in countries that lack free press; 42 per cent of the world's population has a Partly Free press; 45 per cent live in countries where the media environment is Not Free. On this basis, only 13 per cent of the world's population enjoys a Free press.
- Two countries significantly affect the figures – China, with a Not Free status, and India, with a Partly Free status. Together, they account for over a third of the world's population.
- The twelve worst-rated countries and territories in the world in 2018 were North Korea, Eritrea, Turkmenistan, Iran, Syria, China, Vietnam, Sudan, Djibouti, Cuba, Equatorial Guinea and Laos.
- The best-rated were the very small and peaceful countries of: Norway, Sweden, the Netherlands, Finland, Switzerland, Jamaica, Belgium, New Zealand, Denmark and Costa Rica.
- And across the world there has been widespread growing animosity to journalists. Even within democracies, there has been a major rise in threats: Donald Trump, for instance, refers to the media as 'the enemies of the people' (the USA has fallen to 45th on the *Index*). There have also been major declines in Poland, Turkey, Hungary – and the UK.[2]

As we sense how our stories are linked to both belonging and danger, we enter a new frame of thinking: a political economy of global political narratives, their structures and transformations.

Questioning the Narrative State

The 200 or so political regimes across the world (mainly democratic or authoritarian, but also tribal, theocratic, totalitarian, autocratic, monarchic, etc.) exhibit multiple pathways into modernities. Each has its own specific historical trajectory and repertoire of governance, economy and culture (Eisenstadt, 2002). And within each, we can find political stories, performances, and contrasting clumps of narrative realities of regulation, reproduction and ritual (Tilly, 2002, 2006). A plethora of questions can now be raised about how people come to tell very different kinds of stories under these very different kinds of regimes. Who gets to speak and who does not? How is narrative power handled differently across different issues such as 'rights', 'the environment', 'sexuality' or 'health'? How might states abuse their use of narrative: by refusing narrative (banning), forcing narrative (torturing), restricting narrative (silencing)? And what role do freedom and autonomy play in shaping storytelling across cultures? This anticipates wider issues. How do state narratives interconnect across the wider world? How do narratives migrate, take refuge, create narrative diasporas? What roles do media, traditional and digital, play in shaping world networks? And how might digitalism create new forms of digital narrative state? Ultimately, broad questions of belonging and national identity are raised, along with issues of moving beyond the state: towards global narratives of citizenship and cosmopolitanism. In all of this, I take the idea of 'states' in a double sense: states as governance, and states as a condition awaiting evaluation. *How do stories get to be told (listened to, performed) under varying complex infrastructures of state and political domination? And how might some narrative states function better than others?*

Here, we are dealing with the power of state and governance. We can say, with Bob Jessop, that states suggest an 'ensemble of institutions . . . whose socially accepted function is to define and enforce collectively binding decisions in a given population in the name of a common interest or general will' (Jessop, 2008, pp. 9ff.).[3] States can build dominant narrative realities in which a common interest will often take the form of shared stories (e.g. of national identity), which then exert definite (hegemonic) powers over people. They could also empower people. Counter-narratives and movements of resistance often accompany them. My concern here is with the contrasting ways narrative states regulate, reproduce and ritualize stories – and how they create our stories of peoplehood that speak of who we are. And how they are resisted.

People live across a wide range of narrative state arenas and spectrums. The narrative state can be partially defined by its stories and counter-stories, the actions that assemble them, and the powers of stories to provide security (or not) to their peoples. As a society builds up its rhetoric and repertoires, these become a key part of its national culture. This includes national and world literatures to which we belong. Often the key stories (religious, literary, poetic, musical) will help to define the state. And, ultimately, conflicts between states may be conflicts over stories (see R. M. Smith, 2003). Once again, we have to be careful of the stories we tell.

Scenarios: sampling complex narrative state regimes

As we roamed the world with journalists, we could start to see just how differently regulated – and indeed, precarious – many narrative worlds are. Some are extremely dangerous; others are more secure. For some, stories are tightly organized and usually oral. For most, nation states bring a large, complex, often literary and legal, narrative order. As we shift across 200 countries or so, we soon sense a wide spectrum. In what follows I provide a few small sightings of such narrative orders.

Democratic Narrative States

I start with *democratic narrative governance*. All societies, whatever their political shade, will generate a multiplicity of stories. But, on the surface at least, democracies will be the most likely of all to cultivate multiple opportunities for storytelling because they allow stories to circulate and be freely reproduced. Because democracies highlight pluralism, a free press, the will of the people, and citizenship, their stories are most likely to be multiple, open and accessible. The storyteller will become a citizen. And, within democracies, the social movement can take its place and tell its stories of human ideals: of human rights, freedom and social justice. These in turn bridge into a civic culture of associations, organizations, interest groups, etc.

This is a widely extensive form of contemporary state: from a limited focus in the early nineteenth century (mainly Western Europe and North America) through to the current period when it has reached into many parts of Latin America, Africa, Asia and Southern and Eastern Europe. There are roughly 120 possible democracies in the world in 2017 (up from just 40 in 1972), but there are also signs of its current decline in many countries, including the 'illiberal democracies' of Hungary, Turkey, Poland, Brazil and Venezuela. Recently there have been a spate of books that tell the stories of the transformation and possibility of the end of democracy (Graeber, 2013; Levitsky and Ziblatt, 2018; Mishra, 2017; Mounk, 2018; Runciman, 2018).

The story of democracy itself is a long history of muddle. Any student trying to make sense of it will read about the 'ancient democracies' and discover this means nothing like we mean today. After all, they championed slavery, excluded women and usually employed elite rule. For 'modern democracies', students may be taught key modern texts, only to find themselves debating a very wide variety of contrasting, oppositional, even contradictory forms: democracy can be agonistic, aggregative, creative, deliberative, dialogic, feminist, participatory, radical, representative, thin and thick. They may also get confused between those who see democracy as an answer to the question 'How to rule?' and others, such as Dewey, who are more concerned with democracy as a form of society. In one straightforward account, the political scientist Todd Landman suggests circles of thick and thin democracy, with procedural democracy, liberal democracy and social democracy spreading out from a core (Landman, 2013, p. 30). And throughout all of this, a perpetual feature of democracy stories will be that they are 'in crisis'. As I write, I find many books recently published claiming this.[4] Democracy is also a story of Crisis.

Defining democracy as the sovereignty of 'the people', elections and free speech, David Runciman (2015, p. xv) suggests that 'Democracy has triumphed, but it has not grown up.' His prime contrast is between democracy and autocracy: whereas democracy involves regular elections, relatively free press and open competition for power, autocracy means that leaders do not face open elections and the free flow of information is subject to political control. Modern democracies also face serious threats from the war on terror, the rise of China and climate change. Colin Crouch (2004) goes further and speaks of the post-democratic society: 'one that continues to have and to use all the institutions of democracy, but in which they increasingly become a formal shell. The energy and innovative drive pass away from the democratic arena and into small circles of a politico-economic elite.'

The most widespread democratic culture of our times is *the neo-liberal/market narrative state:* a bulwark of intense capitalism, it is seen to be the harbinger of freedom and the key narrative of many Western cultures, the democracies where free speech and open storytelling seem to be the norm. But these neo-liberal states are scarcely free at all and constitute a new form of dominant narrative. As we have seen (chapter 3), *Homo economicus* becomes the key narrative character, making money the central narrative plot. Here is a world dominated by narratives of the market, big business, deregulation; by advertising and the promotional culture; a narrative of financialization, debt and even greed; a story in which public institutions of care (education, health, welfare, etc.) become overtaken by market values, and where values of individualism, self-reliance and individual rational choice, and 'natural competitiveness', become the basic commonsense of our storytellings. This can be a place of massive corruption (Brown, 2015; Dardot and Laval, 2014). An ideology of freedom is swamped by the dominance of money and markets, and a crude materialism regulates life. Accounts outside of it are discredited.

Democracies are surely troubled forms and often exist more as an ideal story than a reality. That said, they do seem to be linked ideally to the long-term stories of the power of all people to be able to tell their tales: with narrative rights, narrative freedom and narrative citizenship.

Narrative citizenship is a sensitizing idea that highlights our rights, duties, values and imaginations as we search for free and equal lives through telling stories. Storytelling is a key to what makes us human, and, as we find the world troubled by failing democracies, authoritarianism and the new digital risk, so it becomes important to think how human beings retain their humanity as narrating animals. Here, I suggest a possibility for development of a Charter for Narrative Citizenship,[5] in which every human and society should cherish the

PRIME GOAL: The nurturing of all human beings as *flourishing, thinking, critical and creative human animals*. It is a core of our humanity.

Flowing from this we look for:

1 The championing of *global narrative freedom* (and narrative rights) for all.
2 The fostering of every human *voice being able to speak freely* about what matters in their lives, including any traumatic experiences.
3 The cultivation of *good narrative skills and practices*: a narrative (and digital/media) literacy that demands good listening, good telling and good dialogue, rather than monologue.
4 The promotion of *dialogues*, especially across groups with different – even opposing – narratives. A major task here is the de-othering of the other and the creation of new dialogic solidarities across differences.
5 The enhancing of affinities to others through *narrative empathy*, creating a sensitivity to the stories of others.
6 The ability to value the importance of *cumulative storytelling and knowledge* that bring into focus the importance of a *just and fair narrative memory*, and an awareness of the problems of epistemic ignorance and injustice.
7 The strengthening of *narrative solidarities* through *the civility of*

talk: the importance of little stories, conversations, the small kindnesses of everyday narrative – online, at work, at play, on street corners, etc.

8 The strengthening of *narrative wisdom* and *narrative trust* in all societies and across all media through an awareness of epistemological, ethical, aesthetic and pragmatic truth.

9 The promotion of narrative institutions – *education, media and digital infrastructures, journalism, art worlds, etc.* – that afford truth, freedom and fairness.

10 The cultivation of a linked digital citizenship and civility alongside a critical awareness of the *limits of the over-mediated life*; the encouragement of an ethical cosmopolitan media, including digital media, in the service of human values.

Authoritarian Narrative States

At the opposite extreme from democracy and narrative citizenship, we find the *totalitarian and authoritarian narrative state*. The most exceptional and extreme narrative state here is the totalitarian narrative state exemplified by Hitler, the Nazis, Fascism and the Holocaust.[6] Hannah Arendt highlights its unique and extreme horror: 'it exploded our traditional categories', making it so vile and threatening that our modernity must persistently keep rethinking its memory (Hayden, 2014, p. 87). This narrative is exceptional; but it alerts us to certain chilling features to look out for. Borrowing some of Arendt's key ideas, the totalitarian narrative state suggests:

• A system of total domination, total ideology and the extinction of all freedoms. Narrative is uniform, monologic, with no plurality.
• A system that functions beyond the state. Anything and everything outside of the total system becomes the enemy, to be removed. All stories have to be within this.
• A narrative that is all-powerful and claims only one way of thinking. It colonizes minds, taking away agentic selves, thinking, reflexivity, intelligence, humanity. As Arendt says: 'it murders the moral person', 'annihilates the juridical person' and 'destroys human individuality' (Arendt, [1951] 1979, p. 455).
• The organization of instruments of terror and violence: there is propaganda and policing for the masses (both public and secret).
• A narrative of widespread organized lying. People come to speak in clichés, can't understand each other's views. They become vulgar, thoughtless and show an inability to think, a refusal to question, a

lack of sense of a past. This is the emerging bureaucratic personality that both Weber and Kafka could already see.
- The presence of radical evil and the banality of evil. Evil is no longer to be found in very bad people, but is rather an absence – a lack of concern, a lack of thoughtfulness, a lack of thinking about others and humanity.
- A climate of widespread fear. Well documented in the cases of Nazi Germany and the Soviet Gulag, whole swathes of people are rendered dispossessed, dehumanized and devalued (*Untermensch* = subhuman). Stories can hardly be told.

Narrative authoritarianism can be seen as a less controlling system. Here, narratives are regulated and restricted, making for a closed monologic story. There are about fifty countries designated as 'Not Free' in this way at present: the most extreme are Syria, Tibet, Somalia, North Korea, Uzbekistan, Eritrea, Turkmenistan, Western Sahara, Central African Republic, Sudan, Equatorial Guinea and Saudi Arabia. Both China and Russia could be included. We can, again, lay out some 'ideal type' typical conditions here. With narrative authoritarianism, we find:

- communications are centrally controlled.
- large surveillance systems regulate and monitor all communications.
- 'free speech' / public speech is severely restricted.
- political mobilization is minimal.
- 'rights' stories will be discredited and unheeded.
- histories across generations are banished and rewritten.
- a culture of secrecy and silencing develops.

There is one dominant story told by one authority (often an autocrat, or even dictator), and this monological state poses special problems for those who dissent. By definition, it will strictly regulate opportunities for storytelling, and one major monologue will dominate and be enforced.

China, with a population of 1.4 billion and tipped to become the dominant country of the twenty-first century, is one of the world's great historical civilizations with a vast landscape of narrative literature over the millennia. It is also a formidable contemporary example of a kind of authoritarian state.[7] Xi Jinping, now president for life with unlimited rule and power, advocates a 'Socialism with Chinese Characteristics for a new era' that has no interest in the systems of Western democracy. It is critical of regional independence and creates a school of thought to make a 'Beautiful China' – a clean environment and greater happiness and well-being.[8] As an authoritarian state, it restricts free speech and public dissent, controls all the major media, regulates digital life centrally and employs large numbers of surveillance regulators and online censors – Garton Ash (2016) estimates between 50,000 and 75,000. This is the land of the Great Firewall, of the suppression of dissidents or any organization outside of the Party; a land with its own developed big-profit internet companies (US companies are largely blocked), with Baidu as a search engine rather than Google, Alibaba rather than Amazon, and Tencent for Twitter (together known as 'BAT'). All are heavily regulated and censored. There is also official guidance on public opinion, and warnings about dangerous concepts such as civil society and Western constitutional democracy. Here, as with many narrative states, including democratic ones, history gets rewritten (for example, the narratives of the Cultural Revolution, the great famine and Tiananmen Square).

That said, many of its people devise ingenious ways of constantly challenging boundaries and resisting dominance. Chen (2014) calls it a 'contentious authoritarianism', wherein a strong authoritarian regime accommodates moderate, widespread and routinized collective movements. When ambiguities and contradictions are spotted, there can be opportunities for protests.[9] A significant subterranean world of alternative stories is likely to be quietly developing. Authoritarianism will not stop ubiquitous counter-stories (innovative, retreatist, ritualistic, rebellious, etc.) but these will be driven into an underground world where stigmatized, secretive, silenced stories have to be very skilfully negotiated. Such stories put people's lives at risk. That said, as I write, China seems to be moving into a more repressive and regulative mode. In 2018, Chinese state media reported the merger of China Central Television (CCTV), China Radio International and China National Radio under a single network to be named 'Voice of China'. The goal of the new platform will be to 'guide hot social issues, strengthen and improve public opinion, push multimedia integration, strengthen international communication and tell good China stories'.[10]

Transforming Narrative Governance

A key issue to consider when thinking about narrative states is the kind of change and transformations that are taking place within them. One major instance of such change is found in those (many) societies that have confronted new possibilities after living perpetually in the shadow of histories of their subordination and repression by former dominant states. Generating what could be called *postcolonial narratives*, they move between four major narrative forms that capture conflicting experiences and traumas. These are:

1 The early founding narratives: usually the stories of the original or Indigenous peoples. These are at risk of being destroyed or lost; and the struggle is to keep them alive in the changing order.
2 The colonizers' stories: the new stories of domination brought by the colonizing state. Here old stories are regulated or outlawed. And the regimes often bring such acts of extreme violence and repression that emerging stories have to be contained and deflated: the world should not know the truth.
3 Resistance narratives: emerging to resist the dominant narratives (see chapter 4). They lead to reform, rebellion and revolution. These become the foundations of emergent subaltern narratives.
4 Transformative narratives: these attempt some sort of reconciliation of these conflicts and tensions, often linked to Truth and Reconciliation Commissions in search of the truth. Many of the forty or so such commissions can be identified with this narrative shape (often these are linked to what have been called 'Transitional States' – but this is a wider term).

A major recognition and understanding of the postcolonial/ neo-colonial narrative state have been advanced in theoretical works by, for example, Frantz Fanon ([1961] 2001), Edward Said (1978) and Gayatri Chakravorty Spivak (1988); by empirical research (for example, on the Partition in India, Apartheid in South Africa, the Cruelties of Latin America (Franco, 2013)); and in the now prolific and wide-ranging neocolonial fiction writing, from works like Chinua Achebe's *Things Fall Apart* (1958) to Ruth Prawer Jhabvala's *Heat and Dust* (1975). Neo-colonial literature has been vital in reimagining these worlds and sometimes suggesting how past antagonisms may be resolved. It has introduced into our understanding some major ideas for thinking about a complex modern narrative state, such as: the core idea of the *subaltern* (the way in which a colonized population loses its voice but may find it again); the *others, otherness and alterity* (in which the colonized become 'the other' of the 'dominant' culture, and what this does to them); *hybridity and border crossing* (in which cultures become a mix of colonizer and colonized); and *diaspora* (in which the colonized are displaced from their own countries and maybe find a new one).

In the long historical *durée*, there are very few countries excluded from these categories! But the modern emphasis is usually on African states, Latin America, the Caribbean and Asia, especially India. Students of the postcolonial have long been aware of these issues, being very critical of the havoc wrought on cultures through power, dominance, and the creation of alterity and the other.

On an even wider level, by the end of the twentieth century, many societies were also facing major changes that started to move them from authoritarian rule to a kind of democracy. Often called transitional states, postconflict states or post-revolution states, their storytelling often centres on confronting the traumas inflicted by a former dominating state. The fall of Galtieri in Argentina, Franco in Spain, and others elsewhere saw new narratives creating opportunities for more democratic generations. The strongest case of this has been storytelling in South Africa, where the breakdown of the discriminatory and Apartheid situation led to a major paradigmatic Truth and Reconciliation Commission, along with a new progressive agenda of human rights, which included gay rights. Indeed, many of these societies have been the homes of Truth and Reconciliation Commissions. This has not, however, always been positive: the situation of new generations in the Soviet Union has become one of the key global activist issues of recent times.

Valuing Narrative Governance: Tales that Rank the World

As we saw above, there are at least 200 states. Most are now ranked in complex world evaluations that show their functioning across a range of major social economic and political dimensions (Cooley and Snyder, 2016). Such international rankings in turn lead to success or failure stories – reports that publish comparative statistics, even as they also tell stories of how states are functioning on many dimensions: human development, peace, democratic progress, levels of violence, economic growth, and even happiness. We seem to be reaching a stage in history where nations and countries are being asked to hold themselves to account. So, here we are starting to find *development stories* that focus on the quality of human lives rather than on the richness of economies (UNDP, 2017);[11] *peace stories* that focus on the state of peace across the world, showing also the amount of war and violence – and how much is spent on these;[12] and *world happiness stories* that put 'well-being' at the centre of the story.[13]

One category that has emerged from all this is the idea of fragile states (variously also called 'weak states', 'failing states' and 'quasi-states'). These stories suggest societies in which we find a combination of: (a) inefficient, corrupt states with low legitimacy; (b) economies not capable of sustaining basic welfare for their members; and (c) a lack of community bonding amongst citizens. As a consequence, people experience a chronic breakdown of their society. An estimated 446 million people live in fragile states, which are usually free from external threats but have major issues of internal violence, conflict and sovereignty (Brock et al., 2012, ch. 1).[14] Here, narratives often develop from former states (often colonized, frequently authoritarian) that have confronted some kind of anomic upheaval with a search for a new order. There has been a major disruption. Stories will, of course, be told. But, at the most basic, such nations provide very limited opportunity structures for storytellings. When states are fragile, stories may well be fragile too. In 2018, among the most worrying countries on 'very high alert' were: Sudan, Syria, Yemen, Central African Republic, Somalia and South Sudan. (Interestingly, there were concerns that some richer countries such as the USA, the UK and Spain were becoming less stable.)

Here we also find what we might call 'stateless stories'. As people move out of fragile and broken states in search of new homes, they often are forced to leave old stories behind and create new stories demanded by new situations: they become refugees at sea, migrants in camps, the displaced trapped in war zones. Displacement is often linked to genocide (Rohingya and Myanmar), civil strife (Syria, Libya, Central African Republic), war (Afghanistan), natural disasters (South Asia, Haiti) and famine (Yemen, South Sudan), generating extreme situations marked by trauma and damage. Forced to live with a deep sense of loss, in fear and pain, what sorts of stories are to be found here? Stateless peoples are denied a national narrative, and even often the world story of basic human rights. Key groups are impacted: children and mothers, young men, old people. They do tell stories, but they are rarely heard. These are the stories of the dispossessed – led to ask 'Where are my stories for living in this world?' And, more disturbingly: 'Do I matter in this world?' (Feldman, 2015).[15] We enter the land of the stateless, and listen to tales of potentially wasted lives.[16]

The Paradox of Narrative Belonging and Othering

Once again, we can see the importance of both narrative belonging and narrative othering. Born into a pre-existing narrative world over which we have initially little control, we face narrative power. We act in relation to some stories and not others, and narrow the vastness of our unique human differences into a major dominant story and a prime 'essential' identity over which we seem to have little choice. We are made into distinct peoples with distinct identities: religious, gendered, political, sexual. Here are imagined communities, nations, states, citizenship and identities to which we come to belong. Belonging to stories helps define nations, establish enemies and send us to war. Stories can give us community even as they seriously limit our lives. Identities can become both the 'ties that bind' and the 'ties that blind'.[17] And such stories then can serve as a way of miniaturizing and narrowing our lives. As we come to identify with friends, family, celebrities and the rest, so we come to belong to certain stories. And these usually contain a sense of the 'other' with whom we are in tension. And this is the broad paradox of narrative belonging. We find or create the stories to which we belong but in the process also create the stories to which we do *not* belong: the narratives of the other.

In the twenty-first century, many claim we live in a world in major crisis. Arrays of political narratives from totalitarianism through the postcolonial to neo-liberalism infuse the earth. There is a realignment of powers: China is likely to become the dominant power by mid-century, and, while this is a country with a long rich narrative tradition, it is also a contemporary state with very strong regulative powers on narratives. It has little time for rights or democracy. We also have much evidence of impending environmental catastrophes that are hurtling many communities into 'the great derangement' (Ghosh, 2016). In many countries there are schismatic wars over ethnicity and religion, fuelled by the intolerance and hatreds generated in niched narratives. The economic system of neo-liberal capitalism has shaped worlds of huge debts, massive inequalities and untold misery. Digitalism is remaking the way we live, bringing many discontents. And so: finding ourselves living in authoritarian states, failed states, displaced states, divisive neo-liberal states, risky digital states, 'the end of democracy' and populist movements, we ask: Where do we belong in all this? And we tell stories of the others who are destroying our lives. There may be little that is new about this. It is the long history of narrative anxiety, anger and resentment (Mishra, 2017).

Narrative states of the world unite! Emerging cosmopolitan opportunities for global storytelling

And yet, in the midst of all these troubles, discontents and 'wicked problems',[18] there has also been another major trend nudging us towards a widening and broadening of our circle of narrative others.[19] Here is the sense of – even a longing for – a potential for more universal *democratic narratives of world openness*. We can see them arising from many sources: global governance, digitalism, transnational movements and cosmopolitanism. There is, for example, a growing extension of *world governance narratives* (notably in the United Nations and INGOs (International Non-Governmental Organizations)) that bring global stories of rights, world health, world cultural heritage, global injustice and global peace. Flawed as many of these organizations may be, they are generating new narratives that are nevertheless infusing the language of politics, creating the possibility of new narratives of global governance. Here also is the rise of new global digitalism that is enabling people to speak more easily across the world. It has brought the possibilities (and dangers) of a new kind of *global digital governance*. As Timothy Garton Ash says, in his compendious book on *Free Speech*: 'Google may not be a country, but it is a superpower. So are Facebook, Twitter and a few other giant information businesses. They do not have the formal law making authority of sovereign states . . . yet their capacity to enable or limit freedom of information and expression is greater than most states" (2016, pp. 47-8). A new kind of transnational digital state is forming, with a new digital language and narrative. More than this, we also see the rise of an array of *transnational movement narratives*, ranging from multi-faith organizations to movements around widespread migration. And with them come new narratives of multi-faith, diaspora and transitional justice: stories of *peacebuilding, state-building, reconstruction*. Central to many of these claims have been stories focusing on human rights.

Cosmopolitan Narratives

Most broadly, we are witnessing the slow rise of *cosmopolitan narratives*. For much of its history, life has been conducted in small, local and parochial groups and communities. Our stories belonged to our family, our tribe, our church, our community. But the changes in recent centuries are gradually bringing a wider understanding of the world and the pluriverse. This makes for us a gradually appearing narrative of 'world humanity': a recognizable 'global we'. *We move to being global humanity* (Mazlish, 2009). Everyday, millions of world stories of humanity are told, and although many still dwell with the parochial, more and more narratives are being forced to confront both our sense of being a small planet in a vast universe and an awareness of a growing range of others who live in the world with us. A major narrative is slowly rolling out for future generations, one that itself has a long history: the cosmopolitan narrative.

Consider, for example, a twenty-first century that now brings an ever growing and quite extraordinary tradition of world literature; transnational cinema; global digital media; world music; international art, archiving and museums; and both local and transnational documentary human testaments that, quite simply, provide a widespread growing network of cosmopolitan world storytelling. Digitalism has enabled what has never been possible before. And this creates an enormous possibility for a spectacular worldwide culture of awareness of human creativities – and our shared vulnerabilities, differences and continuities. A great global civilized conversation and dialogue among the many groups, cultures and civilizations becomes a growing possibility for generations to come. We live in early days of such momentous change, but there surely is a major opportunity here for future human life. And here are major grounds for looking very positively ahead, for never before have we had access to such an impressive worldwide cornucopia of global narratives of possibility (Casanova, 2007; Dallmayr, 2002; De Bary, 2013; Palumbo-Liu, 2012).

Conspicuously, too, in the modern world, as workers, students, tourists, families and refugees face global media, travel, migrate and become displaced, so we start to find in turn a growing opportunity for the stories of some cultures to become more open to each other and 'mix and mingle', influencing each other. Here the search is on for common grounds and dialogues among people moving around the world and learning from each other through emerging world narratives. As Martha Nussbaum puts it:

> If our world is to be a decent world in the future, we must acknowledge right now that we are citizens of one interdependent world, held together by mutual fellowship as well as the pursuit of mutual advantage, by compassion as well as self-interest, by a love of human dignity, in all people, even when there is nothing to gain from cooperating with them. Or rather even when we have to gain the biggest thing of all: participation in a just and morally decent world. (Nussbaum, 2006, p. 324)

There is nothing new in this ambitious world narrative. It has a long history. The key elements – of openness, fluidity, tolerance and an ability for cultures to speak with each other – are themes of cosmopolitanism.[20] Van Hooft (2009) summarizes some of its key contemporary examples: 'International distributive justice; peace; human rights; environmental sustainability; protection for minorities, refugees and other oppressed groups; democratic participation; and inter cultural tolerance. And virtues such as tolerance, justice, pity, righteous indignation at injustice, generosity toward the poor and starving, care for the global environment, and the willingness to take responsibility for change on a global scale.' All these can bring stories of cosmopolitan states.

Troubled as the contemporary world is, we do have in sight a new world where more cosmopolitan and hybrid generations of the diaspora have been created and open a wider range of possibilities and global activisms. Through this, we can start to see the emergence of new global meta-narratives of a critical grounded human cosmopolitanism in the making. I return to this in the final chapter.

7

Narrative Wisdom

Freedom of speech means you can say whatever you want. What you can't do is lie and expect not to be held accountable for it. Not all opinions are equal. And some things happened, just like we say they do. Slavery happened, the Black Death happened. The Earth is round, the ice caps are melting, and Elvis is not alive.

Deborah Lipstadt, the film *Denial*[1]

Only fifty years after the Holocaust, during which humans slaughtered some 6 million people, a movement of Holocaust deniers emerged. Now, as I write, a major new Nazi movement has emerged in Germany. How can it really be possible that, just a couple of generations after the profound horrors and evil of the concentration camps – within living memory – a sizeable group of people can deny them? How can the factual record be challenged, going against tens of thousands of witnesses? What makes people Holocaust deniers? And how can modern Nazis appear? Can nothing ever be learnt across generations? Can there be any 'truth' in what they claim?

Such debates came to a head in the 1990s when David Irving, a prolific writer of books on World War II, and a key spokesperson for Holocaust denial, was named and shamed by the historian Deborah Lipstadt in her 1993 book *Denying the Holocaust*. Irving filed a lawsuit; the case against Lipstadt was brought to a London court; her defence legal team remained focused steadfastly on Lipstadt's claims; a dramatic trial unfolded; they went in rigorous pursuit of the objective facts of the situation and a refutation of any lies; Lipstadt won. A rigorous search for truth is always vital.

But there is also always more to it than this. For example, the mass, violent, dehumanizing slaughtering of some 6 million people has to be seen as a major ethical, moral and political issue for the history of humankind – as does the issue of just how we can most intelligibly talk about and visualize such atrocities and pass this awareness on to future generations. We are not here just talking about truth, but an important range of other human sensitivities: ethics, aesthetics, dialogue, ontology – and power as well. How do we keep vital stories alive, live with them and champion the significance of their truth?

Hannah Arendt once again gives us food for thought: 'No one has ever doubted that truth and politics are on rather bad terms with each other, and no one, as far as I know, has ever counted truthfulness among the political virtues' (Arendt, 'Truth and Politics' in Arendt, 2006, p. 26).

Arendt's claim above is a striking one, worth remembering. Politics is not about truth: it is about power, although it is common enough to claim that we should make 'truth speak to power'. To this, I add that narrative is not about truth either: it is as much about imagination as it is reality, living as it does on a fiction–reality continuum, creating a perpetual reality puzzle. Many of the stories in this book 'struggle' with truth, but storytelling is not meant to be 'science' and only some of our stories (like the news and the documentary) purport to tell us directly about the true real world we live in. The diverse mythologies and storytellings of our multiple, contrasting and contested religious faiths do not usually claim scientific truth – they reach to even higher levels! So, my two core interests, narrative and power, do not necessarily direct themselves to truth. Power and stories can be about many other things: imaginations, influence, creativity, propaganda, deceptions, lies – not necessarily truth.

And yet, as I write, we live in a time of Brexit, Trump, Putin, Xi Jinping, Kim Jong-un; the very notion of truth seems to be at risk as we gather a contemporary awareness of this millennia-old problem. There is nothing new about this, although we have recently been treated to a plethora of books that suggest it is. There are now multiple books showing us *How Mumbo Jumbo Conquered the World* (Wheen, 2005), and many more on *post-truth* and *fake news*. As I write, the Brexit Campaign in the UK notoriously revealed the way politicians can easily propagandize falsehoods and denigrate truth-seekers. We are being told to trust 'experts' no longer – nor 'knowledge' or 'science'. And with President Trump we find a myopic world leader engaged in peddling prejudices, negative values and lies of all kinds, wilfully dismissing issues such as 'global warming' (even banning the phrase) and yet retaining popular support. By August 2018, the *New Yorker* magazine claimed he had lied publicly at least some 4,229 times![2] Trump castigates all media and their news as 'fake news' and 'the enemies of the people', degrading political language to crude tweets. We sense a world where truth and good language are significantly changing. We become extremely critical of the very idea of narrative. But, again to repeat, there is nothing new about this: history is a history of a troubled reality puzzle.

We have seen before the rise of Truth Commissions (in the story of Luz Arce, for example). These have been set up to find out the truth about major past atrocities (with forty since the 1980s), but they nearly always result in controversy and anger. This is not just because the empirical facts may be hard to unearth: it is that there are also always multiple feelings, threatened values and contested memories that inevitably emerge, too. As the search for truth proceeds, it commingles with a field of wider emotionally charged issues: of *recognition, remembrance, revenge, reconciliation, reparation and redemption* – and global social justice. To make sense of a story such as the Holocaust requires a much wider canvas than just 'the Truth'. While it must always pivotally highlight this fact-finding evidence-based and rational mission, it also needs wider panoplies of wisdoms.

Narrative truth

The most implausible thing that can be said about truth it that is plain, or simple, or obvious. The Russian philosopher Bakhtin gives us a key opening idea for thinking about truth. Never a fixed, ready-made thing, it comes to us through conversation, debates, struggles: a serious, questing, dialogue. As he says, 'Truth is not born, nor is it to be found, inside the head of an individual person. It is born *between people* collectively searching for truth, in the process of their dialogic interaction' (Bakhtin, 1984, p. 110).

Truth emerges through *dialogic struggles*. And these, as we have seen, are partially shaped by such things as narrative inequalities, digital risks and narrative states. We have not always thought this. In traditional societies, truth came mainly from the gods and was decreed by religion. As societies modernized, this 'absolute' truth clashed with a new conception of truth: as rationality and scientific debate. And as we have entered a sort of postmodern world that is self-aware of rich diversity and complexity, truth has become much more contested. It is now recognized that truth, voiced by a range of authorities, is a struggle and journey – a becoming, something to aim for, if never quite fully attained (Caputo, 2013,

p. 220). But truth-seeking is a major human virtue, which, the philosopher Julian Baggini pithily suggests, will include: 'modesty, scepticism, openness to other perspectives, a spirit of collective enquiry, a readiness to confront power, a desire to create better truths, a willingness to let our morals be guided by the facts' (2017, pp. 105-6). Problematic as the idea most certainly is, 'some kind of truth' – never simple, straightforward or easy – is ultimately always necessary. Ignorance, lying and deception are the enemies of humanity. A society without some kind of belief in truth would soon fall apart.[3]

Narrative Wisdom

Since antiquity, a useful distinction has been made between truth and wisdom. While truth must ultimately make grand claims to rationality and science, wisdom is more grounded, down to earth and practical. It is acquired slowly through life experience; it is weighted in the stories of everyday life, drawn from practical know-how and knowledge, and developed through personal, embodied (emotional and cognitive) intelligence. It will show a wide-ranging concern and care for the world and its diverse peoples, moving practically towards a sense of compassion, justice, and even inner peace as a virtue.[4] It also knows the importance of responsibility and trust – as the glue that gives institutions a sense of security.[5]

To develop critical narrative wisdom requires rationality and science to give us our impartial understanding of the objective world around us. But we will also need imagination to help us push horizons and break boundaries into visions of better 'realities'. We will need dialogue to grasp a multiplicity of voices, standpoints and arguments. We will need global ethics so that we can develop moral imaginations across cultures, understanding the genealogies of the values that different cultural stories promote. We will need aesthetics to provide a sensitivity to the difference of the beauty of stories: 'truth may be beauty'. We will need reflexivity to locate and ponder our own 'real relation' to it all. We will need pragmatism to help us see the daily workings of stories – their practical goals – as well as to inspect the consequences of our ideas. We will need an understanding of complexity, of the fragility of all our understandings. Ultimately, through all this, we can build up a sense of security with them: we need to trust our stories. When we bring these dimensions together, connecting them to the history of our own experiences, we are starting on a journey towards *a critical cosmopolitan narrative wisdom.* And *we* need this wisdom to help us tie all of this together. It is a goal to strive for – yet one very few of us, if any, will ever reach. We often have to dream the impossible dream. Few of us could ever achieve such skills in appraising narratives. So I am not suggesting here that we must all become advanced philosophers (or philanthropists!). Philosophy speaks its own puzzles, develops its own controversies, and abounds in specialized, difficult terminologies – although it can always help. But critical narrative wisdom teaches us to be more direct.

And so we return to the reality puzzle. Narrative and story must always pose questions about their relationship to truth, fiction, reality, imitation and values. Is there a *really real reality?* Narrative understanding must take us to this further land, helping us build bridges to wider narrative wisdoms that make us connect our stories to a caring about real human lives.

Bridges over troubled waters: truth, wisdom and the reality puzzle

I will start very simply. A basic understanding of narrative requires time and space: to sit and stare, to ponder and puzzle, to appreciate the multiplicities of humanities and care about the world. A virtue for the modern world is surely slowness and simplicity. And yet this modern world does not offer such a space very often, and many people living in hard or busy times will find few opportunities for possibilities like this. It should be the space of universities but so often they have now become frenzied market, metric, managerial machines with little time for slow thinking. Yet the wisdoms of our stories come slowly, are revealed gradually. We grasp our meanings through thinking cautiously, little by little. With a disjointed media market miasma and an ever-pressing speedy and saturating digital deluge dominating our lives, we need to take time and space out to appreciate stories and their value slowly.

A mild, but very important, response to all this may simply be seen as developing a widespread *media and digital literacy* through reflection, dialogue, empathy and education: being able to find time and space to think carefully and critically about what we are given through media and digitalism. Media studies, communications studies and the digital humanities, so often mocked, certainly bring the possibility of providing some major tools for reflection and critical thinking, to help us think seriously about what media narratives are doing to us. Indeed, they ask central questions about how the dominant media actually work in our storied lives and how we can do intelligent readings of them. In this new digital world, we belittle such studies at our own peril. Media and digital education – and a literacy in film as well as literature – become vital cultivations for living in the complex modern world.

Challenging Questions

Moving on, there are certain key questions that always need addressing in thinking about truth and wisdom. Not all will be equally important for each story. Not all stories warrant such attention. But ultimately all do need some consideration. Table 7.1 outlines them.

These are very grand questions but the first, pragmatism, will get us to keep our feet on the ground by encouraging us to be practical – to look at what stories are trying to achieve and appraise them on this. Starting with the practical question – How does this story work? – we look at the detailed workings of our story: its histories, forms, aims, achievements, consequences. Narratives evolve for different purposes: they may aim to inspire, to create imaginations or to give us facts. So here is nitty-gritty grounded stuff – how is the story in the round actually done?

From this, we can move on to the classic question of truth: of science and epistemology. The battle is against ignorance and falsehoods and pursues rationality, knowledge, science. We look at what is increasingly known as virtue epistemology (Battaly, 2018). While there are commonalities across different epistemologies of science – inquisitiveness, open-mindedness, curiosity, rationality, humility,

Table 7.1 Some questions for a narrative wisdom: the puzzles of reality

1 Pragmatic question	So how is the narrative assembled and what is it hoping to achieve? The practical background.
2 Scientific question	So what is the objective, impartial, falsifiable evidence in this story? This is the Big Question: the classical issue of standard truth.
3 Aesthetic question	How do we respond to the story, what do we feel about it? The correspondence with a pleasing logic and style.
4 Value question	And what values and ethics appear in the story? The overall value stance.
5 Standpoint (political) question	Detect the political interests and standpoints revealed in the story. The political hierarchy of credibility, silences, locations. How might different standpoints dialogue with each other?

methodological rigour – there are also major differences. The physical sciences largely study a world 'out there', but the social sciences have to understand the subjective objectively: they have to make sense of the multiplicity of different worlds that human beings inhabit and the values they bring to them. Centrally, the social sciences have to deal with human meanings and values as their very subject matter. They have to confront inter-subjectivity. Stories, in a sense, are the bread and butter of social science – the rawest data we have. And there is now a very substantial amount of 'scientific' work on narratives and story.[6]

All sciences change and have their own internal debates and conflicts. Back in the 1960s, the philosopher of science T. S. Kuhn (1962) introduced the key idea of *paradigm* and showed how the ideas of science get caught up in particular ways of thinking, and need, from time to time, ruptures and revolutions to enable us to see in new ways. Most science is contested from within, through different schools of argument. It helps to know a little about what these are. That said, certain methods stand above these big splits: issues of accuracy, consistency, simplicity, breadth and fruitfulness are important to all. Any story based on research will need to raise these issues of accuracy and science.

We also have to consider aesthetics. This, rather than science, is usually the litmus test for the arts. It detects the forms and qualities of art and writing. Its truth is the best. Just how might a story create pleasure, exhilarate, make your heart soar, give your life meaning, generate anger, joy, despair, grief, hope – however momentarily? Is the story beautifully crafted or is it harsh, ugly, lazy, crude, technically impoverished? Aesthetics suggests there may be some inner logic – it looks for patterns, styles, value, 'the good' in objects, events, writing: good art, good music, good architecture, good theatre and, of course, good stories. What makes for a good story or a good film (and, just maybe, how might this link to a good life?)? Aesthetics helps us make judgements about what is valuable and beautiful in human life and inspects our emotional responses.

There is a very long history of doing aesthetics, from Aristotle, Plato and Plotinus through Hume, Schiller and Dewey and on to Adorno, Goodman and Danto, etc. These days it takes in art criticism and modern cultural studies and practical aesthetics, which connect the world's current troubles and issues to our bodily and emotional imaginings of them (Bennett, 2012). Some of the key criteria suggested to help us in our judgements include: pleasure, a sense of pattern, beauty, harmony, order, symmetry, lightness, irony, design, metaphor, imagination and its horizons, a sense of the ecstatic, a peak experience or a consummate experience, the sublime and the tragic. Wherein lies the value of such experiences?

Another question concerns the values of our stories. We have seen that all stories encode values. What are they? They are present with the producer, the reader, the text and the world. And they persistently raise issues of human vulnerability, relationships, virtue, social justice and cosmopolitanism (see chapter 2, p. 35). Telling stories is never a value-free and value-neutral activity. And so one key dimension for understanding stories is to unpack these values. We can hear the story of Malala or witness the 9/11 terrorism acts and ask: Just how might this drama enhance our moral imagination, foster a communicative ethics between multiple voices holding different values, and ultimately generate a wider sense of global ethics and global compassion for others?

Finally, stories are told because people take an interest, an engagement, a stance in the telling. What are the 'interests' behind this story: who owns this narrative? In this sense at least, all stories are political, as they display multiple standpoints, often in opposition with each other. Does a dominant voice appear through this tension? What are the standpoints and political interests – the often-concealed ideologies – at work in this story? Connecting to the philosophies of ideology and standpoints, the issue of truth also raises the more distinctly political question of *dialogical political standpoints* found in all stories: Whose side are we on?[7]

Reading Refugee Stories: Fire at Sea

Any narrative raises reality puzzles: How can we bring the search for truth and wisdom to it? Take, as an example of early 21st-century life, Gianfranco Rosi's 2016 Oscar-nominated Italian documentary film, *Fire at Sea* (*Fuocoammare*), which quietly tells the tale of a small community in the Sicilian island of Lampedusa going about their daily activities and chores, making everyday sense of them. It focuses especially on the routines and tales of 12-year-old Samuele. At the same time, we see another world struggling off the coast: the desperate plights of stateless refugees who are drowning, dragging their dead in body bags, crying for their loved ones, being rescued. And then there is Pietro, the doctor, alternating between medical care for locals and migrant emergencies. Here we see separate narrative worlds in very close proximity, but neither touching the other. How do we make sense of this documentary film as it faces our truth and reality puzzle, trying to listen to multiple voices in a search for human value: the story of 12-year-old Samuele starting out on his everyday life; a doctor who tries to make sense of the problems of patients on the islands; and the chaotic lives of the arriving refugees. The refugees themselves are escaping the horrors of an abject life, now seeking a new one. One says:

> This is my testimony . . . We could no longer stay in Nigeria. Many were dying. Most were bombed . . . We fled from Nigeria. We ran to the desert. We went to Sahara Desert and many died . . . Raping and killing many people, and we could not stay. We fled to Libya. And Libya was a city of ISIS. And Libya was a place not to stay. We cried on our knees, 'What shall we do?' The mountains could not hide us. The people could not hide us. And we ran to the sea. On the journey on the sea, 200 passengers died. . . . Only 30 were rescued, and the rest died. Today we are alive. (Nigerian refugee, *Fire at Sea*, 2016)

More: here is also a filmmaker, his cameraman and crew seeking to create a kind of overarching canopy of meanings and values. And this story is not isolated and alone. It joins a rich tapestry of refugee stories screaming to the world about our neglect and their agony: it has become the narrative of our time. What kind of truth lies here?

Any serious search for wisdom or a truth about any story will be a lot of work and take time: wisdoms are not lightly or speedily achieved. It helps to start with the most practical questions about the background and purposes of the film. All narratives require contextualization. I read about the filmmaker and his goals, examined the history of the film's reception across the world (very positive), and located it in the wider world context of many refugee stories produced with different goals in this world-historical time of crisis. By taking the story as a whole, I started to look at the truth of this story in the round. It was giving us raw life as filmed, documenting far more of ordinary people's life than that of the refugees – and all as it happened. It gives us a kind of documentary realist truth – a truth we can see. But to make sense of this, we have to have some background about filming, documentaries, the producer and the director; despite its naturalness, there is a clear staging of the narratives. A camera – and maybe a camera crew – intervened. How did all this work? An interview with the director will help: he says, 'it starts with reality – and reality is my main source of telling the story. I don't change that, I stick to that, I don't make people interact with other people that they don't in real life. . . . I use the language of cinema in order to reinforce the reality.'[8]

I looked at a range of other stories – there is no shortage of them, and migrant stories come in many forms, produced for many different purposes. Among others, we find statistical reports and social surveys, journalism and news press accounts, life stories and interviews, documentary and fiction film, poems, art exhibitions, photos and sculpture, blogs, tweets and websites.[9] Pragmatism makes us confront this rich variety of stories. Not all will be seeking objective fact: some may have insight or understanding as a goal; some may be taking a political stance (whose voice is being heard?); some may have a goal of tapping into wider aesthetic truths; some may be inspirational; others may just have a desire to make us think. A pragmatic attitude encourages us to be down to earth: to look at a range of experiences, appreciate the plural world and look practically at what different stories are trying to achieve.

But this is just a start. Rosi's film is not meant to be a scientific story, but as a documentary it clearly makes a claim to be documenting a true reality. Here is a place, Lampedusa, and a refugee crisis. I enter the land of fact-checking and rationality. Some facts are given in the film. 400,000 migrants have landed on the island over the past two decades, and an estimated 15,000 have died on the journey across the Strait of Sicily. All this needs to be checked. There are major fact-checking systems now available, major resources available online which provide such data. I looked especially at the UN Refugee Agency where I was told: 'We are now witnessing the highest levels of displacement on record. An unprecedented 68.5 million people around the world have been forced from home. Among them are nearly 25.4 million refugees, over half of whom are under the age of 18.'[10] This in turn raised the problem of the validity of such statistics. To take this seriously I would need to examine these tables very closely. How can good statistics be maintained in such crisis situations?

Moving on, I asked how I personally responded to the film. This is not a neutral story and it is emotionally charged. We can expect strong reactions. I was quietly shocked. By focusing on an everyday story of a little boy doing boyish things for most of the film, a boy unaware of the refugee crisis on his doorstep, we see the divide between the knowing and unknowing world. Never mind the ignorance in distant lands, it is there just a few hundred metres away. But we are also shown the direct horrors of the refugee life: we momentarily empathize with pain. Compassion enters. Students of aesthetics have a language for all this: we become ironic spectators – a new form of watching the suffering of others from afar.[11] And here the issue of values starts to be raised. Throughout this study, I have stressed how values encode life and narrative, and suggested some of the major human values – others may have different ones (see again table 2.3). Human vulnerability is suggested, along with some core human values – *care, relationships, justice and rights, virtues and cosmopolitanism* – found throughout the film: they are all being negotiated in the everyday life of the island and the refugees. The filmmaker will also have his own ethical issues, but he takes no explicit stance: confronted with a plethora of ethical issues, it is now up to our spectator to decide. Or not. Only the doctor comes with a moral voice, when he says: 'It is the duty of every human being to help these people.'

So, mixed in with all this are ideological questions: the politics of contrasting standpoints. We have to ask: Whose side are we on? The film takes us to a land of narrative inequalities, hierarchies of credibility and narrative injustice: poor peasant stories jostle with dispossessed refugee stories. Refugee stories are grounded in subordinated standpoints: they have some similarities to slave stories – powerless, marginalized, low on world hierarchies of credibility and tellability. And they produce an enormous range of human responses – including human nastiness as a response from many; they are often silenced, and the stories told by the press, for example, are infused with politically conservative values. Refugees can be represented as threats and dangers. Indeed, studies of media responses, for example, do suggest that immigrant stories can be seriously misrepresented in the news (Philo et al., 2016).

And so, going back to at least Plato and Aristotle, we have long had to live with the reality puzzle and the ways in which we try to capture it in our poetics, our rhetoric, our politics. Today, it as if we have learnt nothing across the generations. While tales of lies, ignorance and deceptions live on in everyday life, humanity will always need narrative acts that search for truth and wisdom.

8

Narrative Contingencies

'Those who have a memory are able to live in the fragile present moments. Those who have none don't live anywhere.'

Patricio Guzmán, *Nostalgia for the Light*, 2010

The Atacama Desert in Chile is the driest place on earth; it resembles Mars. In the film *Nostalgia for the Light* (2010), we look through the eyes of two groups who gather there to understand the past. Astronomers gather because the desert provides the best place to observe the universe through clear skies: 10,000 feet above sea-level, they look up and converse with the past light streaming across the millennia. They seek the origins of humanity. But grieving women also gather – to look down into the sands of the desert. They search for the bones of their loved ones killed in the Pinochet regime: harsh heat keeps human remains intact. Here is a home for two endless stories of life and death as both groups look for their past. Chilean director Patricio Guzmán, famed for *The Battle of Chile* and *The Pinochet Case*, ends his mesmeric award-winning documentary affirming the value of story and memory because, as he states, 'Those who have a memory are able to live in the fragile present moments. Those who have none don't live anywhere.' Here is a search for stories of our past living in the present and giving hope for a future.

This chapter asks how stories are born, live and move through the world: how they are created, transformed, flourish, wither, and die. The grandest version of all this draws from ideas of evolution, adaptation and narrative inheritance. In his dazzling study *On the Origins of Stories*, Brian Boyd (2009) traces a long history of storytelling, claiming that stories have universal and evolutionary functions. They help us to pay attention to the detail of the world around us, enhance creativity, foster imagination and enable empathy. Imagined stories, fictions, are vital in sharpening human attentiveness, social cognition and, indeed, social intelligence. Taking us back to the classic work of the *Odyssey* (as indeed many studies do), Boyd suggests the profound significance of stories in sculpting what it means to be human, advocating 'evocriticism' as a way of making sense of literature through linking stories to the 'whole of life' across evolution (p. 384). Likewise, the neuro-anthropologist Merlin Donald (1991) suggests that humans have a natural capacity for narrative that has moved us on as a species. And the world's leading sociobiologist, Edward O. Wilson (2017), now claims that human creativity and stories are central to our evolutionary inheritance.

These accounts have great value. But, like so much of evolutionary thinking, they can be just a little too grand, a little too all-embracing – and a little too apolitical. I am more interested in how stories take shape as people act on them: how their powers move them from invisibility to articulation, from inner worlds to outer ones, from private life to public life, from nothingness to prominence and permanence: from absence to presence to memory. Indeed, how might people act towards them as 'ghosts'? In the closing chapter, I will also ask when a story might ultimately become a sustainable story: one worth building up and taking to a future. These are pretty difficult questions about origins and creativities, silences and absences, drama and animation, remembrances and genealogies.

The challenge is to start with a story, any story, and then tease out the flow of actions around it and its transformations of value and storied meaning. When I was young, I first encountered the writings of Erving Goffman, the twentieth century's most profound micro-sociological storyteller. I enjoyed reading his book *Asylums*, where he looked at the stories of the mentally ill, suggesting that the mad do not suffer from illness as much as they do from contingencies, fates and turning points. The life of the mad, he says, can be seen as a series of social encounters with family, friends, strangers, doctors, nurses, inmates and self. It is these *contingencies* that moved life along. At this time, I was also a young potentially gay man, exploring my own sexuality and unsure whether being gay was a mental illness. Indeed, doctors started treating me for my worries! I saw immediately it made more sense to see my life as a series of contingencies. How people defined me and how I defined myself was what was moving me on. And in this it was the stories that we are told and tell ourselves that matter. Much later I saw how this storytelling shaped by local circumstances also made sense of therapy and sexual violence. And so

I started to sense a basic flow of suffering, surviving and surpassing. Bit by bit, it became clear that stories had their own stories, their own starts and ends – and middles. And they mattered.[1]

The story of stories

And so my sense of story became wider, broader and deeper. While there is a perpetual flow of stories, there will be some critical moments (epiphanies) when human actions put power and storytelling into a full-blown aware dialogue, making some experiences more powerful, as they become more visible and 'tellable' than others. How do political processes bring stories to life, organize their 'tellability', 'visibility' and 'reception' at different moments? And how might it also kill them off? I was led to ask how grounded power and narrative actions moved a story along. Most stories are short-lived: they flitter into the world and vanish. Human stories can only really exist and last if people take an interest in them, act towards them.

Human Stories, Narrative Time, Story Flows

The world is full of human stories we could follow. Many fictional stories have their followers and fans, but these are not my main interest here. I am more interested in *tales of human documentary reality*: of sufferings, troubles and trauma. We have sensed this in some of our earlier stories: of slavery, of Malala, of Rwanda. Ultimately, all narratives dwell perpetually in the actions of moving time–space worlds. Stories are always on the move, continually being animated through actions flowing through moments in the public labyrinth of interconnected networks. Space–time narratives are episodic and contingent, but can speak to many things. Narratives of *historical* time document the past, *chronological* time charts sequences and stages in linear ways, *biographical* time tells a story moving through a life from childhood fairy tales through to late-life wisdom's tales, *generational* time maps the historical age cohorts of lives, *simultaneous time* brings together pasts, presents and futures, and narratives of *transcendent* time speak to time above and beyond mundane life. And where might the speed of *digital* time fit into all this?[2]

My concern here lies mainly with *contingent and episodic* time. This highlights the key moments, epiphanies and turning points of storytelling. Think of the story of any story as a kind of 'journey' or 'career' transformed at critical moments. After all, this metaphor provides one of the most classic genres of storytelling. It suggests how *narrative silence* moves into personal and public tellings, becoming routine and habituated, and ultimately dwindling and vanishing. I speak here of mobilities and their moments, rather than stages: this is no simple linear trajectory (Urry, 2000, 2003).

As people act towards their stories in varying ways across time and space, so they face constraints and opportunities: stories will always keep changing and moving on. Contingencies shape stories. Specifically, any narrative action will depend on many changing events rotating through five key contingencies of time (*when* is it being told?), space (*where* is it being told?), others (*who* is telling and who is being told?), agency (*why* is it being told?) and media (*how* is it being told?). Thus, different stories of migration, sexual violence, war and health crises will be told in different times and places through varying media to differing audiences and with different motivations. They will be shaped by inequalities, digitalism and the state. Some stories (of love, war and peace) have roamed the whole of history, while others have their moments of silence (the long history of child abuse), their moments of visible suffering (world poverty) and their moments of political glory (liberation movements). And right now, we are also on the verge of a new kind of story being told: the non-human story that is being told digitally by robots and algorithms, with no human authors and few human readers. In this chapter, we will remain for a little while longer with the stories of the past few millennia: with human-made stories.

Moments of narrative power

Narrative power can be fragilely framed across critical 'moments' (or 'epiphanies') when key narrative actions of power transform our tellings. They do not necessarily work chronologically: far from being linear or circular, these moments and contingencies can loop into each other, jumping to and fro. Although it helps initially to place them as a kind of sequence, ultimately this will not work: they are always commingling. Table 8.1 suggests some putative moments. Ultimately, reality and narrative can only exist in a present, but this does not stop us playing with both past and future in multiple ways.

This is a very basic schema, but it can be applied across a very wide range of events. What actions brought the story of possible traumatic stress disorder to be part of war stories, abuse stories, atrocity stories (Young, 1997)? How did second-generation survivors of the

Table 8.1 The story of a story: narrative actions and their moments

1 *Before stories*	A void with elements of a story waiting to be told
2 *Creating stories*	The earliest stories struggling to be born and to give value to the world
3 *Living stories*	The moments that stories start on their journeys through life: here there are many moments of narrative actions, ranging from empathy and framing to contesting and mobilizing
4 *Dying stories*	A story starts to come to an end: atrophy, fading, death
5 *Afterlife stories*	A story is remembered: stories become the hauntings and legacies of different generations

Holocaust come to tell the stories of their silenced parents (Stein, 2014)? How do the stories of gay rights change over generations (Plummer, 2015a)? How do people today (a generation on) remember Apartheid in South Africa; and what diverse, troubled stories were told during it (Andrews, 2007, ch. 6)? How can we recall the sides and conflicts of the Vietnam War (Nguyen, 2016)? What stories of today's world cannot be told, for a long time – if ever? How do you activate your grandparents' story? How do we act towards stories throughout life?

Before stories: narrative void

Throughout history, billions of experiences take place in the world every day; only some get put into stories that we act on. Many can never be told, and many told are immediately lost. These days, more stories are digitally saved, leaving their dim traces on the web. But even as this happens, there are always many events, major and minor, outside of our awareness, awaiting notice, often crying out to be told, but lost before they are even uttered. There always remains a vast reservoir of inchoate, putative, unseen stories. So here is our challenge: *to imagine the seemingly unimaginable, since it is as yet unnoticed, unspoken, maybe non-existent.* What can a story possibly be like before it becomes known as a story through human actions?

We start with a void, a world of possible absences, a putative story. Here is the unsayable, the ineffable, the moments of narrative 'being and not being', a world of 'nothingness'.[3] Imagine empty spaces of 'pre-stories': perhaps vast reservoirs of untold darkness and space. Like prenatal babies, the void or the deep, there can be much going on that is unseen: a space of connected parts only very dimly visible. Is this the 'uncertain, shadowy kind of existence' that Arendt talks about ([1958] 1998, p. 50)? This is a curious stumbling world, where we can hardly find the words to think the experience – even though, like shadows, we sense there is something there. Here are murmurings and ambiguities floundering for sense, dimly perceived, scarcely understood at all: the stories we have hardly begun to tell.

Three opening imageries help us grapple towards this unknown. One is drawn from physics and poetics and sees stories like a busy vast pluriverse of twinkling stars that flash into the universe, sparkle along their way, flicker and die. Stories are like stars in the universe, guiding and lighting us on their way as we, and they, come and go. Or we could turn to evolution and biology, and see stories as evolving in ecological environments. As plants depend on soil, water and nurturing to grow, so stories need tender loving care to flourish – without them, they can hardly appear. Nurturing cultivates stories. Whether we see stories as stars or plants, they suggest a naturalness to storytelling. Another imagery suggests stories emerging through contests over resources, drawing from a political economy of conflicting groups. There is a struggle across space and time, over which stories can be told and which cannot. This image senses the ways some stories rise up and others do not: stories may emerge through powers over competitive space, and it brings back into play the idea of narrative inequalities. There is a struggle over story.[4]

These images might help guide us to 1,000 mini-projects of tracking a story and tracing its origin. There is, as usual, an irony to all this – for, once we become sensitive to this issue, we can find vast swathes of putative 'once untold but now told' stories. Child sexual abuse (CSA) stories have long dark, possibly universal, histories, and even today are likely to start life as concealed, shamed, repressed stigma stories. But the past forty years have brought about recurrent storytelling explosions about abuse through the work of media and movement campaigns. In the UK, abuse, violence, corruptions and even deaths in homes and care appear periodically in the news, but most of the time they fall into silence.

But there are many examples. For example, the dimly sensed stories of *Offshoring* described by John Urry (2014) show the secret worlds of the rich and plutocratic islands, ships, planes, tax evasion and corruption where the rich conceal their wealthy worlds. They are rarely public stories. Likewise, most of the extensive world of the abject poor lives today with stories untold. And here too is 'The Environment': while big catastrophic tales may get attention, they rapidly come and go, moving speedily from startling spectacle to silence. Here are the stories of Bhopal, Chernobyl; of catastrophic landscapes, hidden land-mines, polluted nature and bodies mutilated – like Animal. This is a hidden world of long-term multiple damages, millions of people with stories untold, a slow damage and a slow violence, a world of calamities that are ponderously, slowly, long-lasting: 'outside our flickering attention spans – and outside the purview of a spectacle – driven by corporate media' (Nixon, 2011, p. 6).[5] We can look in the present to the past to discover many instances of *stories untold, awaiting, slowly – maybe – becoming told*. But also, maybe, never being told.

Creating stories: originating acts

Men, not man, live on the earth and inhabit the world.... The central political activity is action. To act, in its most general sense, means to take an initiative, to begin, to set something into motion . . . With the creation of man, the principle of beginning came into the world. It is in the nature of beginning that something new is started, which cannot be expected from whatever may have happened before . . . The fact that man is capable of action means that the unexpected can be expected from him, that he is able to perform what is infinitely improbable. And this again is possible only because each man is unique, so that with each birth something uniquely comes into the world . . . nobody was there before.

Arendt, [1958] 1998, pp. 177–8

And so, a story is born. At the heart is the idea of natality so central to Hannah Arendt's work. (And with it, action and the process of 'augmentation', increasing, growing.) Reaching the unique moment of birth, we face issues of the wonders of birthing, of emergence, creativity, of possibilities. And midwives and handmaidens can kick-start an inchoate, 'putative' or latent story into narrative action.

We can initially distinguish four originating actions through which human stories enter the world: here are narrative actions of *creativity, coming out, catastrophe and coercion*. I am sure there are others. They are not mutually exclusive and can be constructed individually or col-lectively. *Creativity narratives* are those most associated with fiction: they require imaginative energy and arrive largely from the powers of the authorial human mind. They come metaphorically out of the blue, conjured up knowingly through imagining new worlds. This is the story most beloved of fiction writers, poets, filmmakers and artists, but there is a necessary element of this in all stories. It is the world of *Middlemarch* and *Star Wars. Coming out / discovery narratives* stories suggest a preexistence; they can be gradually explored. Here are the stories often associated with trauma, abuse, becoming gay, awareness of race, disability, womanhood and the rest. They are the stories of 'Lifting a Veil', 'Coming Out', 'Seeing the Light'; what was once hidden is now made public. These are stories of journeys, of voyages of discovery (De Gloma, 2014). *Catastrophe narratives* are stories that explode into consciousness without much or any warning. These are usually quite shocking stories, as they seem to arise from nowhere and change lives: the shock of a disaster (Katrina, Grenfell), a sudden death (Princess Diana), a crisis attack (personally, Malala; socially, the planes crashing into the Twin Towers). Here there would seem to be no advance warning (often there is but it was ignored) (see Saul, 2013). And, finally, there are *coercion narratives* that are forced, coaxed, manipulated stories, through confession, torture: a person has no choice but to tell the tale, as in the story of Luz Arce in a Chilean detention centre.

These stories, once uttered, become possibilities, opportunities, affordances. They now need to live in the world, to get a life and be negotiated through the world. These early stories set up basic *acts of conversation and identification, establishing dialogue* between the characters in the text, between the author and the text, between the reader and the text, and the author and the other readers. Here are complex acts of, and key processes of, *empathy, role-taking and dialogue.* As we have seen (chapter 2), these are central features of our narrative actions: we come to identify with a story, create a conversation with self and other, make connections between an inner being and an outer world. Stories can easily become stereotyped. But here is mind, self and society at work; and a story that is often an identity story can help tell us who we might be. Sometimes we turn this identification into something substantial, an essence, a stability, a private personhood. In doing this, we might find the collective identities of others will help us. As we become sensitive to a growing wide range of imagined communities, so we learn deeper stories. In locating the nation state, we develop nationalist stories. In locating child abuse, we start to tell abuse stories.

An Aside – Communicating Stories: Mediated/Digital Acts

A story gains life through communication: it has to be spoken, listened to, written, painted, printed, filmed, photographed, digitalized. A major moment in the reading of contemporary stories will be *acts of digital communication*: a story gets activated through media work. So the history of any contemporary story will now increasingly find its starting moments through digital contact – Snapchat, Twitter, YouTube. Media are increasingly hybrid: traditional media merge with digital and media worlds. From childhood onwards, we set up actions and conversations between self and media (television, books, the digital and the rest). As we enter the mediated landscapes of the celebrity, the news story, the hashtag tweet, the entertainment media and the rest, so we generate affective narrative mediations that shape the ways we feel ourselves into our stories.

Imagine: the bits and pieces of unborn stories are everywhere awaiting birth in a world where the power of 'grander, meta-narratives and generic structures' might act as handmaidens waiting to coax them out. Here is the power of journalists, authors, artists, photographers, filmmakers, celebrities of all kinds – and a multitude of everyday folk, all on the edge of telling a story.

Living stories

The story is now on its way. It confronts a great many issues on its journey – a life and story in full swing. And here is where a myriad of little narrative actions happen that give the story a swirling momentum and keep it alive. Here are some of these actions, most of which have been introduced before, and many of which can serve as epiphanies in a person's life:

- *Dialoguing*: continuing conversations with self, other and media
- *Empathizing*: understanding contrasting interpretations of story
- *Framing*: organizing the elements of story – character, plot, etc.
- *Articulating*: finding and clarifying a voice
- *Identifying*: bridging cultural stories with personal identity of self and other
- *Bonding*: finding others, sharing stories, belonging to narrative community
- *Outing:* going public, moving from the personal and private into the public labyrinth
- *Contesting:* conflicting stories are told, stories are challenged
- *Mobilizing:* organizing and energizing the story
- *Dramatizing:* bringing stories alive through performance and performativity
- *Negotiating:* stories change, develop and diversify
- *Globalizing:* moving local stories around the world
- *Routinizing:* stories become habits.

While this is only a schematic listing, it can help to make sense of a great many (not all) stories of lives and their sufferings. To make things clearer, an example will help: gender (and sexual) violence. This is a major story of our times; it has not always been so. I first encountered it in 1976 when I heard Susan Brownmiller deliver a lecture on her new (and bestselling) book: *Against Our Will*. Here she took me into *the narrative void* that I did not know about: a long-silenced world history of men raping women, of abuse, violence and fear. The social conditions – the rise of second-wave feminism – now made the moment ripe for the story to be told. She was brave to tell the story, and it gathered large crowds. A new narrative community was in the making. It was gradually accompanied by a host of linked stories: sexual harassment, child sexual abuse, date rape. And so rafts of new *'discovery' stories* were born. And they became part of a struggle for making women's lives valued.

At the outset, we can see this as *a dialogic, interpretive struggle*: both women and men needing to find a voice, articulate a silence, over matters like sexual consent, sexual violence, sexual power. Women re-appraise their lives in deep conversations with themselves, others and the media. Women come to make sense of their lives through empathizing with others, glimpsing a bigger story that, bit by bit, putting it together, suggests the *framing* of the rape narrative: with key characters, plots, themes. In earlier moments, acts of violence that were once muddled, jumbled and unclear now start to find a coherence. As *new voices and identities are articulated,* a voice is shaped which makes sense of the body, the person, the life. (Men may well do the same.)

Gradually, the story becomes *a collective story* and many women can bond together through a narrative community, gaining strength and coming out together, making their stories more and more visible. New groups and movements can be *mobilized* and *performed.* Here was the emergence of Rape Crisis Centres and the Take Back the Night marches of the 1970s. As they enter the public sphere, the story goes public. At the same time, it also tends to isolate some men, turning them into a possible dangerous 'other' as the story is *contested.* More and more, the story becomes well known, even *ritualized* and made more routine. At the same time, other groups *renegotiate* it – helping to reshape the emerging story of child abuse, secrecy and power. The story also goes *global*: the global women's movement in particular turns it into a worldwide issue that every country has to face. These days, of course, this process is speeded up by Facebook and the like: bringing, for example, the #MeToo

movement, which itself brings along further conflicts and disagreements between women – driving the story further along. There is
never a fixed, pure and stable story.[6]

The stories linger. The stories never end. Each generation has
to revisit. As I write this book in 2017, there has been a major
series of new scandals around sexual harassment, which started in
the Hollywood film industry (linked to Harvey Weinstein), moved
into political scandals, became widespread and global. Some people
spoke as if the story was new! Others with a sense of storied memory
could see this as the failure of the old stories, now coming back to
haunt us. The stories returned: their task was not done. Stories of
sexual violence look like *a perpetual haunting*.

Dying stories

And so a story comes to have a life, diversifies, flourishes. But then?
How do stories fade? In a practical everyday life, we tell stories that
come and go very quickly – stories have a short life. And in these days
of tweets, many are even more short-lived. This is the flittering of
stories. Ultimately, a story can only live if we act towards it. A story
can only survive if it dwells in human actions and, when we stop
acting towards it, it faces a narrative mortality, a narrative death. In
thinking how stories atrophy, fade and maybe die, there are interesting parallels in examining how vast numbers of languages fall into
decline,[7] how books in libraries fade from view, how architectures
tumble into ruins, and even how people disengage and die: ener-
gies spent, all said and done. Like languages, books, buildings and
people, most stories do eventually fade from sight. People no longer
act towards them. In a memorable video,[8] the Liverpool poet Brian
Patten (2007) wanders around the tombstones of a graveyard asking:
'How long does a man live?' And, reading the lines of his much-loved
poem 'So Many Different Lengths of Time', often now read at funer-
als, he replies: 'A man lives for as long as we carry him inside us.' For
as long as a life is remembered, and memories held in common, a life
can live on.

The same is surely true of stories: a story lives for as long as we
carry it with us, and act towards it. One of these key actions is *holding
memories in common*. Looking over the remnants and rummages of
historical tales, we could ask: What are the key actions that lead our
stories towards narrative death? Most *flicker* and die almost instantly:
stories simply come and go in a moment. For a large number, the

story fades over time: we *forget* them. They do not die as much as live in perpetual suspension, awaiting an unlikely return. This raises the acute importance of forgetting and remembering in storytelling. But, for some, this forgetting is much more wilful: it is part of a strategy of *denial*, concealment and repression – we do not want to remember the story. This is often linked to shame. Much has been written about this in recent years regarding a world of past and current traumas: How do the worlds of slavery and Holocaust, Rwanda and Hiroshima come to get denied? (See Cohen, 2001, for the seminal study of the process of denial.) Sometimes testimonials of the past are simply, but wilfully, *concealed*. When the Nazi camps were discovered, there were many signs of last-minute attempts to hide what had been done. Modern British history can be written as a series of serious deep concealment of blunders, wars, treachery and the rest. In a telling account, Ian Cobain's study *The History Thieves: Secrets, Lies and the Shaping of a Modern Nation* (2016) shows massive cover-ups of state activities – from Bletchley Park to its successor, GCHQ. Notably, Cobain shows how all the governmental records in postcolonial states such as Kenya were burnt: their histories obliterated. So many stories are wilfully *destroyed*: books are burned, monuments are toppled, holy places desecrated, architecture and buildings wantonly shattered. There is a long history of banning and burning books, of censorship and libricide (well documented in Rebecca Knuth, 2006). And modern examples of the destruction of past monuments abound.

And so stories face many ways of narrative death: through *forgetting* (stories stay outside of memory); *habitualizing* (stories become taken for granted, clichés – we no longer think about them); through *decaying* (we neglect the stories); through *concealing* (we hide stories); through *denial and repression* (we push the story away); through *destruction* (we destroy the story); through *ceremonial* events (we bury our dead); and through *coercion* (our stories are taken away from us).

Afterlife stories

And yet . . . our stories can remain perpetually unfinished. In the words of Bakhtin, they are 'unfinizable'. We face a certain open endlessness with stories as they re-fashion, re-work and re-value themselves and come back to haunt us, often in new forms as memories that are always partial and often unjust. This is most noticeable in stories of mass social trauma, social injustice and big political horrors and catastrophes: Auschwitz, Stalin's Gulag, Mao's Cultural

Revolution, Hiroshima, Rwanda, Vietnam, the slavery of the USA, the Apartheid of South Africa and now Syria and Myanmar. (It might also be applied to the football fields of Hillsborough, the burning towers of 9/11 and, now, Grenfell.) *Was there ever an ending – can there ever be an end – to our stories of slavery, sexual abuse, AIDS, war trauma, holocaust?* Here is serious unfinished business, and the stories of those who suffered keep resurfacing: they will not die. The imprisoned, tortured and murdered all over the world (and, indeed, also their murderers, slaughterers, torturers) must speak again and again; past lives with stories to be told cannot be forgotten. We live with the partiality of stories, the unfairness of many memories and the perpetual symbolic presence of the living dead. Viet Thanh Nguyen's key study of the Vietnam War and memory opens with the vital comment: 'All wars are fought twice. The first time on the battlefield and the second time in memory.' The many-sided nature of memories leads him to the ideas of just and unjust memories, along with just and unjust forgetting (Nguyen, 2016, p. 4). These are key ideas to help us in thinking about our remembrances of things past: where was justice here?

The Unfinished: Memories, Archives, Ghosts and Acts of Remembrance

And so we come to live in the cosmopolitan graveyards and hauntings of evaluative storytelling. We stand perpetually on the edge of past stories all round the world that can be found in the justice of stories of family and friends, of memorials and museums, of drama, literature, film, photography – and the great growing digital archive. Here lie past and future nightmares and dreams. To hover among these vast narratives on the great bookshelves in the libraries of the world is to be slowly overwhelmed by the presence of authors and their stories throughout history. Shakespeare is full of hauntings; Dickens has his three Ghosts of Christmas; Ibsen's *Ghosts* follows lives ruined by the ghosts of past misdemeanours; Frank Capra's *It's a Wonderful Life* has an angel taking us back to show us how our world of loved ones might look if we had never lived; and Toni Morrison's *Beloved* ([1987] 2004) has the murdered baby walking though the present as an agonized adult of slavery. Indeed, in her seminal text, *Ghostly Matters*, Avery Gordon (2008) has brought the idea of ghosts firmly into social science thinking. To see 'ghosts' and 'hauntings' is to focus on what has disappeared, what goes absent, what may still be lingering – to sense the repressive powers of silencing and premature closures. She speaks directly of the repression and the atrocities directed towards Blacks in America since its inception. The complexities and horrors (and joys) live on today, sometimes in new forms.

Currently, we see it in both the #BlackLivesMatter movement and the #MeToo movement, where past traumas of racial and gender violence are revisited. The Truth Commissions on past cruelties are also places full of these hauntings – as are the museums and archives. The whole of historical storytelling has become a political struggle for value. As Lisa Yoneyama surveys the remnants of Hiroshima, she remarks: 'To perform an act of remembrance and to possess a means of memorialization becomes equivalent to demonstrating power and autonomy' (Yoneyama, 1999, p. 36). And, increasingly, the ghosts of the past enter the digital machine. At the University of Southern California Shoah Foundation's Visual History Archive on the Holocaust, for example, we find housed some 100,000 hours of video, including interviews with over 50,000 Holocaust survivors. Vital stories now live on in the digital archive (Shandler, 2017).

And yet, along with all these memorable ghosts, I am also reminded of a key line at the closing of George Eliot's *Middlemarch*: 'the growing good of the world is partly dependent on unhistoric acts; and that things are not so ill with you and me as they might have been is half owing to the number who lived faithfully a hidden life, and rest in unvisited tombs' ([1871] 2003, p. 838). Never mind the extraordinary stories that do eventually get told – there are infinitudes of stories not even partially told. And with this, we circle back to the void with which we started, a return to untold stories, the tales of the 'lost and forgotten'. Our moments continue to flow: in episodes, in dialogues, in circles and in generations – even as many get lost in the stars.

Narrative Hauntings: Generational Narratives

And so to the notions of hauntings, ghosts and memory must finally be added the more concrete one of generation.[9] Stories change across generations, and *generational narratives* are stories told (or silenced), heard or owned across specific age cohorts. A generation can usually be seen as spanning thirty or so years – thus, a single modern life could possibly be closely aware of five differing generations (with a parent, grandparent – and a child, grandchild), each with their tales to tell (or not). This means a life could live across a range of at least five eras of time, bringing wildly differing tales, tensions and troubles. How might stories be remembered across the generations? Stories can clearly live on: travelling across generations as new voids awaiting discovery, or as memories, even *postmemories*.[10] They also have the power to travel backwards and forwards, as in modern classic time films like *It's a Wonderful Life* (1946), *Back to the Future* (1985) and *Peggy Sue Got Married* (1986).

The sociologist Arlene Stein has written a very moving sociological account of her own generational crisis. Her father was in the Warsaw Ghetto, but he never spoke about it in her childhood. As with so many, escaping the Holocaust created a silence – and the need to create a time and space to rebuild a new life and story, forgetting the horrors of the past. Throughout her childhood, she experienced this silence; but on the death of her parents, she felt the need to confront and make sense of it all. In this, she found herself among a legion of children now wishing to remember – a second Holocaust generation. She wondered: 'How did we get from *there* – a time when speaking of the Holocaust was mainly a private activity . . . to *here*, the rise of a robust Holocaust memorial culture that has broad resonance?' (Stein, 2014, p. 3). And this is part of a much wider story – a broader process of reclaiming and remembering trauma and earlier life.

Sustainable stories and the legacies of stories

We are, it seems, the sophisticated political storytelling animals. Start a tale from any angle, any moment, any contingency, and push it in multiple directions. Power shapes our stories in many ways: there is no one way. And this leaves us with good puzzles. What difference might it make to start with the ends of stories and work backwards: to ask the story to unroll back across generations, or to puzzle over how it comes to be told so uniquely and distinctly at this very moment, right now, in this way and not some other? What came before? How did it unfold to be told in this way, right now? What is its genealogy, its history, its hauntings, its moments? Can there ever be narrative closure? More: enter the story from the side – whose standpoint is here, what other perspectives could be taken, what contrasting directions could it travel in? There is never one unitary and linear story taking one path. Narratives are full of power, potential and possibilities. We have travelled full circle. As T. S. Eliot famously says in *Little Gidding*:

> *What we call the beginning is often the end*
> *And to make an end is to make a beginning.*
> *The end is where we start from.*

Throughout the ages, poets, writers and dreamers have known this story of the story of our changing times and spaces so well. Behind all this, there may well ultimately be values that depict the best of our common humanity: a sort of narrative wealth, a world of resilient and sustainable stories, a perpetual positive narrative power. What might have been learnt from the contingencies and actions of stories past? And what might future stories bring? It is to this that I now turn.

Act 3

Moving On: Acts of Narrative Hope

We need a Narrative Hope:
a perpetual struggle for an imagination
that glimpses a better world
for all generations to come.
Hope lies in the present
as we engage in narrative acts;
setting us in pursuit
of a kinder, caring, fairer
human world of politics.
Careful the tales we tell.

9

Caring for Narrative Futures

Towards a Politics of Narrative Humanity

Careful the tale you tell
That is the spell
Children will listen.

Stephen Sondheim, Into the Woods

And they all lived happily ever after. Or so the story goes. In Stephen Sondheim's marvellous musical *Into the Woods* we are taken into the mystery and excitement of the children's fairy tale where a happy ending is expected. The musical weaves together a merry band of childhood figures: Little Red Riding Hood and a wolf, Jack and a beanstalk, Cinderella and a charming Prince, Rapunzel and her hair flowing from a tower – as well as a baker and his wife without a child. They all have a somewhat frightening Witch to scare them. And as they venture into the woods, their stories clash and unfold. By the end of the first act, wishes do come true, problems are resolved, and all are set to live happily ever after. Then comes the second act. It turns out all is not well: the Prince cheats, a giant kills, people quarrel. Sometimes, it seems, 'people lose their way, halfway through the woods'. There is no happy ending. But a wish and a dream – a sense of purpose – will keep them moving on. And so Sondheim's Witch sings: 'Careful the tale you tell!' (Sondheim, 2011, p. 103).

In narrative, as in life, we must indeed be careful. Much of our contemporary world can readily take us to the dark woods. In this book alone, we have seen a multiplicity of stories of cruelty, ignorance, violence, greed, failed governance, environmental neglect, digital abuse, social injustice and dehumanization. It is not hard to see why people become dark pessimists and perpetual grumblers. Disappointed with life, we give up on good stories. Yet 'dark stories' can force a pessimism of the soul, leaving us to dwell in the narrative of misery, misanthropy and myopia. Famously, in the wake of the horrors of the Holocaust, the brilliant but deeply pessimistic critical theorist Theodor W. Adorno warned us, epigrammatically: 'Writing poetry after Auschwitz is barbaric.' In this final chapter, I want to move beyond barbarism and darkness towards a certain necessary lightness. I want to engage in narrative hope.

Acts of narrative hope

Narrative hope walks a wobbly line: between the new optimists like Steven Pinker (2018) and Hans Rosling (2018), who claim our world has never been better, and the miserabilists who argue there can be no writing poetry after Auschwitz. They speak of the horrendous plight of the Angel of History who looks back to see a world of human carnage[1] – and one which has now entered the time of the Great Regression (Geiselberger, 2017). Narrative hope has to be perpetually and fully aware of this dark abyss of atrocities that humanity has committed in the past and present (and, sadly, may well continue into a future); it does see the need for persistent critique and radical change. But it also knows that there has also always been a long alternative real history of the positive and the good: the value of hope for humanity has been perpetually stressed (Bloch, [1938-47] 1986).[2] And people have not given up on it: just recently, we have seen published Barack Obama's *The Audacity of Hope* (2008), Noam Chomsky's *Hope and Prospects* (2011), Ronald Aronson's *We: Reviving Social Hope* (2017), Michael Albert's *Realizing Hope* (2006), Jonathan Lear's *Radical Hope* (2006) and Rebecca Solnit's *Hope in the Dark* ([2004] 2016). In the wake of the 2016 presidential election, with the arrival of Trump and his politics of self-interest, narcissism, anger and media hostility, it was not long before a book appeared on *Radical Hope*, containing letters to new generations advising them not to give up on hope in dark times (De Robertis, 2017). Likewise, the influential journalist Rebecca Solnit offers us a multitude of small stories of hope while recognizing the horrors of the current world. In one remarkable book, *A Paradise Built in Hell: The Extraordinary Communities That Arise in Disaster* (2009), she listens to stories of bravery and altruism from people facing great tragedy and personal loss in the disasters of the 1906 earthquake in San Francisco, the 1985 Mexico City earthquake, 9/11, Hurricane Katrina in New Orleans in 2005, and more.

She finds a positive force and community at work in the ruins and crisis: people who engaged in acts of hope.

For sure, stories can damage, destroy, dehumanize. But above all they can inform, influence, inspire. They are the beating heart of good education, therapeutic culture, social activism, humanitarian aid, Truth and Reconciliation Commissions and much more. Stories can bring hope and the power of transformation at personal, practical and social levels. As we engage in narrative interactions and build narrative communities, we share stories that may change the world. This has been a persistent theme: stories can remould lives even as they raise political challenges, provoke change and set new political agendas.

A Normative Turn: Politics and Positive Narrative Futures

My closing aim then is to think positively about power, stories and the future.[3] Taking a much more explicitly normative turn, I now ask how actions and dialogues of narrative power might help us develop a politics of narrative humanity. I imagine some of the stories that will help create better narrative realities. To help make this normative turn, I turn to a basic distinction around *positive power* and *positive narrative*. Positive power works to enhance the ways individual and collective human lives and society are shaped and influenced for a better-flourishing world for all. It is empowerment: the power to. In the struggle for human value, positive narrative works to enhance the mechanisms through which we dialogue with each other and tell stories, so that lives, human encounters and social worlds can sense a flourishing *for all*. By contrast, of course, we also have negative power, which is repressive and negative narrative, which is restrictive and harming.

Ultimately, positive power asks the central question about what constitutes valued lives, hopeful lives – even loving, contented and creative lives – and, with this, kind, thoughtful, caring governance. It will look for and tell both good stories and stories of the good. What this means will always be contentious, but I have hinted at these stories throughout. It could well mean making a society a safe, secure and loving place for its members – one where violence, exclusion, inequalities, disease and dehumanization are held at bay for all of its population, as much as is possible; where the most vulnerable are looked after well. It will be one where narratives will generally be trusted: they do what they should do and give us a security in the world. Consequently, the idea of narrative power directs us to core stories of what constitutes a good, flourishing and trusting life, and asks us to consider just how this may be achieved. It brings a politics of narrative humanity.

Sustainable Narratives: Imagining a Narrative Commons

Like many, I often feel estranged from a world where most of our economic, political and media systems can fail us so very badly, causing huge amounts of suffering for large numbers of people. Yet, while we do have much critical thinking about our difficulties, there is often a distinct lack of future narrative visions. Bearing in mind the inevitable ubiquity of human differences, just what do we wish our future world to look like for *all* people? How can *all* people find their way to have as good a life as they can? We start to look for stories that will help us imagine futures where we find better ways of doing, living and talking about the good things we wish for in the world. We ask: Just what might good narrative futures look like?[4] We might even ask whether narrative progress is possible. It is very odd that, while we usually place great emphasis on economic, scientific and technological progress, our concern with the ways our cultures, ethics, humanities and stories move on is frequently neglected (Bod, 2013; Epstein, 2012). And yet, since stories are one key to the struggle over what it means to be human, surely a key question has to be: *How can we use narrative actions to build world stories that support the advance of our world and our humanities?*

It helps to draw a parallel with the arguments that environmentalists make about the sustainability of the commons. The commons suggests 'the wealth we inherit and create together and must pass on . . . to our children . . . a long-term stewardship of resources, which communities manage . . . through shared values' (Bollier, 2014, p. 175). The commons can lead to 'a different way of seeing and being' in the world. Just as the environmental commons is open to all and needs protecting, so a narrative commons suggests there is an ecology of stories cultivated across history though a labyrinth of narrative communities from which we can learn and build. It asks us to look at the life stories of stories and build a sustainable *narrative care* that searches for the human values that lie behind the best of our common humanity. Here is our narrative wealth, our sustainable stories, our shared cosmopolitan human values. The idea of narrative care and sustainability makes us look seriously, globally and critically to the pasts, presents and futures of storytelling – their vibrancy, diversity, longevity, health, resilience.

Many public figures have themselves debased this process – just as the media have frequently become a false friend. Sustainable stories take us back to basics: making us pause to consider the story arcs and story canopies that constitute the big and little problems of human-kind. Here are macro sustainable stories (the big canopies) and micro sustainable stories (the little canopies). Big canopies have to deal with those central problems of human suffering and governance that I have raised throughout this book; they are linked to memories and the cultivation of all kinds of remembrances of things past. Little canopies protect us from the little daily storms and chaos of every-day life: giving us everyday meaning through everyday stories. Here is a home where we can find *a cosmopolitan commons of good stories*; where little narrative acts of truth, beauty and kindness are promoted as a way of life. Sustainable stories are the ones worth building up and taking to the future. These necessarily build from past stocks of stories, reworked for the needs of the present, and imagine the ability of future generations to develop their own new and better stories. Human life is an accumulating flow of progressive stories.

Aware then of the clutter and complexity of our current world, its atrocities, exploitations and inequalities, the ever-present character of our narrative fragility becomes more and more apparent. As we reach a world of growing narrative puzzlement accelerated by digital-ism, many get lost and face narrative saturation, meaninglessness and even fear. In what follows I pick up on just a few of the major strands that enable stories and narrative to connect to hope, the commons and human flourishing.

Here comes the rainbow: creating a politics of narrative humanity

What matters at this stage is the construction of local forms of community within which civility and the intellectual and moral life can be sustained through the new dark ages, which are already upon us . . . I can only answer the question 'what am I to do?' if I can answer the prior question: 'of what story or stories do I find myself a part?'
    Alasdair MacIntyre, *After Virtue: A Study in Moral Theory*, [1981] 2007, my emphasis

The highly regarded communitarian philosopher Alasdair MacIntyre made these claims in 1981; since then, the world he worried about has not advanced very much.[5] His thinking leads us to ask: What communities do we imagine we belong to? These will give us our stories. And one way of thinking about this is through the developing idea of social imaginaries – the 'ways people imagine their social existence' (Castoriadis, [1975] 1987; Taylor, 2004). A politics of narrative humanity aims to build *visions of past, present and future cosmopolitan narrative imaginaries.* It pays attention to our stories of past, present and future existence, helps us think generationally and across time, cultivates imaginaries of better worlds and the cosmos and enables thinking of future stories of hope, dialogue, belonging and human flourishing. Here are the long historical struggles for just narratives of the good and ethical life based on shared human values being built into trusted everyday institutions: stories of providing care, being kind, recognizing the rights and needs of others, developing responsibilities, fostering empathy, enhancing dignity, doing justice, creating freedom, being autonomous, creative of love, trust, dialogue and wisdom. As ever, this may bring a clashing of values, but it is important to seek out a shared world of stories of good and better imaginaries.

Important here is the persistent awareness of the value of intelligence and creativity to humanity, along with a sense of the narrative power of communities in which we struggle to help these develop. From the outset of this study, I have been recognizing issues of human suffering and vulnerability, showing how stories encode human values, and how we come to rely on our embodied, emotional narrative actions to bring them alive. Ultimately, all politics is about this struggle over human values and involves both stories of power and identifying the power these stories have over lives, relationships and personhood. This is part of a much wider and stronger claim: what makes us human is the collective creation, development, recording, and remembering of and connecting with ideas, knowledge, feelings, narrative. Thinking carefully is one key to what really makes us decisively human. And stories have simply been a major way of doing this. Thinking (and knowledge) should not simply be equated with science, though that is certainly part of it. Nor should it be equated with formal education systems, though again these play a key role. What matters here is a focus on all the various means that will *help the thinking, critical, creative human animal to* bring to the world their own original and unique embodied thoughts as they confront a much deeper and wider pre-existing multitude of world knowledge: all the ideas and creativities that have gone before. Much has been achieved in the past, though we are quick to forget this.

As we have seen, the ubiquitous acts of *doing stories* bring vital shape and power to form human life. Born with vulnerability into unique human differences, our stories perform vital roles in our social, relational and personal life. Whether through speaking, reading, writing, digitalizing or simply looking, stories can do many things to make us human. To recall: stories can energize us with empathy, enhance creativity, give meaning and imagination, provide history, repair trauma, assemble identity – and so much more. They can open our minds to mimesis; lend coherence to chaos; help organize knowledge, categories, constructs, information; provide us with all kinds of social maps; give us memory; broaden perspectives and foster wider canvases. They can become our good companions in life. And they can enable us to see the possibilities of change, cultivating a political awareness. And, of course, they can also bring damage too. But, overall, *stories bring the possibility of a reflective, reflexive and remembering embodied just humanity.* We saw it in Malala's battered but fighting young voice; it was present as Death spoke in *The Book Thief*; it is Animal telling us the tales of disability freaks and the environmentally wounded; it is protesters tweeting in Tahrir; it is catharsis in the Twin Towers; it is the story of Frederick Douglass, Toni Morrison and James Baldwin. And the rest. Telling the story can give us power and hope. Here are stories as a way of empowering and living a life – constructive, challenging and creative – and of appreciating that they can do this. The idea of narrative power shows us how stories are also embedded in asymmetrical and hierarchical relations: they bring the potential for exclusion, othering and the dehumanization of life, even as they can also bring the possibility for emancipation, protest and change. All of this starts to suggest the possibility and need for developing a narrative citizenship and a politics of narrative humanity.

Here we build upon many strands of progressive 21st-century politics, suggesting the creation of a politics of narrative humanity that works through hope, dialogue and actions to be attentive to the linkage between stories of past, present and future; to act in the world to rework the dehumanization of life; and to care for narrative flourishing in generations to come. It is a politics that sees human beings as flourishing, thinking, critical, creative and imaginative human animals. An *intellectual dignity* is seen as a core of our shared common humanity, and global narrative freedom and rights are a prerequisite for a good human existence. This means the fostering of an ability for every human voice to be able to speak freely about what matters in their lives.

Narratives Past: Lest We Forget

All stories become historical and generational. There is the long view that digs deep into distant past remnants and ruins to locate the fragments of stories from the many hundreds of generations of our longish past. And there is a shorter view that faces just how a few recent generations have lived stories with their nearest kindred and friends across the changes of remembered lives. Both ways, remembering stories keeps alive the vital cumulative memories of the past. Across the globe, all narrative stories have their own story of birth to death to afterlife. And living a rich human life means becoming aware of this generational and cosmopolitan history of our ever-changing multiple stories.

This means searching through the biographies and communities of the past to sense their continuity with the present. Memory stories are part of what makes us human, and autobiography is a prime tool for creating these. All cultures that survive have long been doing memory work as they pass on the value of classic stories of religions, philosophy, art, literature and music: of Buddha, Confucius, Allah, the Bible, the Greeks, Leonardo da Vinci, Shakespeare, Gaia, onwards. In looking to the past, there are many such stories to treasure – the kindnesses and resiliences of our own grandparents' lives, for example. We also have the stories of our own families, our own hobbies and workplaces, our own communities, our own countries, our own planet. In doing this, we look to *The Company We Keep* (Booth, 1988) and learn to speak seriously of *Handing One Another Along* (Coles, 2010), *Cultivating Humanity* (Nussbaum, 1997) and *Dialogue Among Civilizations* (Dallmayr, 2002).

All this means the regular acquiring of new skills. Every time we confront a problem in the present, from disability to war to racism to marriage breakdown, we can learn from the stories of people who have been here before. Imagine a chorus of ghosts assembling before us to retell their stories, 'lest we forget'. And the past most surely harbours an infinity of stories from which we can learn. Here we start to develop skills to recognize the power of *critical cultural memory*: of people, of groups, of places, of events and of states themselves. As generations move on, how are we to understand the injustices of past worlds – from British slavery and British colonialism to the patriarchies of the past? How best to gather cosmopolitan memory stories of justice and injustice – through biography, archives and oral histories – in order to make sense of them? And this leads us to develop a wider sense of the history of diverse world humanities: to appreciate the significance of a cosmopolitan literacy. How to encourage a reading of human difference through world art, literature, film, documentaries and music, and enhance different languages across them?

In thinking about all of this, we start to realize the importance of narrative communities and their archives. Storytelling is a central force in creating the groups, communities and relationships we dwell within. It is narrative communities and connectivities that ultimately help us to *record life* (the documentary function, telling us our stories), *remember life* (the history function, enabling reflections and memories of our past) and *reimagine life* (the inspirational function, enabling us to envision better worlds). Biographies of all kinds play a key role here. As we ask what historical narrative communities we belong to, we will also sense the struggles over values that they faced in the past and how they acted on them. Such stories can become the Wealth of Nations, providing one key basis for a good life and a good society. Through empathy and dialogue, they provide a canopy for us to identify with others, to sense the long history of belonging to narrative communities and maybe some shared common human values.

Narratives Now: Reworking Narrative Fragility

Narrative life is fragile: all too human, stuffed full of vulnerability and human difference. Riddled with inequalities and digital risk, troubled with issues of truth and reality, lodged in restrictive and regulative states, and permanently haunted by the contingencies of time, narratives will always pose problems. Often, we are haunted by a spectre of narrative dehumanization, a perpetual possibility of turning human beings into non-human beings. Here are societies that silence and refuse to recognize the complex multiplicities and humanities of the voices of their peoples, social orders that trap people into inequalities and exclude them, and digitalism that seeks to turn the human into the machine. Such societies and groups will inevitably fail people by denying their humanity and weakening the chance of a progressive change for a better world. A major goal of a politics of narrative humanity is perpetually to act to repair this fragility, even as we also perpetually work to change it. And in the current time, much of the fragility of our current narrative life is derived from the humanly made infrastructures of capitalism.

It is our narrative actions that bring the power to make stories come alive, repair damage, and rework our sense of the human. Throughout this book, I have started discussions of ways of moving ahead with such problems. This politics of narrative humanity brings into focus a number of key narrative actions. We engage in *making narrative justice* when we look at narrative inequalities and 'othering', raising issues of redistribution and recognition, human rights and social justice. We engage in *humanizing the digital* when we transform digital risks and mediated life through bringing positive human values to them. We engage with *democratizing narratives* when we push society and its governance perpetually to confront issues of freedom and control, citizenship and equality, along with a down-to-earth community engagement that challenges authoritarian modes. We engage in *cultivating narrative wisdom* when we recognize the complexities of the perpetual and universal reality puzzle of truth and falsehood, knowledge and ignorance. And we engage with *sustaining narrative care and human flourishing* when we take the long view of narrative: its history, memory and critical epiphanies of change. For example, we can start to focus on:

Listening to stories of the lives of others across the world whose lives may be different from ours. As society becomes more global, this becomes a prerequisite for good human (and political) functioning, for the good working of all societies that seek a respect and recognition for global human dignity. This will never be easy. But as we open ourselves to hear more tales of inequalities – of the sorrow and suffering of the slaves, the abject poor, the marginalized refugee, the environmentally damaged – so, ironically, we get a glimpse of the possibility of a better world: of what needs to be done. Stories will deepen our imaginations, our sympathies, our critiques of a damaged world. It is why stories, including biographies, are so often used by social movements, by reformers and campaigners, by educators and by humanitarian activists to provide exemplars and case studies to help us all see the need for and possibilities of social change. The silencing of this diversity of human stories is the silencing of humanity and human life. We go in pursuit of *making narrative justice*: concerned with narrative inequalities, narrative exclusion and narrative 'othering'.

Working to humanize the digital world. For too long our digital life has been mainly in the hands of technocrats and big business – its central task has been to expand and make money. Yet human lives are under threat in many ways from digital risks: from cruelty and surveillance to digital saturation and dehumanization. Our long-time classical mode of storytelling may decline as it faces the new digital world of stories and the possibility of a saturated, over-mediated life, lacking wholes and relationships. So a politics of narrative humanity has to bring a firm focus on a digital humanism – on applying human values to digital life – to remind us of the importance of story, dialogue, empathy and human action, and to resist any complete takeover by the digital, and the robotic dominating our humanity. We go in pursuit of an imaginary of a caring, empathetic digital humanism.

Taking seriously ideas of free speech, equality, openness and the participation of all people in storytelling – democratizing narrative. This stands in sharp contrast with authoritarian states, where narratives are closely regulated, controlled, closed. Of course, the idea of democracy has a long, challenged and flawed history as ideals of both community and governance. And it may not work everywhere. But, ultimately, it is the most compatible politics with a flourishing narrative life – seeking a distinctively human form of power for all the people (*demos*) that creates a storytelling that is equal, free, participatory, diverse, yet together. Throughout history, as today, democracies have been persistently thwarted by corruption and ignorance. The corruption flows from wealth, bureaucracies and self-serving elites; the ignorance flows from the failure of societies to provide the critical imaginative education necessary for all to participate well. Actions are needed that will build not just a politics but also a society where the complexities of just what 'the people' are is recognized: there is no unified human mass but a complex amalgam of diverse interests and needs. This is what democracies cultivate. And so *human differences and their stories have to be centre stage.* This challenge takes us to the key narrative institutions of a society, in law, education, medicine, media, social movements, arts, museums and the rest.

Narratives to Come: Building from Grounded Utopias of the Present

And so to a vital sense of futures, where we enter the lands of tentative utopian thinking, of dreaming of better worlds for generations to come. I am not planning here to engage in science fiction – though that is one of many pathways. Nor do I mean the substantial post-humanist literature that takes us beyond the self, beyond the species, beyond human death (e.g. Braidotti, 2013). Instead, I join with Rebecca Solnit's suggestion that 'What we dream of is already present in the world' ([2004] 2016, p. xv). Here utopias are not narratives of a life to come, but narratives of worlds already in existence. Much has already been achieved, and there is much we can learn from. We empathize with the things we value today, tell stories about them and work to make them more plentiful. I am always delighted when I look around to find many wonderful things potentially living and working well in our world: often in human relationships, nature, art, music, social movements, sport and much more. Contemporary stories of these diverse and cosmopolitan experiences do not suggest perfect worlds (there will always be fault lines), but they do suggest pathways well worth developing. People flourish, dialogue with each other, seek better worlds, develop quiet contentment, try to lead 'good lives'. While the critical tradition of looking at stories and their institutions is well established, looking at existing stories to see their shapes in a positive light is much rarer. How can we study existing stories and tease out from them what needs to be celebrated and advanced?

Recently, there have been a number of important accounts of looking for these real grounded utopias in the writings of Rebecca Solnit ([2004] 2016), Erik Olin Wright (2010), Ruth Levitas (2014) and others. From them, we learn to move beyond the older debates on utopias. Drawing from some of their ideas, and knowing about the vulnerability, tensions and fragility of humanity, there are three key strategies. First, we look for stories of the myriad contemporary experiments in living around the world that reveal how some practices are working well for people in groups and society, where life and its institutions are developing positively, *the everyday grounded utopias of the present.* As we tell these stories, we also examine their flaws and scrutinize possibilities for improvements. We start to *tell stories of how these worlds work well, but also how they could be made better.* Finally, drawing from this, we go beyond these into new stories suggesting new evolving sets of practices in the future, and dialogues. We imagine *new stories of flourishing worlds.* Here we get a glimpse of possible better worlds now being developed – the search for grounded utopian practices in everyday living. And the new *s*tories that we create today help us to reimagine a better world including politics and arts, based on what we are doing. Such experiments are ragged: they show problems as much as successes, but they do indicate ways that human worlds move forwards. They will never be grand utopian tales: storytelling tells us we have to live with little and fallible bits of utopian narratives. But they give us stories to help us move on. Here are just three of many examples of the stuff of life on which these bigger future stories can be built.

> Stories that show how people look after and care for each other. We can see this everywhere in stories of the daily practice of care – of how people look after and tend to the needs of their loved ones and dearest, but also in the 'kindness of strangers'. Indeed, vital social institutions are built out of loving care – health, welfare, education, social work, art. A key idea here is that of the idea of the caring democracy. Here too is the evolving story of those relatively few nations that choose to care for all of their people by ensuring that everyone is provided with good

health, vibrant education, a sustainable environment and necessary welfare. They find common value grounds – even a National Health Service. Here are *narratives of cosmopolitan human caring* to build on.

Stories that show how communities and movements across the world come to share and dialogue across different stories. Here are the emerging stories of organizations for world literature and music, multi-faith groups, global politics, global sport, world universities, environmental agencies, humanitarian care, international film festivals. While not necessarily agreeing with each other, people come to live together through practical concerns. These show grounded projects that unite contrasting communities and minimize the potential for conflict through differences. Here are *narratives of cosmopolitan community and communication* to build on.

Stories that show the enormous accumulation of knowledge and wisdom across cultures and history. The former Director of the British Museum Neil MacGregor, for example, surveys all the stories of art and artefacts to tell *A History of the World in 100 Objects* (2012), while the philosophers Dreyfus and Kelly (2011) highlight the importance of great writings and objects which display the bright and shiny things of the past: the powerful sacred qualities about them, their 'whoosh factor', that helps energize, delight, create ecstasy. And there are contemporary glories too: in the emerging Wikipedia and some other global websites, we start to sense a worldwide resource for a common humanity – a widespread cosmopolitan knowledge, art and humanity across the world. Here are *narratives of historical cosmopolitan wisdoms* to build on.

While all have their weaknesses, they all lead us to acts of narrative hope.

An abundance of stories in search of a better world

I started this book with six stories in search of a better world and have made my journey through many narratives before arriving in a troubled, even regressive, world. But I have ended with a fanfare of possibilities: with the importance of acts of narrative hope.

As I was finishing the book, I visited two exhibitions in London in the summer of 2018: both could be seen as narrating our dark world. One was a retrospective on the work of the photographer Dorothea Lange at the Barbican, and the other was a remembrance of the Aftermath of World War I at Tate Britain.[6] Every day, our lives are cluttered with stories, and it matters in the end which stories we choose to engage with. On this particular day, I chose yet more stories of human suffering – and hope.

I have long been interested in the work of the photographer Dorothea Lange, but this was the first time I had the opportunity to see a full chronology of her work. She is most well known for her dramatic photo of Mother and Children ('Immigrant Mother') in the dust bowl of America's 1930s depression, and sure enough here was a room devoted to this powerful story of abject poverty. But it was surrounded by rooms where I was confronted face by face with those others who had suffered the breakdown of human life in other ways: through worklessness, homelessness and neglect, for sure, but also through arriving in Japanese internment camps. There were photos of a beautiful Californian landscape being destroyed by the rapaciousness of man. There were many photos of close-up suffering. Here too was the story of Dorothea Lange – a talented but ordinary woman who devoted much of her life to telling us about the sufferings of her time and the power and politics of seeing. Here, over half a century after her death, is her legacy. In these photos, I saw the faces of the past staring at me, pleading for a better world – then and now: to make visible the past, to tell us a story, to make us think anew, to make us angry, to seek change, to not forget.

I moved on to 'Aftermath'. This was an exhibition designed to mark the end of four years of remembering the centenary of World War I. It depicted the art of the thirty years that followed on from it. This war killed 10 million people, wounding some 200 million others. A first room contained paintings of death and carnage; a second showed the mutilated bodies, wounded and scarred; a third told the stories of memorials built. And on: gradually, I entered rooms which suggested the slow building a of a new order – some of it through a hopeful sense of the past being restored, but much of it suggesting a new cynicism and despair arriving with the advance of capitalism. One famous image – George Grosz's *Grey Day* (1921) – foregrounds a rich businessman building a new capitalism while a wounded soldier staggers in a middle ground. In the background, a sense of an ominous grey world moves along darkly. And this is just before war starts again with World War II. How quickly we move on and forget the wickedness of our ways. Are we condemned to do this all again – again and again? And here a contemporary gallery gives us stories, 100 years on, to play with our memories and compassion – 'lest we forget'.

And so, once again, we have the stories of power and the power of stories. The power to remind us of the inequalities of narrative:

of who gets routinely heard and who does not. Of the fragility of our media to be able to record and tell our stories, especially as we move on to a new electronic and digital age. Of our power to keep vital memories alive through tellings and retellings of our past, even as we look ahead in the present. Of the importance of narrative wisdom: a reality puzzle making us aware of the perpetual and deep struggle for truth and beauty, values and power, all the time. And of the ultimate need for daily narrative acts questioning what it all means to be a human – of the storied values humanity must cherish and help to survive in the face of storied monstrous cruelties and adversities. Living actively, creatively and positively with the power of our sustainable stories of hope is what helps make us truly human.

Notes

Prologue: Going Backstage

1 I have discussed my personal relationships to stories in a number of places. See Plummer, 1995, prologue; 2015b, appendix; 2017.
2 For earlier statements on critical humanism, see Plummer, [1983] 2001; 2013a; 2015b; and forthcoming. Several works have recently made the important case for bringing humanism back into sociology: see Chernilo, 2017; Morgan, 2016; Wilkinson and Kleinman, 2016. Liz Stanley's elegant collection of essays provides a wonderful sense of the field of humanist narrative research at the start of the twenty-first century (Stanley, 2013).

1 Narratives of Suffering: Six Stories in Search of a Better World

1 The term 'polyphony' is borrowed from music and means 'multiple voices'. It is developed in the work of Bakhtin, 1981.
2 Genette ([1983] 1988, p. 13) says story is 'the totality of the narrated events', and narratives are 'the discourse, oral or written, that narrates them'. Widely quoted, it is hardly clear – and also brings in the additional complication of discourse. For my wider manifesto account of stories, see Plummer 2013b.
3 This was one of the great insights of C. W. Mills, 1959, and explored by many, including Iain Wilkinson and Arthur Kleinman, 2016. See also Jeffrey Alexander, 2012a.
4 Hannah Arendt discusses the work of Isak Dinesen in Arendt, [1951] 1979.
5 In 2017, her 2013 speech to the UN on women's education was commissioned and set to music as 'Speak Out' by Kate Whitley for International Women's Day on 8 March. See also Malala's website at https://www.malala.org.

6 See also the Giddens paradox in Giddens, 2010. The importance of the broad critical role of literature in studying the environment is brilliantly captured in Ghosh, 2016, and amplified in Treanor, 2014.

7 A term used by President Trump and widely cited on 12 January 2018 as he talked about migrants from Haiti and Africa.

8 For overviews and discussions of Truth Commissions, see Bakiner, 2016; Hayner, 2010.

9 The writing on this is substantial. See Jill Bennett (2012) who has suggested it as an event which helps define a new approach to aesthetics as people had to work out their own response to the 'visual disaster'. A beautifully written critical account of a visit to the Memorial Museum is by Harvey Molotch (2014). See also Stubblefield, 2015; and the 9/11 Memorial Museum: https://www.911memorial.org.

2 Narrative Actions of Power

1 The literature on narrative is now colossal. There are two major ways of studying narrative. The long-standing classical approach focuses centrally on texts and how they are analysed (e.g., Bal, 1985; Puckett, 2016). A less prominent approach focuses less on the specific texts than the actions that surround them: the social, historical and political role of stories in society, states and everyday life (e.g Andrews, 2007; Gubrium & Holstein, 2009; Jackson, 2002; Tilly, 2002). Both are linked and necessary. This chapter focuses primarily on some key features of the latter.

2 Another distinction often made is between narrative theorists who claim narrative is constitutive of human existence (e.g. Hannah Arendt) and those who see it as a tool for imposing meaning on reality (e.g. Hayden White, [1973] 2014). As will become clear, I hold both views and do not regard them as mutually exclusive. For a stringent account of this, see Strawson, 2004.

3 See Hannah Arendt [1958] 1998, pp. 7-8. For me, Arendt is one of the most interesting writers on narrative power, hard as she is to grasp sometimes because she writes outside of and against traditional thinking. I have found Hayden, 2014, a useful guide, and the film *Hannah Arendt*, 2012, a provocation.

4 The idea of mimesis has a long history, but the classic text is Auerbach, [1953] 2003. A major school of thought – Mimetic Theory – has grown from it, primarily associated with the work of René Girard (1923-2015). For his account of 'mimetic desire', see Girard, 2011, which provides a key selection of his ideas.

5 In psychology, the word 'affordances' is widely used: 'Affordances provided by the environment are what it offers, what it provides, what it furnishes and what it invites' (Gibson, 1979, p. 127). Every narrative invites us to see the world in certain ways and act in certain ways.

6 Some of the ideas for this have been developed in both cultural and

media studies for quite a while (variously called reception theory, audience theory, spectator theory, performativity). See Beck, 2007, on listening.

7 Empathy is another well-developed feature of the human condition. We are the empathetic, dialogical animal. The writing on all this is now very substantial: some claim it is becoming both more prevalent and more central to the distinctiveness of human life, at its best flourishing into compassion, while others are critical of its overuse. See Armstrong, 2011; Bakhtin, 1981, 1984; Baron-Cohen, 2011; Bloom, 2016; Cooley, [1901] 2009; Rifkin, 2009.

8 The foundations of modern self-theory lie in James, [1892] 1961, Cooley, [1901] 2009, and Mead, [1934] 1970; the 'Circle of Others' is well discussed in Forman-Barzilai, 2010; and the nature of 'the other' in Kapuściński, 2006. See also Butler, 2005.

9 This *understanding* of stories, the phenomenological-hermeneutic approach to narrative, is developed in the work of many, including Carr, 1991; Gadamer, 1975; Kearney, 2002; Lara, 1998; and Ricoeur, 1992, 2005.

10 Here I am being shaped by the vital writings of Berger and Luckmann, 1967, and Durkheim, [1895] 1964 – a world of 'ways of acting, thinking and feeling which possess the remarkable property of existing outside the consciousness of the individual'.

11 The difficult idea of a public sphere goes back at least to Kant, Mills and Dewey. Habermas, [1962] 1989, gave the baseline modern formulation. But a quite large academic industry has now emerged to rework the idea. Some examples are: Butler et al., 2011; Fraser and Nash, 2014; McGee, 2009; Volkmer, 2014; Warner, 2002.

12 Bertrand Russell,1975, famously once claimed, in the introduction to his book on power, that 'The fundamental concept in social science is Power, in the same sense in which Energy is the fundamental concept in physics.' For valuable discussions of power, see Dowding, 2011; Hearn, 2012; Prus,1999; Scott, 2001; and Wrong, 1979. From them I have built a sort of interactionist humanist theory of power.

13 I can agree with Foucault,1976, pp. 121-2, that narrative power involves 'a multiplicity of relations of force' that are 'not be sought in the primary existence of a central point' but rather 'produced at every instant, at every point': 'Power is everywhere: not that it engulfs everything, but that it comes from everywhere.'

14 'Contentious politics' is a sociological term associated with the political sociologists Charles Tilly and Sidney Tarrow, 2015, to capture ways actors outside of mainstream politics make claims on authorities and make public performances drawing on standard repertoires of collective actions. It is used in research. By contrast, agnostic politics is associated with political philosophers such as Chantal Mouffe, Bonnie Honig, James Tully, William E. Connolly. As is common, they seem to make

little or no connection with each other at all. But there is an excellent overview by Mark Wenman, 2013.

15 On wider accounts of narrative and power, see Livholts and Tamboukou, 2015.

16 Ultimately, power is derived from a number of sources. Back in the 1970s, Michael Mann's monumental four volumes of historical sociology on the *Social Sources of Power* highlighted four interconnected key sources: ideological, economic, military and political (the IEMP model). He has stuck with this typology for some four decades. In this book I broaden this a little and sense several shifting categories. He was often writing in, and about, a pre-digital era.

17 The study of human values is an important, but largely neglected, one. Sayer (2011) has usefully asked how things come to be valued; Christian Smith (2003) claims we are the 'moral believing animal'; and Kitcher (2011) suggests we have evolved practical moral solutions to life over the millennia.

18 To take each of these values further, see, for example, on (1): Arendt, [1958] 1998; MacIntyre, [1981] 2007; Nussbaum, 2011; Unger, 2007. On (2), see: Armstrong, 2011; Rifkin, 2009; Smith, [1759] 2000; Sznaider, 2001; Ure and Frost, 2014; Yuval-Davis, 2011. On (3), see: Engster, 2007; Gensler, 2013; Sen, 2009; Tronto, 2013; Turner, 2006. On (4), see: Besser and Slote (2018); Treanor, 2014. On (5) see: Appiah, 2006; Attfield, 2014; Tremblay, 2009; Van Hooft, 2009; Widdows, 2011. These are all Western accounts. For a broader sweep, both Malik (2014) and Haidt (2012) are excellent starts.

19 See the discussions in Alexander, 2011a; 2011b; 2012a; 2012b; 2017; and Matynia, 2009, p. 11; Smith and Howe, 2015. In the early twenty-first century, there are two contrasting scholars who apply the dramatic metaphor to politics. Jeffrey Alexander, a sociologist, works within a largely Durkheimian tradition of strong culture, 'cultural pragmatics' and moral value, suggesting the drama of social life. Alexander is a North American liberal and seeks to explain the workings of civil society and democracy, and existing orders, primarily using the analysis of symbolic and binary codes in political speeches and actions – Watergate, Obama, the Egyptian Revolution, etc., have been his concerns. Judith Butler, an influential feminist / queer philosopher, draws from Continental Philosophy and especially Austin's theory of performativity ([1955] 1962), and is a North American socialist feminist radical who is very critical of the neo-liberal order and its patriarchal structure, and seeks transgression and radical social change. She claims that power helps constitute the subject. Her earliest work was on the politics of gender and performativity – for which she became world famous for challenging orthodoxies. More recently, she has been at the forefront of a politics of assembly (social movements), dispossession and precarity, whereby the conditions of livability are destroyed. She locates such themes as pervading and galvanizing contemporary political actions.

20 See the elegant essay by James Wood on Chekhov's *The Kiss* (Wood, 2015, pp. 31-7).

3 Narrative Power as a Struggle for Human Value

1 This is my favourite classification and comes from a gentle, lesser-known work published in 1982 by the late literary critic Langdon Elsbree (1929-2014). The literature here is vast, from Propp, 1968, to Booker, 2004.

2 A distinctive branch of political analysis, Interpretive Political Science, has specialized in this. It is critical of conventional political science and focuses on meanings, discourse, argumentations, ideology, language and narrative. For an overview of this field, see Bevir and Rhodes, 2018. See also the *Journal of Narrative Politics*.

3 There are some marvellous vignettes of some of these systems as narratives in C. Smith, 2003, ch 4.

4 On economic narratives, see the notable work of the economist Deidre McCloskey, 1998.

5 See http://brandirectory.com/league_tables/table/global-500-2014.

6 For further discussions of this narrative self/identity, see: Holstein and Gubrium, 2000; Ricoeur,1992; Smith and Watson, 2001.

7 For a valuable overview of affect, see Wetherell, 2012.

8 In a much-neglected study, Rogers M. Smith (2003a) builds up an important account of how 'stories of peoplehood' define identities and support political life by enabling community building. Ultimately, they become the foundations of nationhood.

9 I draw here from classical theories of self, interactionism, role-taking and dialogue found in the works of Bakhtin (1981, 1984), Berger and Luckmann (1967), Cooley ([1901] 2009), James ([1892] 1961), Levinas (1969), Mead ([1934] 1970) and many others

10 The Russian-language philosopher Mikhail Bakhtin (1895-1975) is one of the most celebrated and influential theorists of narrative theory, introducing the ugly words *polyphony* (originally several melodic lines, but also found in most stories and talk) and *heteroglossia* (the presence of two or more voices or expressed viewpoints in a text or other artistic work). More simply, both capture the idea of multiple voices in dialogue, out of which diverse new strands appear and are part of the wider view of never-ending narrative interaction.

11 'Narrative empathy is the sharing of feeling and perspective-taking induced by reading, viewing, hearing, or imagining narratives of another's situation and condition.' See Keen, 2007.

12 It has been much studied: see, as examples, Alexander, 2012a; Andrews, 2007; Goodson, 2017; Jackson, 2002; Schafer and Smith, 2004; Selbin, 2010; Tilly, 2002; Woodiwiss, 2009; Woodiwiss et al., 2017.

13 See Erickson, [1966] 2004, on witchcraft purges; Douglas, 1966, on

purification rituals; Elias and Scotson, [1965] 1994, on the community; and Young, 1971, on Drugtakers. Other prominent writers on 'othering' include Appiah, Bauman, Eco, Kapuściński, Levi, Levinas, Morrison and Sen.

14 Across his work, Alexander depicts many binary structures: of motives, relationships, institutions, of East–West, of civil society, and revolutionary Egypt.

15 See Solinger et al., 2008, p. 11. For further striking case study illustrations of this process, see the collections of writings in: Crawshaw and Jackson, 2010; Davis, 2002; Inayatullah and Dauphinée, 2016; and Weibel, 2014.

4 Narrative Inequalities

1 A valuable discussion of dehumanization is Smith, 2011. As he remarks, despite the importance of this idea, there has been very little discussion of it; and his book is an extended and readable account.

2 Slave stories were rarely without controversy: the bestselling novel of the nineteenth century in the USA was Harriet Beecher Stowe's *Uncle Tom's Cabin* (1852). For some, it is seen to 'alter the course of history'; for others, such as James Baldwin, it is 'a very bad novel, having, in its self-righteous, and virtuous sentimentality, much in common with *Little Women*'. See http://nymag.com/news/frank-rich/james-baldwin-everybodys-protest-novel-2013-11.

3 This idea was originated by Bernard Bell,1987, p. 3.

4 See www.whitneyplantation.com.

5 See Kendi, 2017. For an account of #BlackLivesMatter, see Lebron, 2017.

6 The late sociologist Charles Tilly (1999) claimed that 'deep and durable' inequalities exist in countries across the world and throughout history. And this means that many lives never get heard.

7 Slavery is another example of this deep and durable historical issue: for a short historical account, see Stevenson, 2015. It can be found in prehistoric hunting societies and in ancient civilization – the Greeks, the Romans, the Persians, the Etruscans. Today, it is estimated some 46 million people live under conditions of modern slavery.

8 Dominance theory was first developed through the critical theorists of the Frankfurt School. More recently, Lovett, 2010, suggests a relationship in which arbitrary power is exerted over people.

9 The 'hierarchy of credibility' was first clearly formulated analytically in Becker, 1967.

10 Figures are disputed; but they are widely documented. For world inequalities, see: Oxfam, 2015; Piketty, 2014. As I write, the most up-to-date account is Alvaredo et al., 2018.

11 For a sample of writings that show the concentration of media power,

see Bagdikian, [1983] 2004; Birkinbine et al., 2016; Chomsky, 1991; Curran, 2002; Freedman, 2014; Noam, 2016.

12 This is a key contrast developed in Greek between 'bare life' (*la vita nuda* or *zoê*) and 'a particular mode of life' or 'qualified life' (*bios*).

13 A recent development in narrative theory has highlighted an ecological approach. See, for example, Gabriel, 2016.

14 As I was writing this book, *I, Daniel Blake* was released and became a major talking point. It is one of millions of films that 'move the world'. In 2017, it was winner of the Palme d'Or at the Cannes Film Festival and won the BAFTA 2017 for Best British Film. On his work generally, see Hayward, 2004.

15 Goffman (1956, 1961a, 1961b) has provided a valuable language for thinking about these many processes. He suggests the importance of role performance, role engulfment, role playing, role improvisation, role distance and role withdrawal. Likewise, in two major works, James C. Scott (1985, 1990) has illustrated how these 'arts of resistance' actually work out in everyday life.

16 The term 'HyperNormalization' was introduced by Yurchak, 2005, to describe the emerging situation in Russia, and then applied to the wider world in the film by Adam Curtis (2017).

17 A valuable introduction to social movements over the past 200 years is Tilly, 2004. A vital work on modern social politics is found in the three volumes by Castells (1996, 1997, 1998). The second volume looks especially at the importance of social movements and identity. Alexander, 2006, situates social movements in civil society. Studies by Andrews (2007), Poletta (2006), Schafer and Smith (2004), Selbin (2010) and Tilly (2002) provide examples of how social movements use stories to bring about change. The role of emotion is highlighted by Jasper, 2018. Plenty of examples of social movements are listed on Wikipedia. For a fascinating and important set of contemporary case studies, see Weibel, 2014.

5 Narrative Digitalism

1 For discussion of this, see Corballis, 2017; Dor and Lewis, 2014; Printz, 2012; Taylor, 2016; Tomasello, 2010.

2 These quotes are from Walter Ong, 1982, pp. 57, 140. In ch. 3, Ong provides a much fuller discussion with many more features.

3 Michael Mann (1986–2013) comments that we know very little about some 99 per cent of our early past history. Goody, 1968, is a series of case studies illustrating the uses of literacy in 'traditional' societies.

4 The ancient Sumerian poem *The Epic of Gilgamesh* is one of the oldest written stories in existence. Along with the *Iliad*, it is much discussed to suggest both continuity with and disruption from contemporary mediated worlds. See, for example, Scranton, 2015.

5　A classic novel on this is Umberto Eco's *The Name of the Rose* (also a film). For a sample of ongoing debates on all this, see Bowman and Wolf, 2008.

6　The classic text is Eisenstein, 1979–82. A critical account is Pascale, 2007. A good read on the history of books in 100 books is Cave and Ayad, 2014.

7　See the work of Turner, 2016.

8　The term 'quantified self' was invented by two *Wired* magazine editors in 2007. For a detailed account, see the work of Deborah Lupton (2016).

9　In this section, I draw from a formidably large body of research which includes: Aiken, 2016; Allen and Light, 2015; Bartlett, 2015, 2018; boyd, 2014; Bridle, 2018; Castells, 1996, 1997, 1998, 2001, 2009, 2012; Chadwick, [2013] 2017; Fuchs, 2014, 2018; Isin and Ruppert, 2015; Koenitz et al., 2015; Margetts et al., 2016; McCosker et al., 2016; Mossberger et al., 2007; O'Neil, 2016; Reed, 2014; Turkle, 2016.

10　See 'Internet Titans' *New Internationalist* 494 (July/August 2016), p. 17. See also Ofcom, Communication Market Report, 2 August 2018: search ofcom.org.uk.

11　See Beck, 2016, listing p. 148.

12　On ideas of digital citizenship, see Allen and Light, 2015; Isin and Ruppert, 2015; McCosker et al., 2016. I see parallels here with an earlier idea of intimate citizenship (Plummer, 2003), which has recently been reworked by Vivienne, 2016.

13　See http://comprop.oii.ox.ac.uk.

14　See Jenny Ughba Korn and other contributors in Rambukkana (2015).

6　Narrative States

1　Richard Lachmann provides a most useful account of the state. He claims: 'The first empires appeared in the Middle East 5,500 years ago. Few states existed until 500 years ago. It is only in the twentieth century that virtually every territory on earth (except for Antarctica) became an independent state replacing the empires, city-states, tribes and theocracies that once ruled most humans' (2010, pp. vii–viii).

2　There is a useful background to this in the Wikipedia 'Freedom of the Press' entry. The most up-to-date information can be found on the Reporters Without Borders home page at https://rsf.org/en. The statistics that I use here come from the *Freedom of Press Reports*: see https://rsf.org/en/ranking.

3　Defining the state is another complex field. Bob Jessop has spent a lifetime studying it. His definition is for openers only, and part of a very expansive debate. See his 2008 classic.

4　See, as examples, *Democracy and its Crisis* (Grayling), *The Crisis of Democracy* (Carfe), *Populism and the Crisis of Democracy* (Fitzi), *Global Capitalism and the Crisis of Democracy* (Harris), *The Crisis of Democracy*

(Li), *Democracy in Crisis* (Merkel) and *Rupture* (Castells). But there are many more. Crisis and democracy is almost a cliché.

5 Although this is a very different set of suggestions, I was inspired in constructing this through the Dulwich Centre's Narrative Justice Charter of Story Telling Rights: https://dulwichcentre.com.au/charter-of-story-telling-rights. I see parallels here with an earlier idea of intimate citizenship (Plummer, 2003), now linked to the growing interest in digital citizenship (Isin and Ruppert, 2015). It also links to a number of the UN's Sustainable Development Goals: see United Nations (2015).

6 The work of Hannah Arendt is the keystone for understanding totalitarianism. See, notably, Arendt, [1951] 1979, as well as Arendt, 1963.

7 A key discussion of the nature of China's politics can be found in the work of Daniel Bell (2016) who sees layers of authoritarianism and democracy, suggests the importance of Confucianism and highlights a 'political meritocracy'.

8 As reported in the *Guardian*, 19 October 2017, p. 17.

9 See Tai, in Weibel, 2014, pp. 396-407.

10 As published by Xinhua, China's official news agency, and reported in the *Guardian*: www.theguardian.com/world/2018/mar/21/china-state-media-merger-to-create-propaganda-giant. For a more sustained discussion on China and internet regulation, see Rawnsley and Rawnsley, 2015; Roberts, 2018.

11 The *Human Development Report* is published annually and contains the Human Development Index. Nowadays, it is also closely allied with the 2030 Agenda and the Sustainable Development Goals (SDGs).

12 See http://visionofhumanity.org/indexes/global-peace-index.

13 See Helliwell et al. (2018): http://worldhappiness.report/ed/2018.

14 The Fragile States Index is funded by the Fund for Peace. In 2015, it found only fifty countries that were 'at least stable'. Many were ranked with warnings and alerts. In 2018, it noted there was some progress, though many richer countries were now becoming less stable. See http://fundforpeace.org/fsi/2018/04/24/fragile-states-index-2018-annual-report.

15 Feldman (2015) argues that for particular individuals to answer this question affirmatively, they must be empowered to jointly constitute the places they inhabit with others.

16 Latest statistical details can be found at www.unhcr.org/uk/figures-at-a-glance.html.

17 Sen, 2006, speaks of the miniaturization of life. A one and only story and identity is very limiting See also C. Smith (2003, p.19), who talks about 'the making, maintaining and transforming of political peoplehood'. While Appiah, 2018, suggests these are the *ties that bind*, Haidt, 2012, suggests they are also the *ties that blind*.

18 A wicked problem is a problem that is impossible to resolve because of its complexity. See Weber et al., 2017.

19 See the new journal *Othering and Belonging*, which deals with these issues: www.otheringandbelonging.org.

20 On cosmopolitanism, see Appiah, 2006, and Delanty, 2018. I discuss many of the issues in Plummer, 2015b, where there are substantial references to the debates and writings on cosmopolitanism. I explore these ideas more in the final chapter.

7 Narrative Wisdom

1 The quote comes from the film. The original study is Lipstadt,1993, and the trial commentary is Lipstadt, 2006, republished as a film tie-in in 2016.

2 See Susan Glasser's 'Letter from Trump's Washington' in *New Yorker* magazine, 3 August 2018: https://www.newyorker.com/news/letter-from-trumps-washington/trumps-escalating-war-on-the-truth-is-on-purpose.

3 The writing on all this is colossal: for general examples, see Blackburn, 2006; Coady, 2012; and Gadamer, 1975. On the current discussion of journalism and media (and Trump), see Kakutani, 2018, and Thompson, 2017.

4 On clarifying the idea of wisdom, see Schwartz and Sharpe, 2011. I also draw from some ideas of Connolly, 2013.

5 Niklas Luhmann's classic work was originally published forty years ago. As he says: 'a complete absence of trust would prevent us getting up in the morning' ([1977] 2017, p. 4). Trust is what holds things together – it provides a security and removes risk and fear. Narrative trust gives security. See also Hosking, 2013, for a history.

6 For examples, see the many 'scientific methodologies' for doing narrative research. Two influential texts here are Riessman, 2007, and Livholts and Tamboukou, 2015. See also Fairclough (2010), who has developed the method of Critical Discourse Analysis.

7 This classic question was posed some fifty years ago by Becker, 1967. It connects gradually to the wider standpoint theory, which I have discussed a little in chapter 4. See: Code, 2006; Harding, 1986; Medina, 2013; Santos, 2014.

8 See the interview with Gianfranco Rosi in the *Guardian*, 9 June 2016: https://www.theguardian.com/film/2016/jun/09/not-even-death-can-stop-200000-migrants-wanting-to-escape-fire-at-sea-gianfranco-rosi.

9 For a small sample of such works, see Sayad, 2004, for a life story; Philo et al., 2016, for contrasting media accounts; Nguyen, 2018, for some literary interviews; Feldman for an analytic account; and the UNHCR website (below) for statistics.

10 The UNHCR website is at www.unhcr.org/uk/figures-at-a-glance.html.

11 This raises important issues of closeness and distance. Here, people are very close, but still have no awareness. An important series of studies has

been made by Chouliaraki (2006, 2013) to examine how we view the suffering of others from a distance.

8 Narrative Contingencies

1 I first started asking such questions with my sexualities research in the 1980s, suggesting some basic moments that fitted well into this flow: the stories of rape, lesbian and gay life, and therapy. For the original discussion of these issues, see Plummer, 1995, p. 49.

2 Time is central in philosophical discussion of narrative. Bakhtin, 1981, for example, speaks of the chronotope when discussing the time–space dimension of narratives. Paul Ricoeur, 2005, traces key issues in memory, recollection, history, time and forgetting. I have also been much influenced by the work of G. H. Mead (1959).

3 Again, the idea of being and nothing is a central one in philosophy, but it is hardly explored in sociology. See Franke, 2014; also Scott, 2018.

4 For an evolutionary theory of the origins of stories, see Boyd, 2009. For a literary-philosophical account, see Kearney, 2002.

5 On environmental stories, see also Ghosh, 2016; Scranton, 2015; Treanor, 2014.

6 On Me Too stories, see the *New York Times*: https://www.nytimes.com/series/metoo-moment. Accounts of Me Too can be found at: https://www.nytimes.com/interactive/2018/06/28/arts/metoo-movement-sto ries.html. For a critique, see Kate Roiphe, *Harpers*, March 2018: https://harpers.org/archive/2018/03/the-other-whisper-network-2.

7 An important comparable case is the extinction of languages: see Nettle and Romaine, 2000.

8 The video can be found at https://www.youtube.com/watch?v=GEoBH 55IdCA.

9 I have discussed issues of generations in Plummer, 2010. Randall Collins, 1998, has studied the networks that organize intellectual narratives across history from Confucius and ancient China through Islam, Judaism, Christendom and on to more recent times. He also suggests creativity is not random among individuals: it builds up in 'intergenerational chains', organized through 'interaction rituals', shared by small networks of people.

10 The term 'postmemory' was introduced by Marianne Hirsch in 1992, originally to help in understanding the relationship between the children of Holocaust survivors and the memories of their parents. It has now been widely expanded and developed in literature. See Hirsch, 2012.

9 Caring for Narrative Futures: Towards a Politics of Narrative Humanity

1 Rebecca Solnit ([2004] 2016, p. 70) alerted me to this. She refers to the famous Klee–Benjamin remarks, and suggests instead the imagery

of the Angel of Past History seeking its wings, from Frank Capra's film *It's a Wonderful Life*. I prefer this because Capra has long been one of my favourite filmmakers.

2 Ernst Bloch ([1938–47] 1986), the key work, comes in three volumes. He was writing during and after World War II and had good cause for despair. More recently I have found Solnit, [2004] 2016, and Van Hooft, 2011, helpful. There is a long philosphical lineage from Pandora's Box through Christianity to pragmatism and on to the work of Richard Rorty (1999).

3 Many works have helped shape my thinking around the future. Three recent ones, taking different stances, are Beck, 2016; Frase, 2016; Urry, 2016.

4 Two main strategies of the past which can still be used are utopian writing and manifestos. I have no space to argue about this. For example, many of our past future visions (often troubling) can be found in the narratives of manifestos: *100 Artist Manifestos* (2011), *The Communist Manifesto* (1848), *The Cyborg Manifesto* (1985), *The Declaration of Rights and of Man and Citizen* (1789), *The Scum Manifesto* (1968).

5 MacIntyre, [1981] 2007, did not suggest it would. His works are deeply critical of the modern and Enlightenment project.

6 Dorothea Lange, 'Politics of Seeing', Barbican, 22 June – 2 Sept. 2018; 'Aftermath: Art in the Wake of World War One', Tate Britain, 5 June – 23 Sept. 2018.

References

Abu-lughod, Lila (1986) *Veiled Sentiments: Honor and Poetry in a Bedouin Society*, Berkeley: University of California Press.

Adie, Kate (2009) *Into Danger: Risking Your Life for Work*, London: Hodder.

Adorno, Theodor W. ([1944] 1991) *The Culture Industry: Selected Essays on Mass Culture*, London: Routledge.

Agamben, Giorgio (1995) *Homo Sacer: Sovereign Power and Bare Life*, Stanford University Press.

Aiken, Mary (2016) *The Cyber Effect*, London: John Murray.

Albert, Michael (2006) *Realizing Hope: Life Beyond Capitalism*, London: Zed Books.

Alexander, Bryan (2011) *The New Digital Storytelling: Creating Narrative with New Media*, Oxford: Praeger.

Alexander, Jeffrey C. (2006) *The Civil Sphere*, Oxford University Press.

Alexander, Jeffrey C. (2011a) *Performance and Power*, Cambridge: Polity.

Alexander, Jeffrey C. (2011b) *Performative Revolution in Egypt*, London: Bloomsbury.

Alexander, Jeffrey C. (2012a) *Trauma: A Social Theory*, Cambridge: Polity.

Alexander, Jeffrey C. (2012b) *The Performance of Politics: Obama's Victory and the Democratic Struggle for Power*, Oxford University Press.

Alexander, Jeffrey C. (2017) *The Drama of Social Life*, Cambridge: Polity.

Allen, Danielle, and Jennifer S. Light (eds.) (2015) *From Voice to Influence: Understanding Citizenship in a Digital Age*, University of Chicago Press.

Alleyne, Brian (2015) *Narrative Networks: Storied Approaches in a Digital Age*, London: Sage.

Altheide, David, and R. P. Snow (1979) *Media Logic*, London: Sage.

Alvaredo, Facundo, Lucas Chancel, Thomas Piketty, Emanuel Sae and Gabriel Zuchman (2018) *The World Inequality Report 2018*, Cambridge, Mass: Harvard University Press.

Anderson, Benedict ([1983] 2006, rev. edn) *Imagined Communities: Reflections on the Origin and Spread of Nationalism*, London: Verso.

Andrews, Molly (2007) *Shaping History: Narratives of Political Change*, Cambridge University Press.

Appiah, Kwame Anthony (2006) *Cosmopolitanism: Ethics in a World of Strangers*, London: Allen Lane.

Appiah, Kwame Anthony (2018) *The Lies That Bind: Rethinking Identity*, London: Profile Books.

Arce, Luz ([1993] 2004) *The Inferno: A Story of Terror and Survival in Chile*, University of Wisconsin Press.

Arendt, Hannah ([1951] 1979) *The Origins of Totalitarianism*, New York: Harvest Books.

Arendt, Hannah ([1958] 1998, 2nd edn) *The Human Condition*, University of Chicago Press.

Arendt, Hannah (1963) *Eichmann in Jerusalem: A Report on the Banality of Evil*, New York: Penguin.

Arendt, Hannah (1979), *Men in Dark Times*, Harmondsworth: Penguin.

Arendt, Hannah (2006) *Between Past and Future*, New York: Penguin Books.

Aristotle (1991) *The Art of Rhetoric*, Harmondsworth: Penguin Classics.

Aristotle (1996) *Poetics*, Harmondsworth: Penguin Classics.

Armstrong, Karen (2011) *Twelve Steps to a Compassionate Life*, London: Bodley Head.

Aronson, Ronald (2017) *We: Reviving Social Hope*, University of Chicago Press.

Attfield, Robin (2014, 2nd edn) *Environmental Ethics*, Cambridge: Polity.

Auerbach, Erich ([1953] 2003, 50th anniversary edition) *Mimesis: The Representation of Reality in Western Literature*, intro. Edward H. Said, Princeton University Press.

Austin, J.L. ([1955] 1962) *How to Do Things with Words*, Oxford: Clarendon Press.

Bagdikian, Ben ([1983] 2004) *The New Media Monopoly*, Boston: Beacon Press.

Baggini, Julian (2017, 20th edn) *A Short History of Truth*, London: Quercus.

Bagul, Babuaro (2018) *When I Hid My Caste: Stories*, London: Speaking Tiger Books.

Bakhtin, M. M. (1981) *The Dialogic Imagination: Four Essays*, Austin and London: University of Texas Press.

Bakhtin, M. M. (1984) *Problems of Dostoevsky's Poetics*, Minneapolis: University of Minnesota Press.

Bakiner, Onur (2016) *Truth Commissions: Memory, Power, and Legitimacy*, Philadelphia: University of Pennsylvania Press.

Bal, Mieke (1985) *Narratology: Introduction to the Theory of Narrative*, University of Toronto Press.

Barkan, Elazar, and Karen Barclay (eds.) (2017) *Choreographies of Shared Sacred Sites*, New York: Columbia University Press.

Baron-Cohen, Simon (2011) *Zero Degrees of Empathy*, London: Penguin.

Barrett, Jennifer (2012) *Museums and the Public Sphere*, Chichester: Wiley-Blackwell.

Bartlett, Jamie (2015) *The Dark Net*, London: Windmill Books.

Bartlett, Jamie (2018) *The People vs Tech: How the Internet is Killing Democracy*, London: Ebury Press.

Battaly, Heather (ed.) (2018) *The Routledge Handbook of Virtue Epistemology*, London: Routledge.

Bauman, Zygmunt (2003) *Wasted Lives: Modernity and Its Outcasts*, Cambridge: Polity.

Beck, Les (2007) *The Art of Listening*, London: Berg.

Beck, Ulrich (1997) *The Reinvention of Politics: Rethinking Modernity in the Global Social Order*, Cambridge: Polity.

Beck, Ulrich (2016) *The Metamorphosis of the World*, Cambridge: Polity.

Becker, Howard S. (1967) Whose Side Are We On? *Social Problems* 14:3 (Winter), pp. 239-47.

Bell, Bernard W. (1987) *The Afro-American Novel and Its Tradition*, Minnesota: University of Massachusetts Press.

Bell, Daniel (2016) *The China Model: Political Meritocracy and the Limits of Democracy*, Princeton University Press.

Bennett, Andy, and Brady Robards (eds.) (2014) *Mediated Youth Cultures: The Internet, Belonging and New Cultural Configurations*, London: Palgrave.

Bennett, Jill (2012) *Practical Aesthetics: Events, Affects and Art after 9/11*, London: I. B. Taurus.

Bennett, Lance W., and Alexandra Segerberg (2013) *The Logic of Connective Action*, Cambridge University Press.

Berger, Peter (1967) *The Sacred Canopy*, New York: Doubleday.

Berger, Peter, and Thomas Luckmann (1967) *The Social Construction of Reality*, Harmondsworth: Penguin.

Besser, Lorraine, and Michael Slote (eds.) (2018) *The Routledge Companion to Virtue Ethics*, London: Routledge.

Bevir, Mark and R. A. W. Rhodes (eds.) (2018) *Routledge Handbook of Interpretive Political Science*, London: Routledge.

Bhopal Survivors' Movement (2009) *Bhopal Survivors Speak: Emergent Voices from a People's Movement*, Edinburgh: World Power Books.

Birkinbine, Benjamin, Rodrigo Gomez and Janet Wasko (eds.) (2016) *Global Media Giants*, New York: Routledge.

Bjorklund, Diane (1998) *Interpreting the Self: Two Hundred Years of American Autobiography*, University of Chicago Press.

Blackburn, Simon (2006) *Truth: A Guide for the Perplexed*, London: Penguin.

Bloch, Ernst ([1938-47] 1986) *The Principle of Hope*, 3 vols., Boston: MIT Press.

Bloom, Paul (2016) *Against Empathy: The Case for Rational Compassion*, London: Bodley Head.

Bod, Rens (2013) *A New History of the Humanities: The Search for Principle and Patterns from Antiquity to the Present*, Oxford University Press.

Bode, Christopher, and Rainer Dietrich (2013) *Future Narrative: Theory, Poetics, and Media-Historical Moment*, Berlin: Walter de Gruyter.

Bollier, David (2014) *Think Like a Commoner: A Short Introduction to the Life of the Commons*, Gabriola Island: New Society Publishers.

Booker, Christopher (2004) *The Seven Basic Plots: Why We Tell Stories*, London: Continuum.

Booth, Wayne C. (1988) *The Company We Keep: An Ethics of Fiction*, Berkeley: University of California Press.

Botkin, Benjamin A. (ed.) (1992) *Lay My Burden Down: A Folk History of Slaves*, University of Chicago Press.

Bourdieu, Pierre (1984) *Distinction: A Social Critique of the Judgement of Taste*, Cambridge, Mass.: Harvard University Press.

Bourdieu, Pierre et al. ([1993] 1999) *The Weight of the World: Social Suffering in Contemporary Society*, Cambridge: Polity.

Bowman, Alan K., and Greg Woolf (eds.) (2008) *Literacy and Power in the Ancient World*, Cambridge University Press.

Boyd, Brian (2009) *On the Origins of Stories: Evolution, Cognition and Fiction*, Cambridge, Mass.: The Belknap Press of Harvard University Press.

boyd, danah (2014) *It's Complicated: The Social Lives of Networked Teens*, New Haven: Yale University Press.

Braidotti, Rose (2013) *The Posthuman*, Cambridge: Polity.

Bratsis, Peter (2007) *Everyday Life and the State*, Boulder: Paradigm Press.

Breed, Ananda (2014) *Performing the Nation: Genocide, Justice, Reconciliation*, London: Seagull Books.

Bridle, James (2018) *New Dark Age: Technology and the End of the Future*, London: Verso.

Brock, Lothar, Hans-Henrik Holm, George Sorensen and Michael Stohl (2012) *Fragile States: Violence and the Failure of Intervention*, Cambridge: Polity.

Brown, Wendy (2015) *Undoing the Demos: Neoliberalism's Stealth Revolution*, New York: Zone Books.

Brownmiller, Susan (1975) *Against Our Will: Men, Women and Rape*, New York: Simon and Schuster.

Butler, Judith (2005) *Giving an Account of Oneself*, New York: Fordham University Press.

Butler, Judith (2015) *Notes Toward a Performative Theory of Assembly*, Cambridge, Mass.: Harvard University Press.

Butler, Judith, Jürgen Habermas, Charles Taylor and Cornel West (2011) *The Power of Religion in the Public Sphere*, New York: Columbia University Press.

Butler-Brown, Tom (2017) *50 Economics Classics*, London: Nicholas Brealey.

Campbell, Heidi A. (ed.) (2012) *Digital Religion: Understanding Religious Practice in New Media Worlds*, London: Routledge.

Caputo, John D. (2013) *Truth: The Search for Wisdom in the Postmodern Age*, London: Penguin.

Carr, David (1991) *Time, Narrative and History*, Bloomington: Indiana University Press.

Carr, Nicholas (2011) *The Shallows: How Today's Online Revolution is Dividing, Diminishing and Disorienting Us*, London: Atlantic Books.

Casanova, Pascale (2007) *The World Republic of Letters*, Cambridge, Mass.: Harvard University Press.

Castells, Manuel (1996) *The Information Age: Economy, Society and Culture*, vol. I: *The Rise of the Network Society*, Oxford: Blackwell.

Castells, Manuel (1997) *The Information Age: Economy, Society and Culture*, vol. II: *The Power of Identity*, Oxford: Blackwell.

Castells, Manuel (1998) *The Information Age: Economy, Society and Culture*, vol. III: *End of Millennium*, Oxford: Blackwell.

Castells, Manuel (2001) *The Internet Galaxy: Reflections on the Internet, Business and Society*, Oxford University Press.

Castells, Manuel (2009) *Communication Power*, Oxford University Press.

Castells, Manuel (2012) *Networks of Outrage and Hope: Social Movements in the Internet Age*, Cambridge: Polity.

Castoriadis, Cornelius ([1975] 1987) *The Imaginary Institution of Society*, Cambridge: Polity.

Cave, Roderick, and Sara Ayad (2014) *A History of the Book in 100 Books*, London: British Library.

Chadwick, Andrew ([2013] 2017) *The Hybrid Media System: Politics and Power*, Oxford University Press.

Chambers, Claire, Simon Du Toll and Joshua Edelman (eds.) (2013, 2nd edn) *Performing Religion in Public*, Basingstoke: Palgrave Macmillan.

Charon, Rita (2006) *Narrative Medicine: Honoring the Stories of Illness*, Oxford University Press.

Chernilo, Daniel (2017) *Debating Humanity: Towards a Philosophical Sociology*, Cambridge University Press.

Chen, Xi (2014) *Social Protest and Contentious Authoritarianism in China*, Cambridge University Press.

Chomsky, Noam (1991) *Media Control: The Spectacular Achievements of Propaganda*, New York: An Open Media Book.

Chomsky, Noam (2011) *Hopes and Prospects*, Harmondsworth: Penguin Books.

Chomsky, Noam (2017) *Optimism Over Despair*, New York: Penguin.

Chouliaraki, Lilie (2006) *The Spectatorship of Suffering*, London: Sage. CUT

Chouliaraki, Lilie (2013) *The Ironic Spectator: Solidarity in the Age of Post Humanitarianism*, Cambridge: Polity.

Cicero (2004, new edn) *Cicero: Selected Works*, Harmondsworth: Penguin Classics.

Coady, David (2012) *What to Believe Now: Applying Epistemology to Contemporary Issues*, Chichester: Wiley.

Cobain, Ian (2016) *The History Thieves: Secrets, Lies and the Shaping of a Modern Nation*, London: Portobello Books.

Code, Lorraine (2006) *Ecological Thinking: The Politics of Epistemic Location*, Oxford University Press.

Cohen, Stanley (2001) *States of Denial: Knowing about Atrocities and Suffering*, Cambridge: Polity.

Coles, Robert (2010) *Handing One Another Along: Literature and Social Reflection. On Character, Courage and Compassion*, New York: Random House.

Collins, Patricia Hill, and Sirma Bilge (2016) *Intersectionality*, Cambridge: Polity.

Collins, Randall (1998) *The Sociology of Philosophies: A Global Theory of Intellectual Change*, Cambridge: The Belknap Press of Harvard University Press.

Connell, Raewyn (2007) *Southern Theory: The Global Dynamics of Knowledge in Social Science*, Cambridge: Polity.

Connolly, William E. (2013) *The Fragility of Things: Self-Organizing Processes, Neoliberal Fantasies, and Democratic Activisms*, Durham: Duke University Press.

Cooley, Alexander, and Jack Snyder (2016) *Ranking the World: Grading States as a Tool of Global Governance*, Cambridge University Press.

Cooley, Charles H. ([1901] 2009) *Human Nature and the Social Order*, New Brunswick: Transaction.

Corballis, Michael (2017) *The Truth about Language: What It Is and Where It Comes From*, University of Chicago Press.

Cornog, Evan (2004) *The Power and the Story: How the Crafted Presidential Narrative Has Determined Political Success from George Washington to George W. Bush*, New York: Penguin.

Cottle, Simon, Richard Sambrook and Nick Mosdell (2016) *Reporting Dangerously: Journalist Killings, Intimidations and Security*, London: Palgrave MacMillan.

Couldry, Nick (2010) *Why Voice Matters: Culture and Politics after Neoliberalism*, London: Sage.

Couldry, Nick and Andreas Hepp (2017) *The Mediated Construction of Reality*, Cambridge: Polity.

Crawshaw, Steve, and John Jackson (2010) *Small Acts of Resistance: How Courage, Tenacity and Ingenuity Can Change the World*, New York: Union Square Press.

Crouch, Colin (2004) *Post Democracy*, Cambridge: Polity.

Curran, James (2002) *Media and Power*, London: Routledge.

Dallmayr, Fred (2002) *Dialogue Among Civilizations: Some Exemplary Voices*, New York: Palgrave.

Dardot, P., and Laval, C. (2014) *The New Way of the World: On Neoliberal Society*. London: Verso.

Davis, Aeron (2013) *Promotional Cultures: The Rise and Spread of Advertising, Public Relations, Marketing and Branding*, Cambridge: Polity.

Davis, Joseph (ed.) (2002) *Stories of Change: Narrative and Social Movements*, New York: SUNY Press.

Deaton, Angus (2013) *The Great Escape: Health, Wealth and the Origins of Inequality*, Princeton University Press.

De Bary, Theodore (2013) *The Great Civilized Conversation*, New York: Columbia University Press.

De Beauvoir, Simone ([1949] 2015) *The Second Sex*, New York: Vintage.

De Gloma, Thomas (2014) *Seeing the Light: The Social Logic of Personal Discovery*, University of Chicago Press.

Delanty, Gerard (ed.) (2018, 2nd edn) *Routledge International Handbook of Cosmopolitan Studies*, London: Routledge.

De Robertis, Carolina (ed.) (2017) *Radical Hope: Letters of Love and Dissent in Dangerous Times*, London: Virago.

Didion, Joan (1979) *The White Album*, New York: Simon and Schuster.

Dodds, Felix, David Donoghue and Jimena Roesch (2017) *Negotiating the Sustainable Development Goals*, London: Routledge.

Donald, Merlin (1991) *Origins of the Modern Mind: Three Stages in the Evolution of Culture and Cognition*, Cambridge, Mass: Harvard University Press.

Dor, Daniel, and Jerome Lewis (eds.) (2014) *The Social Origins of Language*, Oxford University Press.

Douglas, Mary (1966) *Purity and Danger: An Analysis of Ritual and Taboo*, Harmondsworth: Penguin.

Douglass, Frederick ([1884] 1997) *Narrative of the Life of Frederick Douglass, An American Slave, Written by Himself*, ed. William A. Andrews and William S. McFeely, New York: W.W. Norton & Co.

Dowding, Keith (2011) *Encyclopedia of Power*, London: Sage.

Dreyfus, Hebert, and Sean Dorrance Kelly (2011) *All Things Shining: Reading the Western Classics to Find Meaning in a Secular Age*, New York: Free Press.

Durkheim, Émile ([1895] 1964) *The Rules of Sociological Method*, New York: Free Press of Glencoe.

Eco, Umberto (2013) *Inventing the Enemy*, London: Vintage Books.

Edelman, Murray (1977) *Political Language: Words That Succeed and Policies That Fail*, New York: Academic Press.

Edelman, Murray (1988) *Constructing the Political Spectacle*, University of Chicago Press.

Eisenstadt, Shmuel N. (2002) 'Multiple Modernities' in Shmuel N. Eisenstadt, ed., *Multiple Modernities*, London: Routledge, pp. 1-8.

Eisenstein, Elizabeth L. (1979–82) *The Printing Press as an Agent of Change*, 2 vols., Cambridge University Press.

Elias, Norbert, and John L. Scotson ([1965] 1994, 2nd edn) *The Established and the Outsiders: A Sociological Enquiry into Community Problems*, London: Sage.

Eliot, George ([1871] 2003) *Middlemarch: A Study in Country Life*, London: Penguin Classics.

Elkins, Stanley ([1959] 1976, 3rd edn) *Slavery: A Problem in American Institutional and Intellectual Life*, University of Chicago Press.

Ellison, Ralph ([1952], 2015, new edn) *Invisible Man*, London: Penguin Books.

Elsbree, Langdon (1982) *The Rituals of Life: Patterns in Narratives.* Port Washington, NY: Kennikat Press, National University Publications.

Engster, Daniel (2007) *The Heart of Justice: Care Ethics and Political Theory*, Oxford University Press.

Epstein, Mikhail (2012) *The Transformative Humanities: A Manifesto*, London: Bloomsbury.

Erickson, Kai ([1966] 2004, rev. edn) *Wayward Puritans: A Study in the Sociology of Deviance*, Boston: Allyn and Bacon.

Everett, Daniel (2012) *Language: The Cultural Tool*, London: Profile Books.

Fairclough, Norman (2010, 2nd edn) *Critical Discourse Analysis: The Critical Study of Language*, Harlow: Pearson.

Fanon, Frantz ([1961] 2001) *The Wretched of the Earth*, Harmondsworth: Penguin Books.

Faraday, Annabel, and Ken Plummer (1979) 'Doing Life Histories' *Sociological Review*, 27 (November), pp. 773-92.

Feldman, Gregory (2015) *We Are All Migrants*, Stanford University Press.

Figes, Orlando (2008) *The Whisperers: Private Life in Stalin's Russia*, London: Penguin.

Finnegan, Ruth (1970) *Oral Literature in Africa*, Oxford University Press.

Forman-Barzilai, Fonna (2010) *Adam Smith and the Circles of Sympathy: Cosmopolitanism and Moral Theory*, Cambridge University Press.

Foucault, Michel (1976) *The History of Sexuality*, vol. I, London: Allen Lane.

Foucault, Michel (1988) *Technologies of the Self: A Seminar with Michel Foucault*, Amherst: University of Massachusetts Press.

Franco, Jean (2013) *Cruel Modernity*, Durham: Duke University.

Frank, Arthur W. (1995) *The Wounded Storyteller: Body, Illness, and Ethics*, University of Chicago Press.

Frank, Arthur W. (2010) *Letting Stories Breathe: A Socio-Narratology*, University of Chicago Press.

Franke, William (2014) *A Philosophy of the Unsayable*, Notre Dame, Ind.: University of Notre Dame Press.

Frase, Peter (2016) *Four Futures: Life After Capitalism*, London: Verso.

Fraser, Nancy (1997) *Justice Interruptus*, London: Routledge.

Fraser, Nancy, and Kate Nash (eds.) (2014) *Transnationalizing the Public Sphere*, Cambridge: Polity.

Freedman, Des (2014) *The Contradictions of Media Power*, London: Bloomsbury.

Freeland, Chrystia (2012) *Plutocrats: The Rise of the New Global Super-Rich*, London: Allen Lane.

Freire, Paulo ([1970] 2017) *Pedagogy of the Oppressed*, London: Penguin.

Fricker, Miranda (2007) *Epistemic Injustice: Power and the Ethics of Knowing*, Oxford University Press.

Fuchs, Christian (2014) *Social Media: An Introduction*, London: Sage.

Fuchs, Christian (2018) *Digital Demagogue: Authoritarian Capitalism in the Age of Trump and Twitter*, London: Pluto.

Gabriel, Y. (2016). 'Narrative Ecologies and the Role of Counter-narratives: The Case of Nostalgic Stories and Conspiracy Theories' in S. Frandsen, T. Kuhn and M. W. Lundholt, eds., *Counter-narratives and Organization*, London: Routledge, pp. 208-26.

Gadamer, Hans-Georg (1975) *Truth and Method*, London: Bloomsbury.

Garton Ash, Timothy (2016) *Free Speech: Ten Principles for a Connected World*, London: Atlantic.

Geiselberger, Heinrich (ed.) (2017) *The Great Regression*, Cambridge: Polity.

Genette, Gerard ([1983] 1988) *Narrative Discourse Revisited*, New York: Cornell University Press.

Gensler, Harry J. (2013) *Ethics and the Golden Rule*, London: Routledge.

George, Andrew (ed.) (2003) *The Epic of Gilgamesh*, Harmondsworth: Penguin Classics.

Gerbaudo, Paulo (2012) *Tweets and the Streets: Social Media and Contemporary Activism*, London: Pluto Press.

Gere, Charlie (2008, 2nd edn) *Digital Culture*, London: Reaktion Books.

Gibson, James J. (1979) *The Ecological Approach to Visual Perception*, London: Allen and Unwin.

Girard, René (2011) *Mimesis and Theory: Essays on Literature and Criticism, 1953-2005*, ed. Robert Doran, Palo Alto: Stanford University Press.

Ghosh, Amitav (2016) *The Great Derangement: Climate Change and the Unthinkable*, University of Chicago Press.

Giddens, Anthony (2010) *The Politics of Climate Change*, Cambridge: Polity.

Goffman, Erving ([1956] 1966) *The Presentation of Self in Everyday Life*, Harmondsworth: Penguin.

Goffman, Erving (1961a) *Asylums: Essays on the Social Situation of Mental Patients and Other Inmates*, Harmondsworth: Penguin Books.

Goffman, Erving (1961b) 'Role Distance' in *Encounters: Two Studies in Interaction*, New York: Bobbs-Merrill.

Goodson, Ivor (ed.) (2017) *The Routledge International Handbook on Narrative Life History*, London: Routledge.

Goody, Jack (ed.) (1968) *Literacy in Traditional Societies*, Cambridge University Press.

Goody, Jack, and Ian Watt (1968) 'The Consequences of Literacy' in Goody, 1968, pp. 27-84.

Gordon, Avery F. (2008, 2nd edn) *Ghostly Matters: Haunting and the Sociological Imagination*, Minneapolis: University of Minnesota Press.

Gourevitch, Philip (2000) *We Wish to Inform You That Tomorrow We Will Be Killed With Our Families*, London: Picador.

Gottschalk, Jonathan (2012) *The Storytelling Animal: How Stories Make Us Human*, Boston: Houghton Mifflin Harcourt, and Mariner Books.

Graeber, David (2013) *The Democracy Project: A History, a Crisis, a Movement*, London: Penguin.

Greenwald, Glenn (2015) *No Place to Hide: Edward Snowden, the NSA and the Surveillance Society*, London: Penguin.

Gubrium, Jaber F., and James A. Holstein (2009) *Analyzing Narrative Reality*, London: Sage.

Habermas, Jürgen ([1962] 1989) *The Structural Transformation of the Public Sphere: An Inquiry into a Category of Bourgeois Society*, Cambridge: Polity.

Haidt, Jonathan (2012) *The Righteous Mind: Why Good People are Divided by Politics and Religion*, London: Penguin.

Hall, Stuart (1973) 'Encoding/Decoding' in S. Hall, ed., *Culture, Media, Language*, London: Hutchinson, pp. 117–27.

Harari, Yuval Noah (2016) *Homo Deus: A Brief History of Tomorrow*, London: Harvill Secker.

Harding, Luke (2016) *The Snowden Files: The Inside Story of the World's Most Wanted Man*, London: Guardian Faber Publishing.

Harding, Sandra (1986) *The Science Question in Feminism*, Milton Keynes: Open University Press.

Hartsock, Nancy C. M. (1998) *The Feminist Standpoint Revisited and Other Essays*, Boulder, Colo., Westwood Press.

Hatzfeld, Jean (2007) *Life Laid Bare: The Survivors Speak*, London: Other Press.

Hayden, Patrick (ed.) (2014) *Hannah Arendt: Key Concepts*, Durham: Acumen Press.

Hayles, N. Katherine (2012) *How We Think: Digital Media and Contemporary Technogenesis*, University of Chicago Press.

Hayner, Priscilla B. (2010) *Unspeakable Truths: Facing the Challenge of Truth Commissions*, New York: Routledge.

Hayward, Anthony (2004) *Which Side Are You On? Ken Loach and His Films*, London: Bloomsbury.

Hearn, Jonathan (2012) *Theorizing Power*, Basingstoke: Palgrave.

Hegde, Radha S. (2016) *Mediating Migration*, Cambridge: Polity.

Hegel, Georg Wilhelm Friedrich ([1807] 1977) *Phenomenology of the Spirit*, Oxford: Clarendon Press.

Helliwell, J., R. Layard and J. Sachs (2018) *World Happiness Report 2018*, New York: Sustainable Development Solutions Network.

Highfield, Tim (2016) *Social Media and Everyday Politics*, Cambridge: Polity.

Hirsch, Marianne (2012) *The Generation of Postmemory: Writing and Visual Culture After the Holocaust*, New York: Columbia University Press.

Hirschman, Albert O. (1972) *Exit, Voice and Liberty: Responses to Decline in Firms, Organizations and States*, Cambridge, Mass.: Harvard University Press.

Holstein, James A. and Jaber F. Gubrium (2000) *The Self We Live By: Narrative Identity in a Postmodern World*, Oxford University Press.

Horten, Monica (2016) *The Closing of the Net*, Cambridge: Polity.

Hosking, Geoffrey (2014) *Trust: A History*, Oxford University Press.

Hyde, Lewis (2012) *Common as Air: Revolution, Art, Ownership*. London: Union Books.

Idle, Nadia, and Alex Nunns (eds.) (2011) *Tweets from Tahrir: Egypt's Revolution As It Unfolded, in the Words of the People Who Made It.* New York: O/R Books.

Inayatullah, Naeem, and Elizabeth Dauphinée (eds.) (2016) *Narrative Global Politics: Theory, History and the Personal in International Relations,* London: Routledge.

Isin, Egin, and Evelyn Ruppert (2015) *Being Digital Citizens.* London: Rowman and Littlefield.

Jackson, Michael (2002) *The Politics of Storytelling: Violence, Transgression and Intersubjectvity,* Copenhagen University: Museum Tusculanum Press.

James, William ([1892] 1961) *Psychology: The Briefer Course,* New York: Harper Torchbooks.

Jasper, James J. (2018) *The Emotions of Protest,* University of Chicago Press.

Jessop, Bob (2008) *State Power,* Cambridge: Polity.

Kakutani, Michiko (2018) *The Death of Truth,* London: Harper Collins.

Kapuściński, Ryszard (2006) *The Other,* London: Verso.

Karatzogianni, Athina, Dennis Nguyen and Elisa Serafinelli (eds.) (2016) *The Digital Transformation of the Public Sphere: Conflict, Migration, Crisis and Culture in Digital Networks,* London: Palgrave Macmillan.

Karatzogianni, Athina, and Andrew Robinson (2010) *Power, Resistance and Conflict in the Contemporary World,* London: Routledge.

Kearney, Richard (2002) *On Stories,* London: Routledge.

Keen, Andrew (2015) *The Internet Is Not the Answer,* London: Atlantic Books.

Keen, Andrew (2018) *How to Fix the Future: Staying Human in the Digital Age,* London: Atlantic Books.

Keen, Suzanne (2007) *Empathy and the Novel,* Oxford University Press.

Kelly, Lynn (2015) *Knowledge and Power in Prehistoric Societies: Orality, Memory and the Transmission of Culture,* Cambridge University Press.

Kendi, Ibram X. (2017) *Stamped from the Beginning,* London: Bodley Head.

King, Anthony, and Ivor Crewe (2013) *The Blunders of Our Governments,* London: One World.

Kitcher, Philip (2011) *The Ethical Project,* Cambridge, Mass.: Harvard University Press.

Klein, Naomi (1999) *No Logo: Taking Aim at the Brand Bullies.* London: Flamingo.

Klein, Naomi (2017) *No Is Not Enough: Defeating the New Shock Politics,* London: Allen Lane.

Kleinman, Arthur (1988) *The Illness Narratives: Suffering, Healing and the Human Condition,* New York: Basic Books.

Knuth, Rebecca (2006) *Burning Books and Leveling Libraries: Extremist Violence and Cultural Destruction,* Westport, Conn.: Praeger.

Koczanowicz, Leszek (2014) *Politics of Dialogue,* Edinburgh University Press.

Koenitz, Hartmut, Gabrielle Ferri, Mads Jaahr, Diğdem Sezen and Tonguç Ibrahim Sezen (eds.) (2015) *Interactive Digital Narrative: History, Theory and Practice,* London: Routledge.

Kuhn, T. S. (1962) *The Structure of Scientific Revolutions*, University of Chicago Press.

Kuntsman, Adi (ed.) (2017) *Selfie Citizenship*, Basingstoke: Palgrave.

Kristof, Nicholas D., and Sheryl WuDunn (2010) *Half the Sky*, London: Virago.

Lachmann, Richard (2010) *States and Power*, Cambridge: Polity.

Laine, James W. (2014) *Meta-Religion: Religion and Power in World History*, Berkeley: University of California Press.

Lamont, Michèle, Graziella Moraes Silva, Jessica S. Welburn et al. (2016) *Getting Respect: Responding to Stigma and Discrimination in the United States, Brazil, and Israel*, Princeton University Press.

Landman, Todd (2013) *Human Rights and Democracy: The Precarious Triumph of Ideas*, London: Bloomsbury.

Lanier, Jaron (2018) *Ten Arguments for Deleting Your Social Media Accounts Right Now*, London: Bodley Head.

Lara, Maria Pia (1998) *Moral Textures: Feminist Narratives in the Public Sphere*, Cambridge: Polity.

Latour, Bruno (1986) 'The Powers of Association' in J. Law (ed.) *Power, Action and Belief*, London: Routledge, pp. 264-79.

Lazzara, Michael J. (2011) *Luz Arce and Pinochet's Chile: Testimony in the Aftermath of State Violence*. Basingstoke: Palgrave.

Lear, Jonathan (2006) *Radical Hope: Ethics in the Face of Cultural Devastation*, Cambridge, Mass.: Harvard University Press.

Lebron, Christopher J. (2017) *The Making of Black Lives Matter: A Brief History of An Idea*, Oxford University Press.

Lee, Francis F. L., and Joseph Chan (2018) *Media and Protest Logics in the Digital Era: The Umbrella Movement in Hong Kong*, Oxford University Press.

Leiss, William (2005, 3rd edn) *Social Communication in Advertising: Consumption in the Mediated Marketplace*. New York: Routledge.

Levi, Primo (1988) *The Drowned and the Saved*, London: Abacus.

Levinas, Emanuel (1969) *Totality and Infinity*, Pittsburgh: Duquesne University Press.

Levitas, Ruth (2014) *Utopia as Method: The Imaginary Reconstitution of Society*, Basingstoke: Palgrave.

Levitsky, Steven, and Daniel Ziblatt (2018) *How Democracies Die: What History Reveals About our Future*, New York: Viking.

Lipstadt, Deborah (1993) *Denying the Holocaust: The Growing Assault on Truth and Memory*, Harmondsworth: Penguin.

Lipstadt, Deborah ([2006] 2016) *Denial: Holocaust History on Trial*, London: Ecco / Harper Collins.

Livholts, Mona, and Maria Tamboukou (2015) *Discourse and Narrative Methods*, London: Sage.

Lovett, Frank (2010) *A General Theory of Domination and Justice*, Oxford University Press.

Luhmann, Niklas ([1977] 2017) *Trust and Power*, Cambridge: Polity.

Lukes, Steven ([1974] 2005. 2nd edn) *Power: A Radical View*, Basingstoke: Palgrave.

Lupton, Deborah (2016) *The Quantified Self*, Cambridge: Polity.

MacGregor, Neil (2012) *A History of the World in 100 Objects*, London: Penguin.

MacGregor, Neil (2018) *Living with the Gods: 40,000 Years of Peoples, Objects and Beliefs*, London: British Museum / Allen Lane.

MacIntyre, Alastair ([1981] 2007) *After Virtue: A Study in Moral Theory*, London: Bloomsbury.

Malik, Kenan (2014) *The Quest for a Moral Compass: A Global History of Ethics*, London: Atlantic Books.

Mann, Michael (1986–2013) *The Sources of Social Power*, 4 vols., Cambridge University Press.

Margetts, Helen, Peter John, Scott Hale and Taha Yasseri (2016) *Political Turbulence: How Social Media Shape Collective Action*, Princeton University Press.

Marshall, P. David ([1997] 2014) *Celebrity and Power: Fame in Contemporary Culture*, Minneapolis: University of Minnesota Press.

Matynia, Elzbieta (2009) *Performative Democracy*, Boulder: Paradigm Publishers.

Mayer, F. W. (2014) *Narrative Politics: Stories and Collective Action*, Oxford University Press.

Mazlish, Bruce (2009) *The Idea of Humanity in a Global Era*, New York: Palgrave MacMillan.

McAdams, Dan P. (1993) *The Stories We Live By: Personal Myths and the Making of the Self*, London: Guilford Press.

McCloskey, Deirdre (1998, 2nd edn) *The Rhetoric of Economics*, University of Wisconsin Press.

McCosker, Anthony, Sonja Vivienne and Amelia Johns (eds.) (2016) *Negotiating Digital Citizenship: Control, Contest, Culture*, London: Rowman and Littlefield.

McRuer, Robert M. (2006) *Crip Theory: Cultural Signs of Queerness and Disability*, New York University Press.

McKee, Alan (2009) *The Public Sphere*, Cambridge University Press.

Mead, George H. ([1934] 1970) *Mind, Self and Society*, ed. Charles W. Morris, University of Chicago Press.

Mead, George H. (1959) *The Philosophy of the Present*, Illinois: The Open Court Publishing Company.

Medina, José (2013) *The Epistemology of Resistance: Gender and Race, Oppression, Epistemic Injustice and Resistant Imaginations*, Oxford University Press.

Meyers, Philip (2014) *Storytelling for Lawyers*, Oxford University Press.

Mills, C. Wright (1959) *The Sociological Imagination*. Oxford University Press.

Mirowski, Philip, and Dieter Plehwe (eds.) (2015, rev. edn) *The Road from Mont Pelerin*, Cambridge, Mass.: Harvard University Press.

Mishra, Pankaj (2017) *Age of Anger: A History of the Present*, London: Allen Lane.

Molotch, Harvey (2014) 'How the 9/11 Museum Gets Us' *Public Books* (9.1) www.publicbooks.org/how-the-911-museum-gets-us.

Morgan, Marcus (2016) *Pragmatic Humanism: On the Nature and Value of Sociological Knowledge*, London: Routledge.

Morrison, Toni ([1987] 2004). *Beloved*, New York: Vintage.

Morrison, Toni (2017) *The Origins of Others*, Boston: Harvard University Press.

Mossberger, Karen, Caroline J. Tolbert and Ramona S. McNeal (2007) *Digital Citizenship: The Internet, Society, and Participation*, Cambridge, Mass: MIT Press.

Mouffe, Chantal (2013) *Agonistics: Thinking the World Politically*, London: Verso.

Mounk, Yascha (2018) *The People vs Democracy*, Cambridge, Mass.: Harvard University Press

Nacos, Brigitte L (2016, 3rd edn) *Mass-Mediated Terrorism: Mainstream and Digital Media in Terrorism and Counterterrorism*, Lanham, Md.: Rowman and Littlefield.

Nelson, Hilde Lindemann (2001) *Damaged Identities, Narrative Repair*, Ithaca: Cornell University Press.

Nettle, Daniel, and Suzanne Romaine (2000) *Vanishing Voices: The Extinction of the World's Languages*, Oxford: University Press.

Nguyen, Viet Thanh (2016) *Nothing Ever Dies: Vietnam and the Memory of War*, Cambridge, Mass.: Harvard University Press.

Nguyen, Viet Thanh (2018) *The Displaced: Refugee Writers on Refugee Lives*, London: Abrams.

Nixon, Rob (2011) *Slow Violence and the Environmentalism of the Poor*, Cambridge, Mass.: Harvard University Press.

Noam, Eli N. (2016) *Who Owns the World's Media? Media Concentration and Ownership Around the World*, Oxford University Press.

Noble, Safiya Umoja (2018) *Algorithms of Oppression: How Search Engines Reinforce Racism*, New York University Press.

Norris, Pippa (2010) *Digital Divide*. Cambridge University Press.

Nussbaum, Martha (1997) *Cultivating Humanity: A Classical Defense of Reform in Liberal Education*, Cambridge, Mass.: Harvard University Press.

Nussbaum, Martha (2006) *Frontiers of Justice*, Cambridge, Mass.: Harvard University Press.

Nussbaum, Martha (2011) *Creating Capabilities: The Human Development Approach*, Cambridge, Mass.: The Belknap Press of Harvard University Press.

Obama, Barack (2008) *The Audacity of Hope: Thoughts on Reclaiming the American Dream*, London: Canongate.

Olesen, Thomas (2015) *Global Injustice Symbols and Social Movements*, New York: Palgrave Macmillan.

Olesen, Thomas (2016) 'Malala and the Politics of Global Iconicity' *British Journal of Sociology* 67:2, pp. 307-27.

O'Neil, Cathy (2016) *Weapons of Math Destruction*, London: Penguin.

Ong, Walter J. (1982) *Orality and Literacy: The Technologizing of the World*, London: Methuen.

Owen, Taylor (2015) *Disruptive Power: The Crisis of the State in the Digital Age*, Oxford University Press.

Oxfam (2015) *Wealth: Having It All and Wanting More*. Oxford: Oxfam Issue Briefing, January.

Palumbo-Liu, David (2012) *The Deliverance of Others: Reading Literature in a Global Age*, Durham, NC: Duke University Press.

Patten, Brian (2007) 'So Many Different Lengths of Time', in *Selected Poems*, Harmondsworth: Penguin; https://www.youtube.com/watch?v=GEoBH55IdCA.

Peters, Otto (2013) *Against the Tide: Critics of Digitalisation: Warners, Sceptics, Scaremongers, Apocalypticists: 20 Portraits*, BIS-Verlag der Carl von Ossietzky Universität Oldenburg.

Philo, Greg, Emma Briant and Pauline Donald (2016) *Bad News for Refugees*, London: Pluto.

Piketty, Thomas (2014) *Capital in the Twenty-First Century*, Cambridge, Mass.: The Belknap Press of Harvard University Press.

Pilling, David (2018) *The Growth Delusion*, London: Bloomsbury.

Pinker, Steven (2018) *Enlightenment Now: The Case for Reason, Science, Humanism and Progress*, London: Allen Lane.

Pirandello, Luigi ([1921] 2014) *Six Characters in Search of an Author*, London: Penguin.

Plummer, Ken ([1983] 2001) *Documents of Life – 2: An Invitation to a Critical Humanism*, London: Sage.

Plummer, Ken (1995) *Telling Sexual Stories: Power, Change and Social Worlds*, London: Routledge.

Plummer, Ken (2003) *Intimate Citizenship: Private Decisions and Public Dialogues*, Seattle: University of Washington.

Plummer, Ken (2010) 'Generational Sexualities, Subterranean Traditions, and the Hauntings of the Sexual World: Some Preliminary Remarks' *Symbolic Interaction* 33:2 (Spring), pp. 163-90.

Plummer, Ken (2012) 'My Multiple Sick Bodies: Symbolic Interactionism, Autoethnography and Embodiment' in Bryan S. Turner, ed., *Routledge Handbook of Body Studies*, London: Routledge, pp. 75-93.

Plummer, Ken (2013a) 'A Manifesto for a Critical Humanism in Sociology: On Questioning the Social World', in Daniel Nehring, ed., *Sociology*, Harlow: Pearson, pp. 489-516.

Plummer, Ken (2013b) 'A Manifesto for Social Stories', in Stanley, 2013, pp. 209-21.

Plummer, Ken (2015a) 'Liberating Generations: Continuities and Change in the Radical Queer Western Era' in David Paternotte and Manon Tremblay, eds., *Companion to Lesbian and Gay Activism*, Farnham: Ashgate.

Plummer, Ken (2015b) *Cosmopolitan Sexualities: Hope and the Humanist Imagination*, Cambridge: Polity.

Plummer, Ken (2017) 'On the Infinitude of Life Stories: Still Puzzling Queer Tales After All These Years' *QED: A Journal in GLBTQ Worldmaking* 4:1 (Spring), pp. 189-97.

Plummer, Ken (forthcoming) *Manifesto for Critical Humanism: In Search of Hope and Flourishing Life*, Cambridge: Polity.

Poe, Marshall T. (2011) *A History of Communications*, Cambridge University Press.

Poletta, Francesca (2006) *It Was Like A Fever: Storytelling in Protest and Politics*, University of Chicago Press.

Polkinghorne, Donald E. (1988) *Narrative Knowing and the Human Sciences*, State University of New York.

Presser, Lois, and Sveinung Sandberg (eds.) (2015) *Narrative Criminology*, New York University Press.

Prinz, Jesse (2012) *Beyond Human Nature: How Culture and Experience Shape our Lives*, London: Allen Lane.

Propp, Vladimir (1968, rev edn) *Morphology of the Folktale*, Austin: University of Texas.

Prus, Robert (1999) *Beyond the Power Mystique: Power as Intersubjective Accomplishment*, Albany: State University of New York.

Puckett, Kent (2016) *Narrative Theory: A Critical Introduction*, Cambridge University Press.

Rambukkana, Nathan (ed.) (2015) *Hashtag Publics: The Power and Politics of Discursive Networks*, Oxford: Peter Lang.

Rawick, Jules, and George Rawick (1972) *The American Slave: A Composite Autobiography*, Santa Barbara: Greenwood Press.

Rawnsley, Gary D, and Ming-yeh T. Rawnsley (eds.) (2015) *Routledge Handbook of Chinese Media*, London: Routledge.

Reed, T. V. (2014) *Digitized Lives: Culture, Power and Social Change in the Internet Era*, London: Routledge.

Ricoeur, Paul (1992) *Oneself as Another*, University of Chicago Press.

Ricoeur, Paul (2005) *History, Memory, Forgetting*, University of Chicago Press.

Riessman, Catherine Kohler (2007) *Narrative Methods for the Human Sciences*, London: Sage.

Rifkin, Jeremy (2009) *The Empathic Civilization: The Race to Global Consciousness in a World of Crisis*, Cambridge: Polity.

Roberts, Margaret E. (2018) *Censored: Distraction and Diversion inside China's Great Firewall*, Princeton University Press.

Rojek, Chris (2015) *Presumed Intimacy*, Cambridge: Polity.

Rorty, Richard (1999) *Philosophy and Social Hope*, Harmondsworth Penguin.

Rose, Jonathan (2001) *The Intellectual Life of the British Working Class*, New Haven: Yale University Press.

Rosling, Hans (with Ola Rosling and Anna Rosling Ronnlund) (2018) *Factfulness: Ten Reasons We're Wrong about the World and Why Things Are Better Than You Think*. London: Sceptre.

Runciman, David (2015 updated) *The Confidence Trap: A History of Democracy in Crisis from World War I to the Present*, Princeton University Press.

Runciman, David (2018) *How Democracy Ends*, London: Profile Books.

Russell, Bertram (1975, rev edn) *Power: A New Social Analysis*, London: Routledge.

Sachs, Oliver (1985) *The Man Who Mistook His Wife for a Hat and Other Essays*, New York: Touchstone.

Said, Edward W. (1978) *Orientalism*, New York: Penguin.

Sainath, P. (1996) *Everybody Loves a Drought: Stories from India's Poor District*, Haryana: Penguin.

Salmon, Christian ([2007]; trans. 2017) *Storytelling: Bewitching the Modern Mind*, London: Verso.

Samson, Colin, and Carlos Gigoux (2017) *Indigenous Peoples and Colonialism: Global Perspectives*, Cambridge: Polity.

Santos, Boaventura de Sousa (2014) *Epistemologies of the South: Justice Against Epistemicide*, London: Routledge.

Sassen, Saskia (2014) *Expulsions: Brutality and Complexity in the Global Economy*, Cambridge, Mass.: The Belknap Press of Harvard University Press.

Saul, Jack (2013) *Collective Trauma, Collective Healing: Promoting Community Resilience in the Aftermath of Disaster*, London: Routledge.

Sayad, Abdelmalek (2004) *The Suffering of the Immigrant*, Cambridge: Polity.

Sayer, Andrew (2011) *Why Things Matter to People: Social Science, Values and Ethical Life*, Cambridge University Press.

Schafer, Kay, and Sidonie Smith (2004) *Human Rights and Narrated Lives*, Basingstoke: Palgrave.

Schwartz, Barry, and Kenneth Sharpe (2011) *Practical Wisdom: The Right Way To Do the Right Thing*, New York: Riverhead Books.

Scott, James C. (1985) *Weapons of the Weak: Everyday Forms of Power Resistance*, New Haven: Yale University Press.

Scott, James C. (1990) *Domination and the Arts of Resistance: Hidden Transcripts*, New Haven: Yale University Press.

Scott, John (2001) *Power*, Cambridge: Polity.

Scott, Laurence (2015) *The Four-Dimensional Human: Ways of Being in the Digital World*, London: Penguin.

Scott, Suzie (2018) 'A Sociology of Nothing: Understanding the Unmarked', *Sociology* 52:1, pp. 3-19.

Scranton, Roy (2015) *Learning to Die in the Anthropocene: Reflections on the End of Civilization*, San Francisco: City Lights Books.

Sedgwick, Eve Kasofsky ([1990] 2008, 2nd edn) *Epistemology of the Closet*, Berkeley: University of California Press.

Selbin, Eric (2010) *Revolution, Rebellion, Resistance: The Power of Story*, London: Zed Books.

Sen, Amartya (2006) *Identity and Violence: The Illusion of Destiny*, London: Allen Lane.

Sen, Amartya (2009) *The Idea of Justice*, London: Allen Lane.

Shandler, Jeffrey (2017) *Holocaust Memory in the Digital Age: Survivors' Stories and New Media Practices*, Palo Alto: Stanford University Press.

Sinha, Indra (2007) *Animal's People*, New York: Simon and Schuster.

Skeggs, Beverley (1997) *Formations of Class and Gender: Becoming Respectable*, London: Sage.

Smith, Adam ([1759] 2000) *The Theory of Moral Sentiments*, New York: Prometheus.

Smith, Christian (2003) *Moral, Believing Animals: Human Personhood and Culture*, Oxford University Press.

Smith, Christian (2010) *What Is a Person? Rethinking Humanity, Social Life, and the Moral Good from the Person Up*, University of Chicago Press.

Smith, David Livingstone (2011) *Less Than Human: Why We Demean, Enslave and Exterminate Others*, New York: St Martin's Press.

Smith, Philip (2005) *Why War? The Cultural Logic of Iraq, The Gulf War, and Suez*, University of Chicago Press.

Smith, Philip, and Nicolas Howe (2015) *Climate Change as Social Drama: Global Warming in the Public Sphere*, Cambridge University Press.

Smith, Rogers M. (2003) *Stories of Peoplehood: The Politics and Morals of Political Membership*, Cambridge University Press.

Smith, Sidonie, and Julia Watson (2001) *Reading Autobiography: A Guide to Interpreting Narratives*, Minneapolis: University of Minnesota Press.

Snowden, Edward (2014) 'Edward Snowden Interview – the Edited Transcript', *The Guardian*, 18 July.

Solinger, Rickie, Madeline Fox and Kayhan Irani (eds.) (2008) *Telling Stories to Change the World*, London: Routledge.

Solnit, Rebecca ([2004] 2016, 2nd edn) *Hope in the Dark: Untold Histories, Wild Possibilities*, London: Canongate.

Solnit, Rebecca (2009) *A Paradise Built in Hell: The Extraordinary Communities that Arise in Disaster*, New York: Penguin.

Solzhenitsyn, Aleksandr (2003, abridged edn) *The Gulag Archipelago*, London: Harvill Press.

Sondheim, Stephen (2011) *Look I Made a Hat*, New York: Virgin Books.

Spivak, Gayatri Chakravorty (1988) 'Can the Subaltern Speak?' in *Marxism and the Interpretation of Culture*, Urbana: University of Illinois Press, pp. 271-313.

Srnicek, Nick (2016) *Platform Capitalism*, Cambridge: Polity.

Stanley, Liz (ed.) (2013) *Documents of Life Revisited: Narrative and Biographical Methodology for a 21st-Century Critical Humanism*, Guildford: Ashgate.

Stein, Arlene (2014) *Reluctant Witnesses: Survivors, Their Children and the Rise of Holocaust Consciousness*, Oxford University Press.

Steinbeck, John ([1952] 2017) *East of Eden*, London: Penguin Classics.

Stern, Steve J. (2004–10) *The Memory Box of Pinochet's Chile*, 3 vols., Durham: Duke University Press.

Stevenson, Brenda E. (2015) *What Is Slavery?* Cambridge: Polity.

Stiglitz, Joseph (2012) *The Price of Inequality*, London: Allen Lane.

Storr, Will (2017) *Selfie*, London: Virago.

Strawson, Galen (2004) 'Against Narrativity' *Ratio* 17 (4 December), pp. 428–52.

Stubblefield, Thomas (2015) *9/11 and the Visual Culture of Disaster*, Bloomington: Indiana Press.

Sundaram, Anjan (2017) *Bad News: Last Journalists in a Dictatorship*, London: Bloomsbury.

Sunstein, Cass ([2007] 2017) *#Republic: Divided Democracy in the Age of Social Media*. Princeton University Press.

Sykes, Gresham (2007, 2nd edn) *The Society of Captives: A Study of a Maximum Security Prison*, Princeton University Press.

Sznaider, Natan (2001) *The Compassionate Temperament: Care and Cruelty in Modern Society*, Oxford: Rowman and Littlefield.

Tai, Zixue (2014) 'Finger Power and Smart Mob: Social Activism and Mass Dissent in China in the Networked Era' in Peter Weibel, ed., *Global Activism: Art and Conflict in the 21st Century*, Cambridge, Mass.: MIT Press, pp. 396-407.

Taylor, Charles (2004) *Modern Social Imaginaries*, Durham: Duke University Books / Public Space Books.

Taylor, Charles (2016) *The Language Animal: The Full Shape of the Linguistic Capacity*, Cambridge, Mass.: The Belknap Press of Harvard University Press.

Thomas, Elsa Ashish, and Rashid Narain Shukul (2015) 'Framing of Malala Yousafzai: A Comparative Analysis of News Coverage in Western and Pakistani Mainstream English Print and Alternative Media' *Media Asia* 42:3-4, pp. 225-41.

Thompson, John B. (1995) *The Media and Modernity: A Social Theory of the Media*. Cambridge: Polity.

Thompson, Mark (2017) *Enough Said: What's Gone Wrong with the Language of Politics*, London: Vintage.

Tilly, Charles (1999) *Durable Inequality*, Berkeley: University of California Press.

Tilly, Charles (2002) *Stories, Identities and Political Change*, London: Rowman and Little.

Tilly, Charles (2004) *Social Movements: 1768-2004*, Boulder: Paradigm.

Tilly, Charles (2006) *Regimes and Repertoires*, University of Chicago Press.

Tilly, Charles, and Sidney Tarrow (2015, 2nd edn) *Contentious Politics*, Oxford University Press.

Tomasello, Michael (2010) *Origins of Human Communication*, Cambridge, Mass.: MIT Press.

Tormey, Simon (2015) *The End of Representative Politics*, Cambridge: Polity.

Treanor, Brian (2014) *Emplotting Virtue: A Narrative Approach to Environmental Virtue Ethics*, Albany: State University of New York Press.

Tremblay, Rodrigue (2009) *The Code for Global Ethics: Toward a Humanist Civilization*, Montreal: Trafford.

Tronto, Joan C. (2013) *Caring Democracy: Markets, Equality and Justice*, New York University Press.

Turkle, Sherry (2016) *Reclaiming Conversation: The Power of Talk in the Digital Age*, London: Penguin.

Turner, Bryan S. (2006) *Vulnerability and Human Rights: Essays in Rights*, University Park: Penn State University Press.

Turner, Graeme (2010) *Ordinary People and the Media: The Demotic Turn*, London: Sage.

Turner, Graeme (2014, 2nd edn) *Understanding Celebrity*, London: Sage.

Turner, Graeme (2016) *Re-Inventing the Media*, London: Routledge.

Tyler, Imogen (2013) *Revolting Subjects: Social Abjection and Resistance in Neoliberal Britain*, London: Zed Books.

UNDP (2017) *Human Development Report 2016*: *Human Development for Everyone*, New York: UNDP.

Unger, Roberto Mangabeira (2007) *The Self Awakened*, Cambridge, Mass.: Harvard University Press.

United Nations (2015) *Transforming Our World: The 2030 Agenda for Sustainable Development*: https://sustainabledevelopment.un.org/post2015/transformingourworld.

Ure, Michael, and Mervyn Frost (2014) *The Politics of Compassion*, London: Routledge.

Urry, John (2000) *Sociology Beyond Societies: Mobilities for the Twenty-first Century*, London: Sage.

Urry, John (2003) *Global Complexity*, Cambridge: Polity.

Urry, John (2014) *Offshoring*, Cambridge: Polity.

Urry, John (2016) *What is the Future?* Cambridge: Polity.

Van Dijk, Jan (2005) *The Deepening Divide*, London: Sage.

Van Hooft, Stan (2009) *Cosmopolitanism: A Philosophy for Global Ethics*, Stocksfield: Acumen.

Van Hooft, Stan (2011) *Hope*, London: Acumen.

Vivienne, Sonja (2016) 'Intimate Citizenship: 3.0' in McCosker et al., 2016, pp. 147-65.

Volkmer, Ingrid (2014) *The Global Public Sphere: Public Communication in the Age of Reflexive Interdependence*, Cambridge: Polity.

Wacquant, Loïc (2008) *Urban Outcasts: A Comparative Study of Advanced Marginality*, Cambridge: Polity.

Warner, Michael (2002) *Publics and Counterpublics*, New York: Zone Books.

Watt, Ian (1967) *The Rise of the Novel: Studies in Defoe, Richardson, and Fielding*, Berkeley: University of California Press.

Weber, Ed, Denise Lach and Brent Steel (eds.) (2017) *New Strategies for Wicked Problems: Science and Solutions in the Twenty-first Century*, Oregon State University Press.

Weibel, Peter (ed.) (2014) *Global Activism: Art and Conflict in the 21st Century*, Cambridge, Mass.: MIT Press.

Wenman, Mark (2013) *Agonistic Democracy: Constituent Power in the Era of Globalisation*, Cambridge University Press.

Wetherell, Margaret (2012) *Affect and Emotion*, London: Sage.

Wheen, Francis (2005) *How Mumbo Jumbo Conquered the World: A Short History of Modern Delusions*, London: Public Affairs.

White, Hayden ([1973] 2014, 40th anniversary edn) *Metahistory: The Historical Imagination in Nineteenth-Century Europe*, Baltimore: Johns Hopkins University Press.

Whitehead, Colson (2016) *The Underground Railroad*, New York: Doubleday.

Widdows, Heather (2011) *Global Ethics: An Introduction*, Durham: Acumen.

Wilkinson, Iain, and Arthur Kleinman (2016) *A Passion for Society: How We Think About Human Suffering*, Berkeley: University of California Press.

Willis, Paul ([1978] 2018) *Learning to Labour: How Working-Class Kids Get Working-Class Jobs*, New York: Columbia University Press.

Wilson, Edward 0. (2017) *The Origins of Creativity*, London: Allen Lane.

Wood, James (2009) *How Fiction Works*, London: Vintage Books.

Wood, James (2015) *The Nearest Thing to Life*, London: Jonathan Cape.

Woodiwiss, Jo (2009) *Contesting Stories of Childhood Sexual Abuse*, Basingstoke: Palgrave.

Woodiwiss, Jo, Kate Smith and Kelly Lockwood (eds.) (2017) *Feminist Narrative Research: Opportunities and Challenges*, Basingstoke: Palgrave.

Wright, Erik Olin (2010) *Envisioning Real Utopias*, London: Verso.

Wrong, Dennis (1979) *Power: Its Forms, Bases and Uses*. Oxford: Blackwell.

Yoneyama, Lisa (1999) *Hiroshima Traces: Time, Space and Dialectics of Memory*, Berkeley: University of California Press.

Young, Allan (1997) *The Harmony of Illusions: Inventing Post-Traumatic Disorder*, Princeton University Press.

Young, Iris Marion (1990) *Justice and the Politics of Difference*, Princeton University Press.

Young, Jock (1971) *The Drugtakers*, London: Paladin.

Yousafzai, Malala (2014) *I Am Malala: The Girl Who Stood Up for Education and Was Shot by the Taliban*, London: Phoenix.

Yurchak, Alexei (2005) *Everything Was Forever, Until It Was No More: The Last Soviet Generation*, Princeton University Press.

Yuval-Davis, Nira (2011) *The Politics of Belonging: Intersectional Contestations*, London: Sage.
Zenor, Jason (ed.) (2014) *Parasocial Politics: Audiences, Pop Culture and Politics*, New York: Lexington.

Videography: Key Films Mentioned or Discussed

12 Years A Slave, 2013, dir. Steve McQueen
Back to the Future, 1985, dir. Robert Zemeckis
Black Earth Rising, 2018, dir. Hugo Blick
Bread and Roses, 2000, dir. Ken Loach
Capitalism: A Love Story, 2009, dir. Michael Moore
Cave of Forgotten Dreams, 2010, dir. Werner Herzog
Citizen Four, 2014, dir. Laura Poitras
Denial, 2016, dir. Mick Jackson
Fire at Sea, 2016, dir. Gianfranco Rosi
Hannah Arendt, 2012, dir. Margarethe von Trotta
He Named Me Malala, 2015, dir. David Guggenheim
Hotel Rwanda, 2004, dir. Terry George
Human Flow, 2018, dir. Ai Weiwei
Hypernormalization, 2017, dir. Adam Curtis
I, Daniel Blake, 2017, dir. Ken Loach
I Am Not Your Negro, 2016, dir. Raoul Peck
Inside Job, 2010, dir. Charles Ferguson
Into the Woods, 2014, dir. Rob Marshall
It's a Wonderful Life, 1946, dir. Frank Capra
Kes, 1969, dir. Ken Loach
Lo and Behold: Reveries of the Connected World, 2016, dir. Werner Herzog
Nostalgia for the Light, 2010, dir. Patricio Guzmán
Peggy Sue Got Married, 1986, dir. Francis Ford Coppola
Run Lola, Run, 1998, dir. Tom Tykwer
Shake Hands with the Devil, 2007, dir. Roger Spottiswoode
The Book Thief, 2013, dir. Brian Percival
The Name of the Rose, 1986, dir. Jean-Jacques Annaud
Tweets from Tahrir: The Arab Awakening, 2012, via Al Jazeera: https://www.youtube.com/watch?v=4yljfoq2qas
Versus: The Life and Films of Ken Loach, 2016, dir. Louise Ormond
Victim, 1961, dir. Basil Dearden

Index